CONTENTS

PART I. BEFORE 1849: HUDSON IN COMMAND AT DERBY

1. Early Developments in the Midland Counties — page 13
2. Focus upon Derby — 39
3. George Hudson lays siege to Derby — 57
4. Hudson's Derby Empire — 66
5. The Birmingham and Bristol Line — 96

PART II. 1849-1868: RECOVERY AND EXPANSION

6. John Ellis to the rescue — 131
7. The Leicester and Hitchin Extension — 140
8. Midland Trains at King's Cross — 162

PART III. 1862-1868: THE LONDON EXTENSION

9. The London Extension (Parliamentary Campaign) — 185
10. The London Extension under construction — 204
11. The Pancras Extension and the St Pancras Branch — 232
12. St Pancras Station under construction 1866-1873 — 252

PART IV. 1868-1874: CONSOLIDATION AND EXPANSION

13. Early days on the London Extension — 270
14. Towards a Golden Future — 297

APPENDIX — 309

BIBLIOGRAPHY — 311

INDEX — 313

CHAPTER I

EARLY DEVELOPMENTS IN THE MIDLAND COUNTIES

For close on a thousand years the Erewash, a tributary of the River Trent, has formed a natural county boundary between the shires of Nottingham and Derby. Furthermore, the valley of the Erewash has long been the scene of active mining operations, and coal mining was very well established there even in early Stuart times. At that period inland communications were still in a medieval state, and output was restricted to what could be easily transported to the nearby towns. Consequently, only the rich and the extremely well to do could afford a luxury like coal, and during winter the less privileged sections of the population shivered in dutiful silence. In such circumstances, scope for major expansion within the industry remained technically impossible until, during the last quarter of the eighteenth century, plans were made to canalize many of the smaller rivers within the Trent basin. Typical examples of this policy were the canalization of the rivers Erewash and Soar, and the opening of two broad waterways—the Loughborough Navigation (9¼ miles) in 1778, and the Erewash Canal (11¾ miles) the following year—enabled the proprietors of the pits near the head of the Erewash Valley to market their products in Loughborough, well beyond the Trent. Ten or twelve more years produced a Parliamentary campaign for extending the broad waterway system southward from Loughborough to Leicester, a commercial and manufacturing centre of long-standing importance. There the coal markets had been dominated for generations by the north Leicestershire pits scattered around Coleorton and Moira, the fuel being brought to the county town by packhorses—a thoroughly slow and expensive system.

In preparing to exploit both the new waterway and the Leicester coal markets, the promoters of the new scheme were subjected to a barrage of abuse from the north Leicestershire coalmasters, who conducted their smear campaign in such a vociferous fashion that Parliament eventually stepped in with the time-honoured expedient of establishing a compromise between the contesting factions. In this instance provision was made for the construction of a branch canal leading westwards across the Charnwood Forest to the north Leicestershire pits, Parliament's intention being that both parties should have equality of access to the county town. Amid great excitement, the two waterways were opened for traffic on October 27, 1794, when coal-laden barges from both the Erewash Valley and the north Leicestershire pits reached the West Bridge at Leicester simultaneously. This was the signal for cut-throat competition to begin, and this continued with undiminished ferocity until the extremely severe winter of 1798-99. Without preliminary warning, snow and ice were suddenly followed by a disastrous thaw. In Leicestershire both the reservoir and the earthworks of the Charnwood Forest extension were badly breached, and overnight the surrounding countryside was inundated by the escaping water. Inspection showed the breached works to be beyond repair and, eventually, an Act of Abandonment was obtained in 1838. At Leicester a new monopoly was instantly created, this time in favour of the Erewash Valley men, a monopoly which remained unchallenged for over thirty years.

The tremendous expansion in British industrial output demanded by the Napoleonic Wars only became technically possible with the universal application of James Watt's steam engine to manufacturing machinery of all types. At the close of the eighteenth century England broke out in a nationwide rash of 'manufactures', and so almost overnight the existing demand for domestic coal was supplemented by a new and colossal demand for industrial fuel. In this way, the Napoleonic Wars precipitated an unprecedented boom for the broad canals and they were soon being extended in all directions. In the vicinity of Leicester alone, new waterways were being pushed eastward to Melton Mowbray and Oakham, and a new series of extensions thrust progressively southward from Leicester until, in 1814, connection was made at Norton with the Grand Junction Canal. Consequently, Leicester, already a large scale manufacturing centre rapidly expanding in its own right, now found itself astride a great national waterway linking the Thames with the Trent and the Mersey. The new junction at Norton also brought Leicester into contact with the complicated network of canals centred upon Birmingham.

With the help of the broad canals, the coal industry rapidly profited upon the wartime boom. In 1808, for example, 270,000 tons were shipped down the Erewash Canal, of which two-thirds found its way across the Trent and then southward to Leicester. Canal stocks soared to fantastic levels and stayed there for well over twenty years, that of the Loughborough Navigation reaching £1,240, the dividend being £87 6s 8d. The canal financiers were then so confident about their future that in 1804 hardly anyone gave serious attention to Trevithick's tiny steam locomotive hauling 25-ton loads around Pen-y-Darren Ironworks at 5 m.p.h., at a fuel consumption of 25 lb. per mile. Nor did an improved version fitted with flanged wheels and put to work the following year arouse much more than passing comment. In fact, British commercial interest was then riveted upon Nelson's efforts to smash the long stranglehold of the French blockade upon continental ports and inland centres. Here, in England, it was seen that even vaster profits would accrue from a reduction in manufacturing costs and, ton for ton, it was often more profitable to transport raw materials and finished goods instead of moving coal. So a new trend appeared whereby factories were built on the coalfields proper, and upon sites well removed from the traditional centres. This trend was even accentuated by Murdoch's gas lighting system which made nightwork possible—something unknown hitherto. The whole pattern of British industry was changing, and perhaps for the first time there appeared signs suggesting that the canals were approaching their zenith.

The end of the Napoleonic Wars in June 1815, with the Battle of Waterloo, was followed by a postwar period of completely false prosperity for British industry, and the eighteen twenties suddenly produced collapse and stagnation. However, more progressive elements were only too keenly aware that a far more efficient and quicker method of transporting bulk loads was desperately needed. As early as 1818 a scheme was promoted for building a railway between Stockton and Darlington in the County Durham. Reaction to this proposal was so spontaneous and enthusiastic that within a week no less than £25,000 had been subscribed. The first serious setback occurred when Parliament rejected the Bill in 1819, but despite this the promoters persevered and their measure subsequently received the Royal Assent in 1821. A further Act of 1823 authorized the company to employ engine power for haulage purposes. It was at that stage that George Stephenson was appointed engineer to the new concern at a salary of £600 per annum, out of which sum he was also required to pay his assistants. Construction work for the Stockton & Darlington Railway took about two years, the line being officially opened on September 27, 1825. At the outset passenger vehicles were horsedrawn, whereas the company's goods and mineral trains were steam hauled, the brunt of the work being shouldered by the Stephenson 'Locomotion No. 1'. This pioneer railway was an instant success, and it provided an example that was soon repeated on differing scales all over the United Kingdom.

Such a lively lead produced instant repercussions throughout the North. Across the Pennines, in Lancashire, commercial and financial interests were actively campaigning against the fact that manufactured goods took as long in transit by canal between Manchester and Liverpool as they did to cross the North Atlantic from Liverpool to America. This grossly restrictive state of affairs led to the formation, in 1821, of the Liverpool & Manchester Railway Company with the declared object of breaking the monopoly wielded by the Liverpool & Manchester Canal Company. Local economic conditions were then at their worst with the 'March of the Blanketeers' and the 'Massacre of Peterloo' still fresh in the memory. The new railway was assailed from all sides. Ferocious opposition came from the turnpike trusts, the coaching interests, a considerable section of the Press, local landowners, and, at government level, by the Parliamentary disciples of the theory of *laissez faire*. The fiercest reaction of all came from the proprietors of the Liverpool & Manchester Canal whose opposition is reputed to have been bought off with no less than one thousand of the railway company's shares. Regardless of the odds, the railway promoters struggled on, and, in 1826, their unremitting efforts were finally rewarded with an Act of Incorporation. However, shortly before this success, the company's original surveyor, William James, fell ill and became bankrupt. At this stage, and upon the instigation of an influential financier, Joseph Sandars, George Stephenson was appointed to fill the vacancy. In spite of the humiliations heaped upon him at the Parliamentary stage, and his subsequent estrangement from some of his most promising pupils, notably Locke, George Stephenson scored a resounding triumph in conquering Chat Moss. During the famous Rainhill Locomotive Trials of 1829 he scored yet another triumph when his entry *Rocket* romped home an easy winner. *Rocket* was also supposed to have been the first locomotive fitted with a multi-tubular boiler, and she certainly provided a 'shop window' for displaying the products of the Stephenson locomotive works lately established at Newcastle.

Hard on the heels of the incorporation of the Liverpool & Manchester Railway Company an extremely ambitious scheme appeared in 1823 for linking London with Birmingham. For its day such a bold pioneer attempt to promote a trunk line well over one hundred miles long was a mammoth project and ten years were to elapse before the new concern was granted its Act of Incorporation, at which stage the tiny, isolated Leicester & Swannington line was already in operation. Incidentally, the construction works for this David and Goliath of the early British railway system were executed by Robert Stephenson, since his father was then engrossed in building new coal mines in both Leicestershire and Derbyshire.

In 1828, when the Liverpool & Manchester line was about half built, one of the partners controlling the Whitwick collieries in Leicestershire, a certain William Stenson, visited the mining areas of the north-east. In both the Stephenson engines being built at Newcastle and the operational potential of the Stockton & Darlington Railway Stenson was quick to see a means of recovering the age-old monopoly of the Leicester coal markets which had been surrendered to the Erewash Valley men thirty years previously. Basically, Stenson's scheme envisaged a railway linking the collieries around Swannington in north Leicestershire with the county town. Upon returning to the district he wasted no time in surveying the most likely route, the details of which he set out in a letter to his friend John Ellis, a wealthy Quaker manufacturer of Beaumont Leys near Leicester.

1. Beaumont Leys, near Leicester
(Home of John Ellis)

Thoroughly interested by Stenson's proposals, Ellis quickly set off across country to consult George Stephenson regarding the feasibility of the scheme. Although then busily engaged upon the Liverpool & Manchester line, Stephenson returned with Ellis to Leicester to examine the scheme in greater detail, and at the meeting held at the 'Bell Hotel' on February 12, 1829, the engineer agreed that Stenson's route held distinct possibilities. Due to prior commitments he declined the post of engineer to this new line, and nominated instead his son Robert, adding his own personal guarantee that the work would be executed in a thoroughly satisfactory manner. In examining Stenson's proposed route, George Stephenson had noticed with great interest the commercial potential offered by the construction of such a line. Coal was abundant around Swannington, Whitwick and Bagworth, there was granite at Bardon Hill, and brickworks already existed at Snibston. The new line, he estimated, would cost about £75,000 to build. Of this sum four-fifths was raised locally; the remainder Stephenson undertook to raise in Liverpool from an influential party of merchants and financiers who were, by now very favourably impressed by the prospects held out by the Liverpool & Manchester line now approaching completion. In this way, then, the 'Liverpool Party' obtained its initial grip upon the earliest railway scheme to appear in the midland counties.

The Leicester & Swannington Act received the Royal Assent on May 29, 1830, that is about eight months after the opening of the Liverpool & Manchester Railway. Under the direction of Robert Stephenson, construction work began the following October. It was completed during the summer of 1832, by which time the Stephenson 0.4.0 *Comet* had been shipped by sea from Newcastle, up the Humber and the Trent, and along the broad canals to West Bridge, Leicester. Steam was raised there for the first time early on Saturday, July 12th. The first section of the

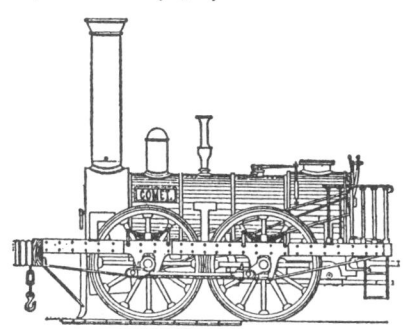

2. Stephenson's *Comet*
Built for Leicester & Swannington Railway, 1832

line was officially opened on Thursday, 17th, with George Stephenson on the footplate of the *Comet*. Of course, these proceedings provided ample scope for a noisy, even tumultuous celebration, the departure of the first train to run south of Manchester being accompanied by the report of specially cast cannon. Soon after this there came yet another loud bang of a quite different nature caused by *Comet's* chimney fouling the roof of Glenfield Tunnel. But this was only a relatively minor setback, and within a month coal was being delivered regularly to Leicester at 10s per ton, and the townspeople there were congratulating themselves upon saving £40,000 per annum, that is, sufficient to offset their parochial taxes.

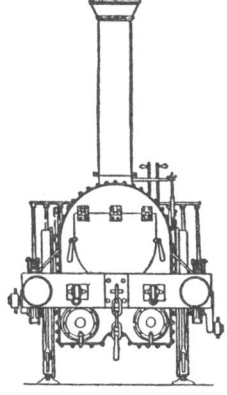

3. *Comet's* chimney
Fouled roof of Glenfield Tunnel during inaugural celebrations

North of Leicester, the Erewash Valley men were far from jubilant. Two of their number had been present at the official opening of the Leicester & Swannington line which instantly threatened their monopoly. In fact, their trade was shattered almost overnight and the market value of the local canal stocks plunged headlong. From the former pinnacle of £705, Erewash Canal stock crashed to virtually nothing, and with that the £47 dividend simply evaporated into thin air. Unemployment was already rife in the valley, but the local coalmasters fought tenaciously to extricate themselves from their difficulties, and as a matter of urgency they called a conference, to which the canal interests were also invited. Before the advent of the Leicester & Swannington Railway the canals had carried some 160,000 tons of coal to Leicester annually, for which services they extracted the following tolls and wharfage charges:

Erewash Canal	11¾ miles	2s	per ton
Loughborough Navigation	9¼ „	3s	„ „
Leicester Navigation	14¾ „	1s 8d	„ „
Total	35¾ „	6s 8d	„ „

i.e. 2¼d per ton, per mile.

In order to recover the initiative at Leicester, an effective reduction in the market price of 3s 6d per ton would be required at once. Even at this advanced stage, the canal people still seemed unable to grasp the critical nature of the situation, for they proposed that the coalmasters should reduce their prices by 2s per ton and that each of the three canals should reduce their rates by 6d per ton, thereby providing a total reduction of 3s 6d. On their side, the coalmasters counterproposed that each of the four interested parties should make an equal sacrifice of 1s per ton, thus achieving a total reduction of 4s at Leicester, as well as increasing the overall reduction by 6d per ton. This, they argued, would give the north Leicestershire men plenty to think about—but the canal people were far too shortsighted to appreciate the wisdom of the suggestion, and very shortly afterwards the meeting broke up with nothing accomplished.

Despite this new setback the Erewash coalmasters were far from being floored, and at their weekly meeting held at the Sun Inn, Eastwood, Nottinghamshire, on August 16, 1832, it was resolved that every attempt must be made 'to lay a railway from these collieries to the town of Leicester'. Furthermore, a committee of seven was immediately appointed to expedite that resolution.

Within a month the scheme was beginning to take definite shape, and at a special meeting held at the Sun Inn on October 4th, a subscription list for £32,000 was raised by the coalmasters that 'a railway be forthwith formed from Pinxton to Leicester as essential to the coal trade of this district'. Simultaneously, a separate meeting of intending shareholders was held at Leicester under the chairmanship of E. M. Mundy, who held a £5,000 interest in the subscription list then being raised at Eastwood.

The survey of the proposed line was entrusted to the engineer William Jessop, whose report dated February 1833, disclosed that an appeal to Parliament that session was impracticable, and so the scheme was kept under constant review at Eastwood during the course of that year. In the autumn it was suggested that by extending the original line from Leicester to Rugby a junction could be effected with the newly sanctioned London & Birmingham trunk line, thereby opening up new markets for Erewash Valley coal within the metropolis itself. This proposal met with instant support, particularly as the additional construction costs should not prove unreasonable, and without further ado Jessop was instructed to extend his survey some twenty miles to Rugby.

Almost immediately after this development, the character of the original project was further modified at the instigation of the Lancashire financiers who had lately been attracted to the scheme. It now received the name of 'Midland Counties Railway' and in November 1833 the new company issued a prospectus stating that 'the railway is intended to connect the towns of Leicester, Nottingham, Derby with each other, and with London, a junction for this latter object being designed with the London & Birmingham Railway near Rugby. A branch will also extend to the Derbyshire and Nottinghamshire collieries and to the termination of the Mansfield Railway at Pinxton. From a very careful estimate of the sources and amount of income on this railway, it appears that a clear annual return of twenty per cent may be expected from the capital invested in it'. This statement is very significant for it shows clearly the influence of the local promoters being rapidly overshadowed by the might of the Lancashire financiers.

As the expanded scheme would obviously require still more capital, the original figure of £32,000 was virtually quadrupled to £125,000; but even this was not nearly enough to justify an appeal to Parliament during the following session, and during 1834 the 'Liverpool Party' increased the capital to £600,000. As the northern financiers were now providing the largest proportion of the capital, they were able to call the tune. In the summer of 1835 they suggested that *their* nominee, 'Charles B. Vignoles', should be asked to make a completely fresh survey of the route 'to find out the very best line to join the London & Birmingham Railway, combining as much as possible the communication to the west with the best line to London'. Vignoles' report, presented in January 1836, revealed a number of hitherto unsuspected deficiencies, so that the company's capital was further increased to £800,000, of which almost fifty per cent came from Lancashire alone, although subscriptions amounting to £2,000 were received from as far afield as South America and the West Indies.

Before leaving this all important question of finance, mention should be made of the commercial and official representatives of Northampton who now attempted to rectify their earlier *faux-pas* in forcing the London & Birmingham people to take their trunk line well clear of the town and through the incredibly difficult Kilsby Tunnel. In November 1835 they sought to persuade the Midland Counties board to divert their new line from Leicester through Market Harborough and Northampton to a junction with the 'Birmingham line at either Blisworth or Roade, instead of at Rugby, as already arranged. To offset partly the extra costs involved, Northampton Corporation offered to take a large block of Midland Counties shares, and they also pointed out the distinct possibility of a large traffic both in cattle and agricultural produce. Still, this offer was declined for two main reasons—firstly, the very small locomotives of the day would be taxed to their utmost by the severity of the gradients in the vicinity of Market Harborough and Kibworth, and secondly, Rugby was much more suitable as the point of junction with the London & Birmingham Railway relevant to the traffic then anticipated between Leicester and the hardware city.

At the Parliamentary stage, the Midland Counties Railway Bill provided for a capital of £1,000,000 with borrowing powers for one-third more, the costs of construction then being estimated at £800,000. Counsel described Leicester, Derby, and Nottingham as very important manufacturing centres engaging in large scale techniques, and fully dependent upon good communications between each other, and also further afield to Birmingham, London, and the West Country. Until the coming of the railway there were three main methods of transport: the coach for passengers and light valuable goods; the canals for goods and raw materials; and, overland, the fly waggons. The conditions then prevailing were clearly demonstrated by the fact that there were only three coaches each day in each direction between Nottingham and Leicester. Leicester was a woollen trading centre selling wool to Yorkshire dealers and receiving machinery from the northern counties. The water journey from Leicester to the West Riding encompassed the Leicester and Loughborough Navigations, the rivers Trent and Aire, and often took the better part of a month. Leicester was also an important worsted and stocking centre, and ninety-five per cent of its raw materials came from the West of England, largely via Birmingham. Between Bristol and Birmingham the overland transits took as much as ten days, whereas by water they took nearly a month; and where the load was of any size a consignment would be split into separate lots and dispatched via devious routes. Between Birmingham and London overland freight was charged 30s a ton—the canals virtually doubled the mileage.

South of Leicester lay Market Harborough. Although only fifteen miles separated these two towns the journey took two days and goods were charged at 10s per ton, the carriers considering such a short journey to be scarcely worthy of their attention. Between Leicester and London the canals charged £2 15s per ton for haberdashery, the waggons charged £3, and the coaches £9 6s 8d. Between Leicester and Derby bulk loads were transported along numerous waterways at about £1 per ton, and for similar reasons widespread expansion of the trade in the particularly fine quality Mansfield stone was being stifled at the very source.

At Nottingham the lace trade was dependent upon raw materials obtained from Devon and Somerset. With communication west of Bristol virtually impossible, many delicate fabrics were even sent by sea via London—a decidedly risky and expensive business.

This, then, is a very brief résumé of the evidence laid before the Parliamentary committee on behalf of the Midland Counties promoters, and although a very strong case had clearly already been made out in favour of the line, there were many hurdles yet to be cleared. Formidable opposition to the Bill came from many quarters, particularly from powerful local interests. In promoting their original scheme for a line to Leicester, the Erewash Valley men were attempting to break the monopoly of the Erewash Canal, the Loughborough Navigation, and the Leicester Navigation. Backed up by the proprietors of the Derby and the Nottingham canals, that trio spared no effort in seeking the rejection of the Bill. Extremely bitter opposition also came from the North Midland Company, whose Bill for a line linking Derby with Chesterfield and Leeds was also receiving consideration that session. This party had been badly frightened by the utterances of Charles Vignoles the previous summer (1835) when suggesting that the Erewash Valley line could profitably be extended northward to a junction with the North Midland at either Clay Cross or Chesterfield. The North Midland people were well aware that if this idea were put into practice, Parliament might very well refuse to sanction a 'parallel line' of twenty miles between Derby and the point of junction. Such a 'decapitation' would not only deprive the North Midland of a very remunerative section of its main line, but also of its end-on connection with its partner, the Birmingham & Derby. Furthermore, both the North Midland and the Birmingham & Derby were 'Stephenson' lines, and at that time there was a strong rumour circulating in railway circles that George Stephenson was most anxious for the North Midland Railway to secure independent access to Derby so that the coal produced from his latest collieries at Clay Cross should find its way westward to the rapidly developing industrial area around Birmingham, and way beyond to the West, rather than southward down the Erewash Valley toward Leicester and London.

The Commons Committee, under the chairmanship of Mr Gisborne, spent seventeen days considering the evidence pertaining to the Midland Counties Bill, and in Parliamentary circles it soon became clear that the fate of the Bill was dependent upon the outcome of the controversy raging over the Erewash Valley section of the scheme. That was the signal for the 'Liverpool Party' to reveal its true colours. To ensure the preservation of their own interests, namely the establishment of railway communication between London, the West Riding, and the northeast of England, they cold-bloodedly abandoned that section of the line running down the Erewash Valley from Pinxton to where it joined the main line immediately north of the Trent. In sanctioning the Midland Counties Railway in that form Parliament also inserted a clause whereby no construction work was to begin on the Leicester and Rugby section of the line for another twelve months, thereby providing adequate time in which the needs of Northampton could be kept under continuous review. It was in this form that the Midland Counties Act received Royal Assent on Tuesday, June 21, 1836.

The first Annual General Meeting of the now fully incorporated Midland Counties Railway Company was held at Loughborough on June 30, 1837. It was here that Charles Vignoles received his formal instructions to prepare for the commencement of construction works. Progress was very rapid, and by the end of the year the following contracts had been let:

1. Derby to the parish of Long Eaton: contractor Wm. Mackenzie of Liverpool, formerly confidential assistant to Thomas Telford.
2. Long Eaton to Nottingham: contractors Taylor, Johnson & Sharpe.
3. Long Eaton to Leicester: contractor Wm. Mackenzie.

Between Leicester and Rugby the line was subsequently undertaken by a contractor named McIntosh who had, reputedly, amassed no less than £1,000,000 within a few years of working as a sub-contractor in Scotland.

In order to obtain the earliest possible return on the Company's financial outlay, the easiest sections were tackled first, so that by the close of the year the two contracts between Derby and Nottingham were in full swing. But a few weeks later, in the spring of 1838, all contracts were advancing rapidly. Of the total labour force of 3,500 men and 325 horses then hard at work, no less than 1,000 men were concentrated on Mackenzie's contract. A particularly lively incident occurred at Spondon during the following August. Here the railway works necessitated the diversion of the canal, thus involving the suspension of navigation, chargeable at the rate of £2 an hour. Just as Mackenzie was preparing to pay up, the canal authorities were suddenly obliged to drain part of their waterway for essential repairs. Seizing his chance, the contractor instantly withdrew men from other parts of the line for concentration at the vital spot. This news spread throughout the district, and in next to no time at all the local population turned out in great strength to enjoy the free show provided by relays of two or three hundred men 'fed most bountifully, and labouring most energetically to complete the novel task within the given time'. The observations of the canal people can be well imagined.

Very interesting light is thrown upon the planning and administrative arrangements of the day by the chairman's speech to the shareholders in June, 1838, during the Second Annual General Meeting, also held at Loughborough. T. E. Dicey explained that very early in the year negotiations had been opened between the boards of the Midland Counties and the North Midland companies concerning the intended future interchange at Derby of through passenger traffic between London and the West Riding. This traffic, alone, had been estimated to be worth £99,000 annually. These discussions had progressed so satisfactorily that a seven years agreement had been prepared and ratified by the Midland Counties shareholders that March. Now, at the end of June, Dicey continued, a separate agreement had been reached by the boards of all three lines converging upon Derby for the construction of contiguous stations there, and at Rugby a station was to be built for the joint use of the London & Birmingham and Midland Counties companies at their point of junction. In conclusion, Dicey stated that contracts had just been let for the rolling stock and the permanent way needed for the Nottingham and Derby section of the line.

In amplifying his chairman's remarks, Vignoles provided some very interesting details about the works. Upwards of half-a-million cubic yards of earthworks were being made, he said, the cuttings would attain a maximum depth of thirty feet, and the embankments a height of twenty feet, the embankment on the approach to Nottingham being three miles long. The permanent way would be the best laid to date, using fifteen foot double-headed rails weighing seventy-seven pounds per yard secured by wooden keys, and at the ends by joint chairs. In the cuttings the rails would be carried upon blocks of Derbyshire millstone grit of five cubic feet, with sleepers on embankments, and longitudinal timbers upon the viaduct across the River Avon near Rugby, and again at Knighton.

Before leaving the preliminary construction works, brief mention should be made of the contractor's locomotives. There were eight of them, and in all probability they were delivered to the working sites by way of either the River Trent or via the Trent & Mersey Canal. These eight were: *Fox* and *Rob Roy* (built by Jones, Turner & Evans of Warrington), *Mersey* (built by Galloway of Manchester), *Aphrite*, *Etna*, *Navy*, *Trent* and *Vivid* (builders unknown). Comparatively little seems to be known about these machines, but *Fox* and *Rob Roy* were later absorbed into the locomotive stock of the Midland Counties Railway, subsequently receiving that company's numbers 46 and 47, respectively. Furthermore, *Fox*, alias M.C.R. No. 46, even seems to have been 'inherited' by the Midland Railway in 1844, but the fate of *Rob Roy* is obscure.

Of the three railways then converging upon Derby, the Midland Counties was the first in the field by a ten-week margin, the initial section, that is between Nottingham and Derby, being officially opened on Thursday, May 30, 1839. Both the local and the national spirit of the occasion is caught in the press report describing the opening ceremony. As the new railway station at Nottingham had been built in 'the Meadows', a short distance from the town centre, some of the guests were conveyed in the new railway omnibus *British Queen*. It was a really sunny day, the bells of St. Mary's church were pealing merrily, and at the station music was provided by the band of the 5th Dragoon Guards, then stationed in the town.

4. Nottingham Station
(Midland Counties Railway), 1839

The whole affair was extremely well organised, about 500 guests being admitted to the trains by numbered tickets corresponding to numbered seats. The carriages were divided into four trains comprising three rakes of six coaches apiece, and one rake of two. Each of the coaches carried the company's coat of arms on its centre panels, as well as a flag hoisted upon the roof, either a Union Jack or an Ensign. The interiors are described as 'the most comfortable yet, being fitted up in the first class with lace and stuffed in the best possible manner'. There were also four 'locomotive engines standing off at some little distance'. These are described as the *Hawk*, *Mersey*, and *Sunbeam*, all with five feet six inch driving wheels, and the *Ariel* with only five feet wheels. Later on, as the locomotive fleet expanded, names were supplemented by numbers and thus *Ariel*, *Hawk*, and *Sunbeam* received Midland Counties numbers 1, 3, and 4 respectively.

'At half past twelve o'clock exactly, the *Sunbeam* engine with its train of four first-class and two second-class carriages was set in motion; and proceeded steadily along the line, amid the cheers of the thousands who were assembled near the spot. At twenty-five minutes to one the engine *Ariel* was attached to the largest train, and the word being given, it moved away in the most beautiful manner possible.' At the departure of each train the band of the 5th Dragoon Guards played 'God Save The Queen', the intervals between the departing trains being filled with the playing of martial airs.

The *Ariel* made a really remarkable run:

Beeston	arr.	12.42	p.m.	
Long Eaton	,,	12.48	p.m.	(6½ m. in 13 mins.)
Sawley	,,	12.52½	p.m.	
Breaston	,,	12.55½	p.m.	(Stop for water)
,,	dep.	12.58	p.m.	
Spondon	arr.	1.11½	p.m.	
Derby	,,	1.19	p.m.	(15½ m. in 44 mins.)

Of course, when the *Ariel* reached Derby, the *Sunbeam* was already there, the arrival of all the trains being welcomed by a 'large concourse of well-dressed spectators'—these being drawn, presumably, from the more affluent members of local society, since the summer of 1839 was punctuated by 'Chartist' disturbances.

After staying at Derby about an hour, *Ariel* left again for Nottingham at 2.31 p.m., 'moving very cautiously over the canal bridge, after which steam was "laid on", and at a tremendous pace away flew the whole at the rate of more than thirty miles an hour on the way back to Nottingham', which was reached in forty-two minutes. There, the guests partook of a 'cold collation' (i.e. a stand up cold buffet). 'A sumptuous entertainment' was provided with more music played by the band. Following the speeches and toasts, the guests were whisked back from Nottingham to Derby in exactly thirty minutes (i.e. 31 m.p.h.), the first six and a half miles to Long Eaton being covered in nine minutes (40 m.p.h.). As if demonstrating that this performance was no mere flash in the pan, *Ariel* made the second return trip from Derby to Nottingham in thirty-one minutes—a wonderful day's work for such a tiny engine.

Regular traffic commenced on the following Tuesday, June 4th, with fares fixed at 4s by first-class carriage, and 2s 6d by second. Weekday services comprised four trains in each direction, leaving Nottingham at 7 a.m., 11 a.m., 3 p.m. and 7 p.m., and leaving Derby at 8 a.m., 12 noon, 4.30 p.m. and 8 p.m. On Sundays there were only two each way, leaving Nottingham at 7.30 a.m. and 7 p.m., and leaving Derby at 8.30 a.m. and 8 p.m. Thus, it will be easily seen that the company's three locomotives—namely, the *Ariel* by the Butterley Company, the *Hawk* by Stark & Fulton of Glasgow, and the *Sunbeam* by Jones, Turner & Evans of Warrington—were very well able to handle this initial traffic. With only five-foot wheels, *Ariel* was quite possibly a goods loco. *Mersey*, of course, was a contractor's engine and, presumably, withdrew from the scene soon after the opening celebrations. Of course, the opening of the Birmingham & Derby Junction line between Hampton-in-Arden and Derby that August brought both Nottingham and Derby through railway communication with London, the trains of both companies using a temporary platform at Derby, pending the construction of the joint station by the North Midland company.

At the time the first section of the Midland Counties Railway was brought into operation, works on the remaining sections between Long Eaton and Leicester, and Leicester and Rugby were proceeding day and night, particularly south of Leicester where many of the works proved heavy. Immediately south of Long Eaton, the line had to be carried across the River Trent and then straight through Red Hill. Work on the bridge was started in June, 1838, the foundation stone being laid without any formal ceremony at the end of the year by its designer, Charles Vignoles. This beautiful structure embraced three spans of 100 feet flanked by ten twenty-five-foot flood arches on the north side, and two on the south. Two stone piers forty feet long, ten feet wide, and twenty-two feet above the level of the water were built from stone obtained in the nearby quarries at Long Eaton, and these carried a twenty-seven-foot roadway. The Butterley Company supplied the ironwork for the glorious Gothic style spans, the bridge being completed by the autumn of 1839.

5. Early Midland Counties Railway train crossing Vignoles' beautiful bridge spanning River Trent, 1840

Immediately south of Vignoles' magnificent bridge, the horse-shoe-shaped tunnel through the Red Hill was built by the contractor, Wm. Mackenzie: 133 yards long, it measured twenty-four feet seven inches from rail level to roof, twenty-three feet wide at rail level, with a maximum width of twenty-six feet six inches, and cost about £50 per lineal yard. The arch of the tunnel was carried through first and the side walls were underpinned and put in afterwards, a popular method of the day to economize on the timber used to support the centering. Incidentally, during the excavations two Roman coins of the Augustian and the Vespasian eras, as well as several skulls, were found near the south end of the tunnel, and the remains of a Roman camp nearby.

By the spring of 1840 the administrative headquarters of the Midland Counties Railway Company were to be found at Leicester, where the station buildings have been described as 'handsome, with the directors' board room and general offices on the upper floor'. There, the traffic facilities consisted of simply one long platform served by a platform loop-line equipped with crossover roads in the centre and a junction at each end. In this way the solitary platform accommodated both up and down stopping trains, leaving the main lines free for through traffic. This was a very popular arrangement during early Victorian times; the old Great Western station at Reading is another broadly similar example of this practice. Even to this day a single platform for up and down trains still survives at Cambridge like a ghost from the past.

6. Leicester station — the administrative headquarters of the Midland Counties Railway in 1840

The Midland Counties extension from the parish of Long Eaton to Loughborough and Leicester was officially opened on May 4, 1840, and, naturally enough, this event provided further scope for more celebrations. With its locomotive sheds and carriage sidings, Nottingham again provided the starting point for the company's inaugural train which set out for Leicester, arriving there at noon. Allowing for passengers to stop and admire Vignoles' handsome bridge across the Trent and the magnificently castellated portal of Red Hill tunnel immediately south of the river, and then a formal stop at Loughborough, the train most probably left Nottingham at 10 a.m. For this special occasion it consisted of four first-class and six second-class carriages drawn by the Bury locomotive *Leopard*, afterwards Midland Counties Railway number 11. Among those on board were 'several directors, also Messrs Vignoles and Woodhouse (the engineers) and W. E. Hutchinson (the Midland Counties Superintendent). Three guards in new uniforms were seated on the carriage roofs, the train being decorated with beautiful banners and a number of flags'. At Leicester station itself the first floor balcony had been specially reserved for the ladies who waved most enthusiastically as the special train drew in to the accompaniment of the assembled brass bands and, of course, the cheers of the crowds. The weather was fine and sunny, and it seems that everyone present enjoyed a very lively time. Undoubtedly, the brewers and the caterers enjoyed a very busy time.

Having stayed at Leicester for about an hour, the inaugural train left for Derby at 1 p.m. Whether or not it completed a triangular trip by running across from Derby to Nottingham isn't clear, but certainly a dinner was given later on in the King's Head Hotel, Derby, after which the revellers went home by train, reaching Leicester at 9 p.m. Normal passenger traffic commenced the following day, May 5th.

A fortnight after the opening ceremony, on May 20th, six trucks laden with coal from George Stephenson's new collieries at Clay Cross arrived at Leicester (Midland Counties), thereby challenging the virtual monopoly enjoyed by the Leicester & Swannington Railway since 1832. Also, on the new Midland Counties extensions coal wharfs had already been built at Loughborough, Syston, Wigston, Crow Mill, Ullesthorpe, and Rugby where the provision of such facilities must have proved a boon to farmers who had formerly been obliged to send their heavy teams to the coal markets at Leicester. There, Stephenson's Derbyshire coals were now beginning to arrive in quantity at 12s per ton, and perhaps these were the early signs of the large scale political railway struggle which would subsequently develop and remain centred around Leicester during the next five or six years.

South of Leicester work on the third and final section of the Midland Counties main line was fast approaching completion. Exactly a fortnight after the official opening of the extension from Long Eaton to Loughborough and Leicester, and with only one set of rails laid down, the contractor's loco *Vivid* hauled a special train carrying the company's directors from Leicester to Rugby and back, on May 18th. At Rugby special arrangements had already been made for Midland Counties passenger trains to be accommodated at a single bay platform there, but their goods and mineral trains were to run past the northern side of the station to a second junction adjacent to the London & Birmingham milepost 82½, as measured from Euston Square, of course. From that milepost, the distance to Derby Junction (i.e. the junction with the North Midland line immediately north of the joint station) was 49½ miles, from Trent Junction to Nottingham 7¼ miles, and the avoiding line from Sawley Junction to Long Eaton just 1 mile, a combined total mileage of 57¾ miles.

Between Leicester and Rugby Junction, the third and final section of the Midland Counties main line was opened for public traffic on Tuesday, June 30, 1840. Apart from the fact that the directors made a private inspection trip along the completed line on Monday, June 29th, there was no formal ceremony whatever. In fact, a local press report states that 'On Tuesday at about 7.30 a.m. a train of four or five carriages reached the station (i.e. Leicester) on its way to the north, and was followed by four other trains in the course of the day'. Southbound traffic to Rugby began running on Wednesday, July 1st, and thus coincided with the opening of the North Midland extension from Masborough to Leeds, as well as the York & North Midland line from Burton Salmon to Altoft's Junction and the Hull & Selby Railway. The 6.30 a.m. ex Leeds, comprising six carriages carrying passengers mostly bound for London, reached Leicester at 2.45 p.m. (i.e. 35 minutes late), whilst the 6.30 a.m. ex Hull consisting of seven coaches reached Leicester an hour late at 3.30 p.m. There were also two other trains that evening, but throughout the day all of the trains ran well behind their scheduled times.

After such an unpromising start, the new extension quickly recovered to settle down into its normal working stride. On the following day (Thursday, July 2nd) the trains were far more punctual; the mid-day special down train ex Rugby (twelve first and second-class carriages and two horse boxes) was only two minutes late, and at 2 p.m. the up train from York and Hull, although ten minutes late in leaving Derby, pulled into Leicester on time—very smart going indeed in view of the tiny Bury engines used. Within a week the punctuality of both the connecting services from the north and the Midland Counties trains had greatly improved, and there was also a very marked increase in the volume of traffic flowing along the new line. In fact, one of the trains reaching Rugby consisted of eighteen carriages, 'including some private ones', although the largest yet seen, one of twenty-two coaches, 'passed along the line on Thursday morning', that is on July 9th.

Along the whole route between Leeds, York, and Hull in the north and Rugby Junction in the south, the newly opened system of railway communication received extensive publicity in the local press. The accompanying timetable summary taken from the *Leeds Mercury* dated July 4, 1840, shows quite conclusively that by the fast morning trains York was now brought within ten hours' journey time of the capital. It is most important to add, though, that this wonderful feat also depended on the fact that south of Rugby Junction the fast morning trains made only three intermediate stops on the journeys to and from Euston Square, that is at Weedon, Wolverton, and Tring; these trains being hauled by London & Birmingham engines specially set aside for the task. From its very first day of operation, the new Midland Counties extension was competing with the Birmingham & Derby Junction line opened the previous year between Derby and Hampton Junction. As the Midland Counties route from Derby to Rugby was about ten miles shorter than the earlier joint route via Hampton, and because of the institu-

7. The original Leicester, Swannington and the Midland Counties lines at Leicester

tion of through bookings to and from London by the more important Midland Counties trains, much of the through London traffic was quickly attracted to the new route. All this naturally stimulated a competitive atmosphere, and at first there was some evidence of sporting rivalry between the two concerns diverging southwards from Derby. Within six months or so this sporting element disappeared and was replaced by more sinister, cut-throat competition. Now, this occurred as Britain entered a period of trade recession, and from about 1841 onward the rivalry between the Midland Counties and the Birmingham & Derby Junction companies was conducted with bitter ferocity on both sides. In February 1842, the Midland Counties board initiated the new system of half-yearly meetings which had been suggested the previous summer; a dividend at the rate of four per cent per annum was also declared, although this fell to three per cent by the following August. Only three months later, in November 1842, a packed special meeting of the shareholders heard James Heyworth propose the appointment of a Committee of Investigation to enquire into the company's affairs and administration. This resolution was successfully opposed by the directors, but in February 1843 a fresh proposal was carried by a majority of three to one. Other proposals made that spring envisaged amalgamation of the Birmingham & Derby Junction and the Midland Counties concerns, but the subsequent negotiations failed over the question of terms. The cut-throat competition was promptly resumed, and continued well into the summer of 1843 until a Writ of Mandamus granted to the Midland Counties by the Court of Queen's Bench compelled the Birmingham & Derby Junction board to equalize their fares between Derby and Hampton Junction.[1]

By the summer of 1843 the contestants were close to complete exhaustion, a fact which did not escape the attention of George Hudson, who had been intently studying the progress of the war being waged south of Derby. Indeed, during the next few months the supremely ambitious Hudson was to utilize that deadly struggle for furthering his own ends by leading a campaign for the creation of the Midland Railway by the amalgamation of all three lines radiating from Derby; but, before considering this in closer detail, it is necessary to summarize the history of the Stephenson lines linking Birmingham with Derby, Sheffield, Leeds, and York.

[1] For details see Chapter 3 (5).

MIDLAND COUNTIES RAILWAY,
FROM LONDON TO DERBY, SHEFFIELD, LEEDS, YORK, AND HULL, AND FROM LONDON TO LEICESTER AND NOTTINGHAM.

THE PUBLIC are respectfully informed that this Railway, from its junction with the London and Birmingham Railway at Rugby, by way of Leicester and Loughborough to Nottingham and Derby (where it joins the North Midland Railway to Sheffield, Leeds, York and Hull), will be OPENED for the Conveyance of Passengers, Parcels, Gentlemen's Carriages, Horses, &c. on WEDNESDAY, the 1st of July next, and that the Trains, with those of the London and Birmingham, North Midland, York and North Midland, and Hull and Selby Railway Companies, in connection with them, will arrive and depart as under, until further notice:—

BETWEEN LONDON, LEICESTER, NOTTINGHAM, DERBY, SHEFFIELD, LEEDS, YORK, AND HULL.

Departure from London.	Departure from Rugby.	Arrival at Leicester.	Arrival at Nottingham.	Arrival at Derby.	Arrival at Sheffield.	Arrival at Leeds.	Arrival at York.	Arrival at Hull.
	6 45 a.m.	7 45 a.m.	9 15 a.m.	9 15 a.m.	11 45 a.m.	1 30 p.m.		
6 0 a.m.	9 40 a.m.	10 45 a.m.	12 15 p.m.	12 15 p.m.	2 45 p.m	4 0 p.m.	4 30 p.m.	6 0 p.m.
9 30 a.m.	1 0 p.m.	1 45 p.m.	3 15 p.m.	3 15 p.m.	5 30 p.m.	6 45 p.m.	7 15 p.m.	8 45 p.m.
1 0 p.m.	4 40 p.m.	5 45 p.m.	7 30 p.m.	7 30 p.m.	10 15 p.m.	11 30 p.m.	12 0 p.m.	
5 0 p.m.	8 40 p.m.	9 45 p.m.	11 0 p.m.	11 0 p.m.				
8 30 p.m.	12 30 a.m.	1 30 a.m.	3 0 a.m.	3 0 a.m.	5 15 a.m.	6 30 a.m.	7 0 a.m.	8 30 a.m.

SUNDAY TRAINS.

	6 45 a.m.	7 45 a.m.	9 15 a.m.	9 15 a.m.				
8 0 a.m.	12 5 p.m.	1 15 p.m.	2 30 p.m.	2 30 p.m.	5 15 p.m.	6 30 p.m.	7 0 p.m.	
	6 30 p.m.	7 30 p.m.	9 0 p.m.	9 0 p.m.				
8 30 p.m.	12 30 a.m.	1 30 a.m.	3 0 a.m.	3 0 a.m.	5 15 a.m.	6 30 a.m.	7 0 a.m.	8 30 a.m.

BETWEEN HULL, YORK, LEEDS, SHEFFIELD, DERBY, NOTTINGHAM, LEICESTER, AND LONDON.

Departure from Hull.	Departure from York.	Departure from Leeds.	Departure from Sheffield.	Departure from Derby.	Departure from Nottingham.	Departure from Leicester.	Arrival at Rugby.	Arrival at London.
				7 0 a.m.	7 0 a.m.	8 30 a.m.	9 45 a.m.	1 30 p.m.
	6 15 a.m.	6 45 a.m.	8 0 a.m.	10 45 a.m.	10 45 a.m.	12 10 p.m.	1 25 p.m.	6 0 p.m.
7 30 a.m.	9 0 a.m.	9 30 a.m.	10 45 a.m.	1 10 p.m.	1 10 p.m.	2 30 p.m.	3 30 p.m.	7 0 p.m.
11 0 a.m.	12 30 p.m.	1 0 p.m.	2 15 p.m.	4 45 p.m.	4 45 p.m.	6 0 p.m.	7 15 p.m.	11 30 p.m.
				7 45 p.m.	7 45 p.m.	9 15 p.m.	10 15 p.m.	
5 15 p.m.	6 45 p.m.	7 15 p.m.	8 30 p.m.	11 0 p.m.	11 0 p.m.	12 15 a.m.	1 23 a.m.	5 30 a.m.

SUNDAY TRAINS.

				7 0 a.m.	7 0 a.m.	8 30 a.m.	9 45 a.m.	1 30 p.m.
	7 45 a.m.	8 15 a.m.	9 30 a.m.	12 15 p.m.	12 15 p.m.	1 30 p.m.	2 55 p.m.	7 30 p.m.
				7 45 p.m.	7 45 p.m.	9 15 p.m.	10 15 p.m.	
5 15 p.m.	6 45 p.m.	7 15 p.m.	8 30 p.m.	11 0 p.m.	11 0 p.m.	12 15 a.m.	1 23 a.m.	5 30 a.m.

Passengers may be booked through, between any of the above places and London, at the Booking Offices of the respective Stations, with the exception of Leicester.

Passengers to or from any intermediate Station, on the London and Birmingham Railway, may be booked through between the above places and Rugby.

N.B. The Trains leaving London at half-past 9 a.m., Hull at half-past 7 a.m., York at 9 a.m., Leeds at half-past 9 a.m., Sheffield at a quarter to 11 a.m., Derby and Nottingham at 10 minutes past 1 p.m., and Leicester at half-past 2 p.m., WILL BE FORWARDED TO AND FROM RUGBY BY SPECIAL ENGINES, stopping only at Weedon, Wolverton, and Tring.

BY THESE TRAINS THE JOURNEY BETWEEN LONDON AND YORK WILL BE PERFORMED IN TEN HOURS.

The Railway between LONDON, LEICESTER, LOUGHBOROUGH, NOTTINGHAM, and DERBY, will be OPENED on TUESDAY, the 30th of June, 1840.
By order,
Leicester, June 24th, 1840.
J. F. BELL, Secretary.

8. Midland Counties Railway timetable, 1840

CHAPTER 2

FOCUS UPON DERBY

At the official opening of the Liverpool & Manchester Railway in September 1830, George Stephenson's personal triumph was marred by two sombre incidents—the fatal accident which befell William Huskisson, and the extremely hostile reception accorded the Duke of Wellington by the angry crowds which broke through the lines of militia as the inaugural train entered the Manchester terminus; upon official advice, the Duke beat a strategic retreat. Despite these setbacks, another month found George Stephenson undaunted and taking a very keen interest in the works for the new Leicester & Swannington Railway then being started by his son, Robert. However, his main preoccupation at that time was the commercial development of the coal measures at Snibston, Leicestershire, and, in partnership with the wealthy Liverpool financiers Sir Joshua Walmesley and Joseph Sandars, he set about purchasing the land in 1831. By the summer of 1832 coal from the new pits was being shipped by canal southwards to London and eastward along the newly opened railway line to Leicester.

Soon, the new pits at Snibston became so important that George Stephenson transferred his residence across country from Lancashire to Alton Grange. During his early days there he received visits from many influential friends such as George Carr Glyn, the London banker, Charles Sturge and William Beale of Birmingham, John and Joseph Ellis of Leicester, and William Vickers of Sheffield. It was largely from their combined suggestions that in 1834 George Stephenson projected a number of very important lines from which sprang a vast network of railway communication to the east of the Pennines. Initially, the backbone of the whole scheme was a line rather more than seventy miles long linking Leeds with Chesterfield and Derby. South-west from Derby the communication was to be continued through Burton and Tamworth into Birmingham which, for the past ten years at least, had been earmarked as the focal point of numerous other projects. Of these the London & Birmingham had been built by Robert Stephenson, and as Chairman of that now nationally important concern, Glyn was very anxious to reap the financial benefits to be derived from George Stephenson's plan to provide through communication between London and Yorkshire, particularly the industrial areas of the West Riding. Glyn thus planned a 'cut-off line' joining Rugby, Leicester, and Derby to connect with Stephenson's newly projected North Midland line, but in this he was forestalled by the Liverpool Party then busily promoting their Midland Counties Railway over much the same route, but in the opposite direction. They, too, had carefully digested Geordie Stephenson's proposals for reaching Leeds and perceived that only a few minor modifications were necessary to profitably adapt the essentially local Erewash Valley line into a vital link in the chain of communication now being forged between London and the North. By 1835, William Jessop, the original Erewash Valley engineer, had been replaced by the Liverpool Party's nominee, Charles Vignoles, and their greatly expanded scheme was now forging ahead under its new title of Midland Counties Railway.

For the Stephensons, both father and son, the autumn of 1835 was an extremely busy season. Under Robert Stephenson's direction the construction works for the London & Birmingham Railway were already striding eastward across the Midland plain towards Rugby and the broad uplands of Northamptonshire, although at Kilsby the tunnel was about to prove far more difficult than had been realized. In a very different way, George Stephenson was also attempting to race the clock. With a considerable number of Bills to be introduced into Parliament in readiness for the 1836 session, speed and mobility were all important. Consequently, his surveys for the Birmingham & Derby and the North Midland lines were made from his famous yellow post chaise. Despite the pressing urgency, nothing was skimped, and in achieving such masterful results the engineer owed much to the competence of his personal secretary, Charles Binns.

In its original form, the Birmingham & Derby project was a straightforward scheme that lived up to its name. Trouble first appeared when Charles Vignoles (Engineer to the Midland Counties Railway Company) called for an extension of the original Erewash Valley line northward from Pinxton to a junction with the North Midland Railway's main line at either Clay Cross or Chesterfield. This instantly aroused the bitter enmity of the North Midland party, and the story goes that they promptly induced the Birmingham & Derby people to compete with the Midland Counties for the through traffic between Yorkshire and London by projecting a double-track branch six and a half miles long (i.e. the Stonebridge Branch) from a junction with their main line at Whitacre to a junction with the London & Birmingham Railway at Hampton-in-Arden. Shortly before all three Bills were debated in the House, a truce was arranged whereby the Erewash Valley extension from Pinxton would be suppressed if the Stonebridge Branch were similarly withdrawn. At the very last moment, however, whether by accident or by design, the advertisement for the Midland Counties extension appeared in the local press. This produced an uproar in the two Stephenson camps, especially as there was no time available for retaliation. To their great credit, though, the Birmingham & Derby solicitors were equal to the occasion. Using a simple ruse, they immediately deposited a Bill for a nominally separate company called the Stonebridge Junction Railway Company, the alignment of which absolutely coincided with that of the former Birmingham & Derby Branch. When laid before Parliament, the Birmingham & Derby and the Stonebridge Junction companies were united under the new title of Birmingham and Derby Junction Railway Company which then received its Act of Incorporation on May 19, 1836, just a month ahead of its rival the Midland Counties.

Hostility between these two concerns reached such a pitch that in 1837 the Birmingham & Derby people went so far as to seek an amendment to their Act providing for a new branch from their main line and running direct from Tamworth to Rugby. This scheme proved unsuccessful, and every energy was then devoted to completing the original branch from Whitacre to Hampton. On the other hand, virtually nothing was done about the western end of their main line between Whitacre and Birmingham.

Construction work commenced in August, 1837, contemporary with the initial section of the Midland Counties line between Derby and Nottingham. Within a year all the land needed for the line between Derby and Hampton-in-Arden had been acquired at a cost of only £10,000 in excess of the original estimates. The work proved relatively straightforward due to the favourable nature of the countryside. For all practical purposes the cuttings and the embankments cancelled out each other, no tunnel was needed, and the ground traversed provided some excellent materials for the permanent way. About half the line proved to be almost flat, and so the works advanced at a very rapid pace indeed, the most important engineering items along the line being the Walton Viaduct (about 400 yards long, and carried on 1,000 piles), and the viaduct across the River Anker near Tamworth. This incorporated eighteen spans of thirty feet, and an oblique arch having a span of not less than sixty feet.

9. The Anker Viaduct (B. & D.J.R.) near Tamworth in 1839

The Birmingham & Derby Junction Railway was officially opened between Derby and Hampton Junction (thirty-eight and a half miles) on Monday, August 5, 1839. There was no spectacular public ceremony. Whether this was due to the recent Chartist troubles, or simply an economy measure is hard to say—but a train of nine coaches with a party of directors on board left

Birmingham at 10 a.m. behind the company's brand new 2.2.2 locomotive *Birmingham*. This special train followed the London & Birmingham main line as far as Hampton Junction where it was reversed in readiness for the remainder of the run to Derby. Many stops are reported to have been made along the new line for the benefit of the directors wishing to inspect the works. The train reached Derby at 2 p.m., the arrival being greeted with cheers from the assembled spectators, and after this 'a most sumptuous cold collation was provided in the King's Head Hotel, with Mr Wallis's accustomed liberality'.

10. Hampton Junction (B. & D.J.R.) in 1839
(Original loco shops in middle distance, London & Birmingham Railway's main line to left)

The Birmingham & Derby Junction works were hardly finished at this stage. At Normanton, just south of Derby, for example, a heavy cutting was still incomplete, and only one track had been laid there for a distance of about 200 yards. At Hampton 'a commodious house is already built, and a first-class station is in the course of erection which, we believe, will be used by both companies'—i.e. the B.&D.J. and the L.&B. The local press also gives a very good idea of the rolling stock then in use on the new line. 'The carriages are similar in most respects to those already in use on the London & Birmingham and the Grand Junction lines; the first-class are very handsomely finished, the bodies of the carriages being painted a bright yellow, and the only external ornament which they bear is the arms of the company which are elegantly emblazoned on the panel of the centre doors. Each carriage bears a number instead of a name, a practice which is now adopted on many of the railways recently opened.' The report also states that no second-class carriages were ready for the inaugural trip, but that they were to be enclosed, and would therefore be an improvement upon those of the London & Birmingham company. 'The third-class carriages are painted a dark brown, they are built in a very substantial manner, and each, it is calculated, will accommodate about forty persons.'

Ordinary passenger traffic began running on the Birmingham & Derby Junction exactly a week later on Monday, August 12th. Henceforth, through[1] railway communication was established between London, Tamworth, Burton, and Derby, at which point the trains were met by properly organized services of road coaches linking Derby with Chesterfield, Buxton, Manchester, Sheffield, Leeds, and York. At first there were five trains each way daily between Derby and Birmingham (six between Derby and Hampton); within a week, however, this was reduced to three, and then increased to four by October. As no effort had been made to complete the main line west of Whitacre, trains for the hardware centre used the Stonebridge Branch and then the London & Birmingham line west of Hampton Junction, for the use of which the London & Birmingham received £180 in tolls each week.

11. B. & D.J.R. 2.2.2 loco *Derwent* supplied by Sharp's, 1839

The B.&D.J. locomotive stock comprised twelve 2.2.2s with 5 feet 6 inch wheels supplied in batches of three by four different

[1] Through Bookings (W.E.F. Monday, August 12th, 1839):

Ex Derby	11.30 a.m.	4.15 p.m.
Arr. Euston Sq.	6.15 p.m.	11.30 p.m.
Ex Euston Sq.	8.45 a.m.	2.00 p.m.
Arr. Derby	3.30 p.m.	9.00 p.m.

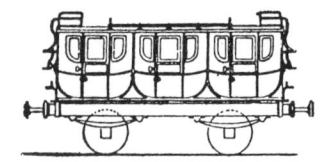

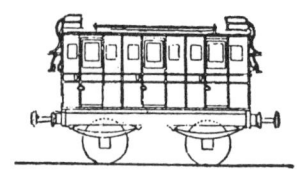

Fares — £1 15s. (first class); £1 4s. (second class)

12. 1st and 2nd class coaches, B. & D.J.R., 1839

makers; two 0.4.2s hauled the decidedly slender freight traffic. The company's locomotive shops were originally located close to the junction with the London & Birmingham Railway at Hampton and from the beginning they were under the personal control of a young locomotive foreman named Matthew Kirtley, then only twenty-six years old. However, with the opening of B.&D.J. direct line between Whitacre and Birmingham in February 1842, the shops at Hampton were closed and transferred to Birmingham the following June, by which time young Kirtley had already been appointed Locomotive Superintendent.

Thereafter, the Stonebridge Branch lost its former share of the Birmingham traffic, though for some time yet the mail trains to and from Birmingham continued to connect with the London & Birmingham trains at Hampton. Within about a year the branch was reduced to single track, which was quite adequate for the through London services then taking about seven hours for the run from Derby.

As with the Birmingham & Derby line, the route for the North Midland Railway was surveyed by George Stephenson in September 1835. North of Chesterfield, Stephenson was confronted by two possible alternatives—firstly, the line could be taken through the massive hills of South Yorkshire to serve Sheffield, Barnsley, and Wakefield or, secondly, a chain of river valleys could be utilized to carry the line well to the east of those centres. In the first case the work would be difficult and expensive due to the need for very lofty embankments and a chain of tunnels; on the other hand, the valley route would preserve very satisfactory gradients. Once again, George Stephenson's keen eye had spotted the existence of tremendous reserves of mineral wealth absolutely ripe for development. Using all his shrewdness, Stephenson made his choice, arranging for the North Midland line to be carried down the centre of the valleys, the track being elevated only to the extent necessary to ensure complete protection from winter flooding. In this fashion, the North Midland Company would tap the huge number of collieries that within a few years would riddle the sides of the valleys at all levels, as well as preserving the maximum gradients of 1 in 330 which were so well suited to the tiny Stephenson engines. In order to place Sheffield in touch with this main line of communication, a short line, five and a half miles long, and to be called the Sheffield & Rotherham Railway, would effect a junction with the North Midland at Masborough.

In making such arrangements, George Stephenson unleashed a torrent of criticism, and in the spring of 1836 the North Midland Bill received a very bad mauling at the Parliamentary stage. There, Charles Vignoles, with the influential backing of Lord Wharncliffe, had much to say in favour of extending the Erewash Valley line up to Chesterfield and then pushing northwards through the hills to Sheffield and Leeds. Had the scheme materialized, the construction costs would have been fantastic since cuttings and embankments in excess of ninety feet would have been necessary. The only alternative to these proposals would have been about ten miles of extremely expensive tunnelling. By far the fiercest opposition came from the proprietors of the Aire & Calder Navigation when the measure was before the House of Lords, and the hostility of the canal interests was only overcome by projecting a deviation of 2 miles 36 chains from the Parliamentary line by carrying the railway across Hunslet Moor, well away from the south bank of the River Aire, on the final approach to Leeds. It was thus only after a really vicious struggle that the North Midland Bill received the Royal Assent on July 4, 1836, at which stage the Sheffield & Rotherham Railway scheme was also sanctioned.

At the beginning of 1837 the preparatory arrangements were very well in hand. The executive engineer's office had already been installed at Chesterfield, and once again George Stephenson had moved his residence, this time to Tapton House, just outside the town. At Derby it had been found that the site originally chosen for the grand terminus was prone to flooding and so, in May 1837, a further Act was obtained authorizing the purchase of suitable land from Derby Corporation. At Leeds arrangements were also well in hand for the acquisition of more land for enlarging the Hunslet terminus.

The construction works for the North Midland line were split into twenty-eight contracts numbered from Derby northward. These included more than 200 bridges and seven tunnels, of of which the longest tunnel, and the most difficult, was the Clay Cross Tunnel (No. 8 contract), 1,760 yards long. Due to the anticipated difficulties, this was about the first contract to be let, being awarded to Edward Price upon the recommendations of the Stephensons and F. Swanwick (the resident engineer). An immediate start was made and the work was executed from six shafts and the two entrances (fourteen headings in all), the removal of the soil being facilitated by the use of fifteen horse whinneys. By the autumn of 1838, 400 lineal yards had been completed and it was confidently forecast that the tunnel would be finished by the end of 1839. However, it was later found that the hill was made up of wet coal measures from which tremendous volumes of water had to be constantly pumped. On the ridge above the workings huge bonfires were kept blazing twenty-four hours a day, and at night these were the wonder of the neighbourhood which attracted sightseers from miles around to watch the navvies toiling in the glare of the flames.

An immediate start was also made at Derby, and by the summer of 1838 it was the scene of tremendous activity. The Nottingham Turnpike was being lowered, the embankment for the railway was taking shape, whilst the ground was being marked out for the joint passenger station, the three goods stations, and the engine sheds.

A few miles north of Derby, at Wingfield, 350,000 cubic yards of earth works were already being hacked out for the new line, and, at Milford, 168 lineal yards had already been excavated for the 860 yard long tunnel. Near Ambergate, the railway was to pass clean through the lofty embankment carrying the Cromford Canal. To meet statutory requirements prohibiting lengthy interference with navigation along the canal, the piers for the new aqueduct were laid very deep down and then built up to support an iron trough cast to the exact shape of the canal. Having been floated into its exact position, the trough was sunk without causing the least disturbance to navigation. At Chester-

13. Bull Bridge, North Midland Railway, 1840
Note railway pierces canal embankment (Cromford Canal) then crosses River Amber

field, the earthworks were practically completed that autumn (1838), while at Rotherham several spans of the thirty-arch viaduct across the River Dun were also finished, it then being confidently expected that by the end of the year the rail connection with the Sheffield & Rotherham line would be firmly established. The construction of huge cuttings and embankments at Oakenshaw involved the excavation and tipping of 600,000 cubic yards of rock, a further 400,000 cubic yards being removed to form the cutting at Normanton. Because of persistently wet weather from June 1839 onward, all of these works proved extremely difficult; work on the tunnels was also seriously hampered and as late as March 1840, F. Swanwick was reporting to a meeting of the Company held in the London Tavern, Derby, that all seven tunnels were complete, except for the portals, with a single line of rails laid right through.

When the North Midland line was approximately half built,

14. Ambergate tunnel
(North Midland Railway), 1840

the complementary Sheffield & Rotherham Railway was opened for traffic on October 31, 1838. The departure of the inaugural train from Sheffield was timed for 10.10 a.m., but according to the local press there was a delay of a good thirty minutes pending the arrival of Earl Fitzwilliam and his party. However, several trips were eventually made, although many of the spectators had to be kept off the track at numerous points. Of course, the Sheffield and Rotherham was a Stephenson line, and it boasted three locomotives delivered from the Stephenson factory at Newcastle by way of the River Humber and the navigations. The first-class carriages are reputed to have been built by Richard Melling & Co. of Green Hayes, near Manchester, and the second-class vehicles were obtained from Bolton specially for the occasion.

Regular traffic began running on the following day, November 1st, when more than a thousand people were carried. That afternoon, a train hauled by the 2-2-2 *Victory*, with George Stephenson on the footplate, made a particularly good run. This was the 4 p.m. from Sheffield, the 5½ miles to Rotherham being covered in 9 minutes 45 seconds, whereupon George Stephenson expressed his opinion that the run could easily be made in seven or eight minutes, once the embankments had consolidated. An excellent service was instituted with trains leaving Sheffield at hourly intervals between 8 a.m. and 8 p.m., and returning from Rotherham at hourly intervals from 9 a.m. to 9 p.m.

The stations for the North Midland Railway were built to the designs of F. Thompson by Thomas Jackson, the celebrated Pimlico builder of the day. At Leeds, for example, the station offices, viewed from the front, were 179 feet long and 28 feet 6 inches deep, with a 6 foot arcade extending their whole length. Mounted at the main entrance was the company's coat of arms (embracing those of Leeds, Sheffield, and Derby), the work of a Birmingham sculptor named Thomas. Behind the station offices, the train shed was 113 feet 6 inches wide with a 'landing stone' 267 feet long on either side, between which were laid six lines of rails interconnected by turntables at each end. The roof, pitched in four sections, was covered by blue slates and skylights extending the full length, and the whole structure was supported by rows of neatly fluted columns. These had been produced by Messrs Braham & Co. of the London Works near Birmingham, and were very similar to those used at Derby. Due to the continuously bad weather, the contract for the erection of the Hunslet terminus was only let to Jackson as late as February 1840, that is about only four months before the North Midland Railway was opened for traffic.

At Derby the North Midland people had undertaken to provide one huge joint passenger station for the accommodation of the trains of all three companies there, so that from the very outset long distance passengers travelling to and from the North received the full benefit of the interchange facilities. One of the largest of the period, the station roof at Derby was arranged in three bays—two of 42 feet span apiece, and one of 56 feet—with an average length of 450 feet, although one reached a total length of 1,050 feet.

Distinctly separate from the usual station offices and buildings provided for each of the three companies, the North Midland had its own board rooms and principal offices which were particularly handsome in design. Again, the three companies had separate goods stations and engine sheds of which the North Midland shed was easily the biggest. In plan it formed a sixteen-sided polygon 190 feet across. The whole structure was 50 feet high. Inside, sixteen lines converged upon one central turntable; outside, the roundhouse was flanked by the carriage houses and workshops, these being 180 feet and 160 feet long, respectively. Thus, in 1840 the North Midland sheds provided the nucleus from which sprang the huge Midland Railway locomotive establishment of later years, and although Derby was then laid out in three well-defined camps, there were already signs that within the foreseeable future the North Midland might very well emerge again as the senior member of the trio.

When finally completed in the summer of 1840, the North Midland Railway had two local summits. Of these, the more southerly was some 360 feet above sea level close to the southern end of Clay Cross Tunnel. North of that point the line fell steadily to Masborough before climbing to the second summit at Royston and then finally descending to Leeds. Against the engineer's estimate of £1,250,000 and the Parliamentary estimate of £1,500,000, the total cost came out at £3,000,000, whilst the works took three years to complete. Construction of the line had employed 10,000 men, the track being finally laid on sleepers for about two-thirds of the total distance, the remainder on stone blocks.

Due to the extraordinarily wet weather which persisted in South Yorkshire from the late summer of 1839, right through the winter, and into the following spring, the North Midland Railway was opened in two sections. Of these the first to be brought into use was the forty-mile stretch between Derby and Rotherham. Without any formal ceremony whatever the ordinary passenger services came into operation on Monday, May 11, 1840, exactly a week after the Midland Counties opened their extension across the River Trent to Loughborough and Leicester, and about eighteen months after the Sheffield & Rotherham commenced work. At Masborough, through carriages which had left Sheffield at 5.53 a.m. (i.e. twenty-three minutes late) were attached to the first North Midland train for Derby. Now, early that morning the rails had been very slippery and the traffic was unexpectedly heavy so that at Chesterfield, where George Stephenson and his guest George Hudson climbed aboard the inaugural train was sixty-five minutes late. For the long climb up to Clay Cross Tunnel, the train was assisted by a pilot as far as the north end of the tunnel. Shortly afterwards, however, when about three-quarters of the way through the tunnel, the engine stalled through lack of steam. Whilst a man was sent back on foot to recall the pilot loco., some of the more excitable passengers had already climbed down from the train and begun wandering about in the tunnel until, above the babel of voices, Geordie Stephenson's Northumbrian accent could be heard bemoaning the lack of organization and urging the jay-walkers to resume their places. The pilot engine duly returned to the rescue, and after the loss of fifteen minutes the journey was resumed, the train eventually rumbling into Derby at 9.30 a.m. instead of 7.45 a.m. as scheduled.

In the down direction matters went much more smoothly with the first train leaving at 9.15 a.m. It consisted of four first, and four second-class coaches hauled by two engines, the pilot being a Stephenson machine with Robert Stephenson on the footplate, the other being built by Mather, Dixon & Co. Despite the wet and boisterous weather, correct time seems to have been kept as far as Chesterfield and Masborough, but for some obscure reason Sheffield was only reached at 11.54 a.m., that is twenty-four minutes late. In the afternoon, the original up train left Derby at 1.22 and subsequently reached Sheffield at 4.13 p.m. In the evening, an informal dinner was given at the Angel Hotel, Chesterfield, to mark the day's events.

The opening of the final section between Leeds and Masborough about seven weeks later was a much more formal affair as it also marked the official opening of the entire North Midland Railway. On Wednesday, July 1st, a train of thirty-four coaches carrying about 500 guests left Hunslet Lane at 8.2 a.m., and it was such a heavy one that the train was double-headed by the Stephenson engines Nos. 60 and 61 (with Messrs Swanwick and Richardson on the footplates). Assistance was also provided in the rear by two other locos., one being built by Kitson and the other by Tayleur. Presumably, these two banked the train up to the local summit at Royston.

Between Leeds and Masborough the engines took in water at Methley, Oakenshaw, and Barnsley, and southward from Oakenshaw the North Midland train was followed by the York & North Midland inaugural train comprising four first-class carriages drawn by the locomotive *Hudson*. This train left York at 7.45 a.m. carrying a party headed by the former Lord Mayor of York and Mrs Hudson, the journey to Oakenshaw taking just an hour.

Masborough was reached at 10.24 a.m., where a number of coaches (9.15 ex Sheffield) were attached to the North Midland train which, at this stage, was well behind time. Chesterfield was reached at 11.25 a.m., that is fifty-five minutes late, and it was there that the train of four engines and about forty carriages was split into two sections consisting of two engines and thirty-four carriages, and six coaches also double-headed—precisely why isn't clear. Like the other principal stations, Chesterfield was gaily decorated with evergreens, and during the fifteen minute stop there passengers were entertained by the music provided by a 'capital band'.

This time there was no hitch at Clay Cross summit, and the train negotiated the mile-long tunnel in four minutes, emerging from the southern portal on the stroke of noon. A seven-minute stop was also made at South Wingfield (12.14 p.m.) where there were more evergreens and more music; two minutes were spent at Ambergate (12.33), four at Belper (12.45), and thereafter the train ran direct to Derby, making a triumphal entry there at 1.7 p.m. So, inclusive of stops, the 72¾ miles from Leeds had taken 5 hours 5 minutes, an average speed throughout of about 14 m.p.h. Very shortly after, *Hudson* arrived with the York & North Midland train amid renewed cheers from the crowds of guests and onlookers.

Just like the intermediate stations the terminus at Derby was also beautifully decorated with evergreens. The guests there were provided with 'a splendid déjeuné consisting of meats, jellies, confectionery, fruits, &c., &c., with wines of the very best quality', and there was also plenty of music to keep things going. This reception lasted about an hour and a quarter, during which time six more carriages were added to the inaugural train for carrying local guests from Derby forward to Leeds on the return run.

With the band playing the national anthem as it left, the train set out for Leeds at 2.30 p.m., and although many miles of the journey were run off at 30 m.p.h., it still managed to run late. By some freak it failed to stop at Oakenshaw, and so the guests from Wakefield found themselves taken on to Leeds, which was reached at 7.30 p.m., that is about an hour late. At eight o'clock a 'Cold Dinner' for 400 guests was given in the Music Hall, Albion Street, and 'an abundance of champagne was provided'. Special tables for the ladies were set out in the orchestra, and music was supplied by the band of the 4th Royal Irish Dragoon Guards.

Afterwards, trains carrying guests returning to York and Sheffield (and Oakenshaw, too, presumably) left Hunslet Lane at about 10.30 p.m., and despite the long day there must still have been plenty of high spirits left (including the bottled sort) because the guests from Derby did not roll home before 5 a.m. on Thursday, July 2nd. As the last of the revellers dispersed preparations were already well in hand for dealing with the 'Western Mail' train ex Birmingham. This left Derby at

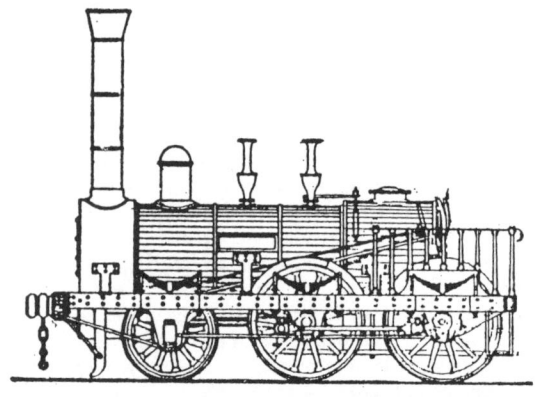

15. North Midland Railway goods engine by Stephenson

5.55 a.m., and after providing a connection for Sheffield, finally reached Leeds in 3 hours 20 minutes.

A contemporary press report, commenting on the opening of the first section of the North Midland Railway in May 1840, states that the company already possessed 'forty first-rate locomotive engines by R. Stephenson & Coy. of Newcastle-on-Tyne; Chas. Tayleur & Coy. of Manchester; Mather, Dixon & Coy. of Liverpool; Fenton, Murray & Jackson of Leeds; Shepherd, Todd & Coy. of Leeds; Thompson, Cole & Coy. of Bolton; Longridge & Coy. of Bedlington, near Newcastle; R. & W. Hawthorn of Newcastle. The engines are not distinguished by names, but by numbers . . .

'The carriages for passengers are of a chocolate colour. The firsts are lined with a light drab cloth and lace, and so well padded as to be extremely comfortable. On the pannels of the doors are painted the arms of Derby quartered with those of Leeds and London, and the words North Midland Railway. The second-class carriages are covered, but without cushions, and open at the sides. We believe it is intended to have third-class carriages altogether open, but not of the stand up kind.'

The North Midland Railway got off to a quite hectic start. Opened for traffic as far as Masborough on Monday, May 11th, Wednesday, May 13th, saw a pilot engine strike the rear of a train standing at Belper. Two horse boxes were destroyed, and the horses were thus walked back to Derby. On the same day, a dog was killed at Belper, and three sheep suffered a similar fate at Eckington on Thursday, the 14th. Some idea of the traffic using the line that July is revealed in a report stating that four trains totalling eighty-six coaches from the North Midland Railway reached Euston Station during the busiest day of the week, 'but the heaviest was cleared in ten minutes'.

NORTH MIDLAND RAILWAY.

OPENING OF THE LINE THROUGHOUT.

THE PUBLIC is respectfully informed, that on and after WEDNESDAY, the 1st of July next, the TRAINS of this COMPANY, in connection with those of the London and Birmingham, Birmingham and Derby, Midland Counties, York and North Midland, Hull and Selby, will START and ARRIVE according to the following Table, until further notice:—

DEPARTURE AND ARRIVAL OF TRAINS BETWEEN HULL, YORK, AND LONDON.

	DEPARTURE FROM				ARRIVAL AT
Hull.	York.	Leeds.	Sheffield.	Derby.	London.
—	6 15*	6 45	8 0	10 45	6 0†
—	7 30*	8 0	9 15	12 0	6 45†
7 30*	9 0	9 30	10 45	1 10	7 0†
11 0*	12 30	1 0	2 15	4 45	11 30†
—	—	4 30†	6 0	8 30†	Western Mail to Birmingham.
5 15†	6 45	7 15	8 30	11 0	5 30*

SUNDAY TRAINS.

—	7 45*	8 15	9 30	12 15	7 30†
—	—	1 30	2 45	5 0†	—
—	—	4 30	6 0	8 30	Western Mail to Birmingham.
5 15	6 45	7 15	8 30	11 0	5 30

DEPARTURE FROM			ARRIVAL AT		
London.	Derby.	Sheffield.	Leeds.	York.	Hull.
—	5 55	8 0	9 15	—	—	Western Mail from Birmingham.
—	9 30	11 45	1 0	—	—
6 0	12 45	2 45	4 0	4 30	6 0
9 30	3 30	5 30	6 45	7 15	8 45
1 0	8 0	10 15	11 30	12 0	—
8 30	3 15	5 15	6 30	7 0	8 30

SUNDAY TRAINS.

—	5 55	8 0	9 15	—	—	Western Mail from Birmingham.
8 0	3 0	5 15	6 30	7 0	—
—	7 0	9 15	10 30	—	—
8 30	3 15	5 15	6 30	7 0	8 30

	First Class.	Second Class.
	£. s. d.	£. s. d.
London to Hull	2 17 6	2 1 0
— York	2 14 6	1 17 6
— Leeds	2 10 6	1 15 0
— Sheffield	2 2 6	1 10 0
Derby to Hull	1 5 0	0 18 0
— York	1 2 0	0 14 6
— Leeds	0 18 0	0 12 0
— Sheffield	0 11 0	0 7 0

N.B.—Passengers may be booked through, or for any of the above places, at the several Railway Stations

☞ Half an hour is allowed for refreshment at Derby.

NOTE.— Those hours marked (*) signify Morning, and those thus (†) Afternoon.

16. North Midland Railway timetable, 1840

CHAPTER 3

GEORGE HUDSON LAYS SIEGE TO DERBY

The second half of 1840 produced a completely new phase in the historical background of the future Midland Railway. Although the three companies radiating from Derby were then in full-scale operation, their respective dividends were distinctly disappointing. The year 1841 produced no improvement, and in 1842 things went from bad to worse. By 1843 this thoroughly unsatisfactory state of affairs paved the way for the spectacular rise of George Hudson, the financial wizard of the age.

Born at Howsham, Yorkshire, in March 1800, George Hudson, the son of a farmer, received precious little education in the academic sense. At the age of fifteen he found himself apprenticed to a York draper, and his natural ability and industry were such that upon completion of his apprenticeship he was made a partner in the firm. Next, a legacy of £30,000 inherited at the age of twenty-seven enabled him to set up a joint-stock bank, from which development it was but a short step to participation in the earliest wave of railway promotion that swept through the country following the huge success so rapidly established by the Liverpool & Manchester Railway opened in 1830. Thereafter his progress was meteoric.

The distinct possibility of York developing into a highly important railway centre was quickly revealed during the early eighteen-thirties by the numerous projects for which routes were already being surveyed. Eighteen thirty-three produced a very ambitious scheme devised by Nicholas, Wilcox Cundy called the Grand Northern Railway. This was to link London with Bishop's Stortford, Cambridge, Lincoln, Gainsborough, and York—a distance of about 190 miles. Next, and acting on behalf of a Lincolnshire party, James Walker executed a survey during 1834 for a line between London and York as part of the wider Northern & Eastern scheme. This in its turn was followed early in 1835 by Gibbs' survey for quite a similar line from Whitechapel through Dunmow, Cambridge, Sleaford, and Lincoln to York. Meanwhile, the Railway Committee of York Corporation had been spending the better part of a year giving very careful consideration to various projects designed to connect their city with neighbouring centres. Prominent among these was a line fostered by Robert Baxter and Edmund Denison for linking York with Doncaster, then on southward across Lincolnshire toward Cambridge and London.

Fate now lent a hand. In the summer of 1835 it so happened that Hudson visited Whitby when, quite by chance, George Stephenson was also there on holiday. Seizing this golden opportunity of obtaining an introduction to the now famous engineer, Hudson obtained first-hand knowledge of Stephenson's immediate plans for linking Birmingham with Derby, and Derby with Sheffield and Leeds, and also of his longer term ambition to extend the line of communication to Newcastle and Berwick. It was in that last-mentioned scheme that George Hudson saw yet another glorious opportunity, and before the meeting drew to a close he had persuaded Stephenson to utilize York instead of Leeds as his base for extending the line of communication northward.

On returning to York, Hudson's boundless enthusiasm encountered little difficulty in persuading the Corporation's Railway Committee to adopt the plan for placing their city astride Stephenson's great chain of railway communication for linking London with the Scottish border. All that was necessary to achieve this end was the construction of quite a short line of barely twenty-five miles connecting their city with Stephenson's trunk line at Normanton, some ten or eleven miles south-east of Leeds, and as the new Stephenson line from Derby to Leeds had already been christened the North Midland Railway, the obvious choice of name for Hudson's connecting line must surely be the York & North Midland Railway.

Including the chain of Stephenson lines through Normanton and Derby, there were then four major schemes under active consideration for linking York with the capital, and all four appeared before Parliament in 1836. Once in London, the contesting parties wasted no time in organizing themselves into a series of groups judged most likely to inflict defeat upon their respective opponents. By far the most powerful of these groups was that of the London & Birmingham and its allies the Midland Counties and the four Stephenson lines—that is the Birmingham & Derby, the North Midland, the Sheffield & Rotherham, and the York & North Midland. George Stephenson's authoritative assertion that his group of lines would provide perfectly satisfactory communication between London, the Midlands, the West Riding, York, and the north-east undoubtedly carried a lot of weight at the Parliamentary stage. It was that very statement, together with the opposition raised by the jealous and hostile landowners which secured the downfall of Gibbs' Grand Northern Railway during the second reading of that Bill. The Northern & Eastern Bill was a little more successful in that it reached the Committee stage, but then it was reduced to a scheme for a relatively short line linking Stratford with Cambridge. With such potentially dangerous opposition safely removed, the four measures forming the Stephenson chain emerged triumphantly from the legislature during the summer of 1836.

The opening in July 1840 of what might very well be termed the Hudson-Stephenson route between Hull, York, Leeds, Sheffield, Derby, and Rugby brought the north of England into direct railway communication with the capital, and practically overnight the section of the London & Birmingham main line south of Rugby Junction became the most remunerative in the country. At their London terminus, Euston Square, the London & Birmingham company subsequently provided a new train shed to the west of their original station, and upon land most probably acquired at the instigation of George Carr Glyn in anticipation of such developments. Specially reserved for the Derbyshire and Yorkshire traffic, these platforms were known to generations of railwaymen as 'the York', although the general public probably knew them much better by their official designation of platforms 9 and 10. At the time of writing, the original platform awnings have been dismantled as part of the current reconstruction of Euston station.

Between Rugby and Derby matters were very different. From the word 'go' the Birmingham & Derby Junction Company found itself locked in something tantamount to mortal combat with its great rival the Midland Counties. In fact, when the former line was opened from Derby to Hampton Junction in 1839, George Stephenson had publicly stated that the two concerns were competitive. He also hoped they would come to terms, 'but if they did not the Birmingham & Derby was quite powerful enough to crush its rival'. Now that both lines were open for traffic, passengers travelling via the Birmingham & Derby route between London, Sheffield, Leeds, and York were to be charged £2 7s first-class, and £1 11s 6d second-class, that is 3s 6d less than the rates advertized by the North Midland Company in conjunction with the Midland Counties.

Against this, the Midland Counties line, via Leicester, was about ten miles shorter than the Birmingham & Derby route via Hampton-in-Arden. The latter company possessed a very capable manager, a young man of twenty-eight named James Allport, and to overcome the disadvantage of the longer route Allport produced a scale of differential fares. Whereas the ordinary fares between Derby and Hampton were 8s first-class, and 6s second-class, through passengers for London were to be charged 2s and 1s 6d, that is a mere quarter of the normal rate. There was one very serious snag inherent in this arrangement, though, due to the fact that for the section of the journey between Hampton and Rugby the London & Birmingham charged 5s and 3s 6d; so, even if the Birmingham & Derby carried their through London passengers absolutely free over the whole 38½ miles between Derby and Hampton, the Midland Counties could still levy 5s and 3s 6d for their 49½-mile run between Derby and Rugby.

The long-term effects of the prolonged struggle were ruinous to both concerns, and a halt was only called when, in the summer of 1843, the Midland Counties procured a Writ of Mandamus from the Queen's Bench Division compelling the Birmingham & Derby Company to abandon their differential scales between Derby and Hampton. This was virtually the beginning of the end, and to all intents and purposes cut-throat competition with the Midland Counties ceased. The Birmingham & Derby also opened the remaining section of its main line from Whitacre Junction to Lawley Street, Birmingham early in 1842, thereby saving the tolls formerly paid to the London & Birmingham for the use of their line between Hampton and Birmingham. Thus, the once famous Stonebridge Branch was now shorn of its former importance, and reduced to single track the following year.

North of Derby, the North Midland Railway also was in financial difficulties during the early eighteen-forties, despite the fact that it enjoyed a complete monopoly. By 1842 no less than twenty-six passenger and freight trains were running between Derby and Leeds daily, and there was additional mineral traffic derived from George Stephenson's collieries at Clay Cross.

Near Ambergate, a rich ironfield was already being exploited and the line from the kilns there was being carried southward into the midland counties and used for agricultural purposes, therby ousting the markedly inferior local product. The company's financial difficulties stemmed from two main sources— its excessive working expenses (forty-seven per cent of the gross receipts), and the serious debts already accumulating from premature expansion. At Normanton, for example, a new joint station had become necessary to accommodate the rapidly increasing traffic converging upon that junction from the North Midland, the York & North Midland, and the Manchester & Leeds systems. Far to the south, at Derby, Robert Stephenson was conducting a prolonged series of experiments designed to achieve much greater locomotive efficiency and economy; one successful result of his efforts was the appearance of his famous long boiler goods engine during the course of that year. Naturally enough, all these improvements had to be paid for, and to meet the heavy costs involved the North Midland board proposed raising £300,000 by shares. These were to be issued to existing shareholders at thirty-five per cent discount and in direct proportion to the number of shares already held, but if these new shares were not fully taken up, the balance would be offered to the public. Quite obviously, then, expansion was impoverishing the company. A rigid economy drive had already been instituted with the result that by August 1841 reductions both in staff and working expenses produced a saving of about £13,000, this sum being further increased by Robert Stephenson's generosity in proposing that his salary as Locomotive Superintendent to the Company be reduced from £1,000 to £600, and the considerable balance owing to him for locomotives supplied should be halved. In pursuance of their economy drive, the North Midland board vetoed the suggestion made by F. Swanwick (the Company's engineer) that a branch line should be built to tap the vast coalfields lying to the west of Swinton and Wath. However, in failing to recognize the potential importance of this type of traffic, the board left the door absolutely wide open, enabling the Great Northern to cash in to great advantage many years later.

The year 1842 was one of depression, and in the Midlands and the North there were widespread misery and industrial stagnation. As the early part of the year produced such unsatisfactory results, the North Midland shareholders began to clamour for the appointment of a committee of seven members 'to examine the position and future management of this Company'. Such demands presented George Hudson with yet another golden opportunity which he seized with both hands. As a large-scale holder of North Midland shares, he took a very active and prominent part in the work of the Committee of Enquiry which duly reported back to the shareholders in November 1842. In replying to the Committee's suggestions regarding further possible economies, William Newton, the North Midland chairman, stated that such policies would endanger public safety. At this, uproar broke out; Newton left the chair, and the meeting was closed. Subsequently, George Hudson and five other new directors were elected to succeed the outgoing six. Even so, the North Midland company was in such financial straits that in the following spring (1843) thirty first and thirty second-class carriages were advertised for sale, being described as 'surplus to requirements'.

Before this critically dangerous stage was encountered, George Hudson had already perceived that the key to the salvation of all three companies converging upon Derby lay in the strength and economies to be derived from complete integration by amalgamation. Therefore, during the summer of 1843 he renewed his proposals for a three-way merger, and due to the exhausted condition of both the Birmingham & Derby Junction and the Midland Counties concerns his earlier suggestions now penetrated with much greater effect, for the Midland Counties Railway amalgamation was proposed by John Ellis on September 21st, and seconded by William Hannay. Yet, some very hard bargaining over terms was still necessary before the Birmingham & Derby Junction shareholders voted their concurrence. By the end of the year, Hudson and his party triumphed to the extent of seeing their 'Grand Midland Amalgamation Bill' deposited in the House in readiness for the Parliamentary session of 1844, but with success now seemingly so close at hand, Hudson could clearly be heard warning his supporters against complacency and the challenges which would surely appear in the new year.

Many other factors were also influencing the destiny of the embryonic Midland Railway. During the late summer of 1843, the London money market underwent a number of extremely important changes which rapidly produced very far-reaching effects upon the British railway system as a whole. At that time, the slump of the early 'forties was fast receding, the gold bullion reserve kept at the Bank of England had trebled, the Bank Rate was two and a half per cent and Consols stood well above par. Also, recent failures in some South American markets had released a tremendous amount of capital which was promptly diverted into the London Market in search of suitable outlets. In such circumstances, City circles began to give increasingly serious consideration to railway promotion as a solution to their problems, a lead which met with a simply astounding response from the investing public. Almost overnight a wave of speculation in railway stocks and shares appeared, mounting higher and higher. There now began a fantastic scramble for railway shares of any description—and with the 'wide boys' at work, some of the schemes foisted on to the more gullible sections of the public simply beggared description. This was the birth of the fantastic 'Railway Mania'.

Some idea of the situation can be gained from the fact that at the beginning of 1844 Parliament found itself confronted by applications for the presentation of no less than sixty-six Bills seeking sanction for the construction of 900 miles of new lines. In a good many cases the new lines threatened the interests of the established companies, which promptly retaliated by projecting a very large number of branch lines having the dual functions of creaming off the traffic potential from the disputed districts as well as serving as feeders to the existing systems. With the arrival of spring, Lincolnshire became the arena for half-a-dozen such schemes. It was at Hudson's instigation that, in March 1844, the North Midland Board projected a line from their main line at Swinton to run across country via Doncaster and Gainsborough to Lincoln, and there to link up with the Nottingham, Newark & Lincoln branch of the Midland Counties Railway. Robert Stephenson was to be the engineer for each of these schemes which were jointly advertised as the Lincolnshire Junction Railway. By such means Lincoln was to be linked with George Stephenson's trunk route in a manner providing through communication with the West Riding, Nottingham, Derby, Birmingham, Leicester, and London.

Within a few weeks George Hudson's personal prestige received yet another tremendous boost, when on May 10th his Great Midland Amalgamation Bill received Royal Assent. Henceforth, the Midland Railway was a *fait accompli*. Within little more than a year the frontiers of Hudson's railway 'empire' had been most skilfully pushed southward by well over a hundred miles, firstly from Normanton to Derby, then southwestward to Birmingham and southward to Rugby Junction, at which centres they now rested cheek-by-jowl with the frontiers of George Carr Glyn's domains as represented by the trunk line of the London & Birmingham Company. Not only was Derby the obvious choice for the headquarters of the new Midland Railway Company, it also provided Hudson with a southern springboard for launching his next major offensive.

17. Clay Cross, North Midland Railway, in the eighteen forties

CHAPTER 4

HUDSON'S DERBY EMPIRE

Amid scenes of tremendous jubilation, the directors of the newly sanctioned Midland Railway Company held their first formal meeting on Friday, May 24, 1844. This supremely important function was held in the station offices at Derby, and very prominent among those assembled upon such an auspicious occasion were the stalwarts who had contributed so much to the success of George Hudson's campaign—Beale, Ellis, Holdsworth, Hutchinson, Lewis, Murgatroyd, Newton, Peyton, Taylor, and Waddingham. In just this very way, then, the new concern well and truly represented the old constituent companies. With the election of a Chairman the first item on the agenda, the name of George Hudson was immediately proposed and seconded by Taylor and Holdsworth, respectively; and without further ado it was 'unanimously resolved that Mr Hudson be the Chairman of this Board'. Secondly, in response to the nominations of Beale and Waddingham, John Ellis was elected Deputy Chairman. Thirdly, both Chairman and Deputy Chairman were declared to be ex-officio members of all committees.

From the very first moment of its existence, the Company's entire eastern flank was menaced by highly competitive projects, the most serious of which was Edmund Denison's scheme launched on May 3rd for providing a 'direct line' between London and York. Constantly alert to this threat, Hudson swung straight into action. The very next day (May 25th) he headed a Midland delegation to Euston Square for immediate discussions with a similar body representing the London & Birmingham Company. There, it was promptly agreed that as from Monday next (May 27th) passengers for Derby and the North would be allowed to make through bookings by the 6.30 a.m. train from Euston Square. Secondly, every London & Birmingham down train would convey Midland carriages between Euston Square and Rugby, where they were to be passed by the siding from the down Birmingham platform to the Midland down line. Thirdly, two Midland composite carriages were to be conveyed by the 11 a.m. and the 5 p.m. trains from London, one for Leicester and Derby, the other for Nottingham. Hudson's fourth point that the Midland Board considered that they were paying a disproportionate share of the expenses incurred by the two companies at Rugby Station, was parried for the moment by Glyn's decision to refer this question to the next full meeting of the Birmingham Board. Lastly, as the London & Birmingham Company then had the very quaint habit of making differential charges in respect of both up and down traffic on the basis of a fixed charge for tolls, and a fluctuating charge for haulage, Hudson suggested a flat rate for both tolls and haulage, but this was similarly referred by Glyn for consideration by the full board.

In those early days of Hudson's chairmanship, relations between Derby and Euston Square were often most cordial, a point which Hudson exploited to the full. In the summer of 1844 a Midland committee comprising Messrs Hudson, Ellis, Beale, and Waddingham were charged with the task of ascertaining whether in view of the competitive schemes now appearing, the London & Birmingham would be prepared to join the Midland in an alliance both defensive and offensive in character. This suggestion was most favourably received, and the joint policy proved amply justified with the appearance on June 11th of the new London & York prospectus.

The general public had scarcely digested that announcement when exactly a week later yet a new railway feat hit the headlines. The completion before schedule of a vital part of the Newcastle & Darlington Junction line enabled a special train, with George Stephenson among the passengers, to leave Euston Square for the North at 5.3 a.m. on June 18, 1844. At Rugby Junction it turned on to Hudson's 'East Coast Route', and travelling via Leicester, Derby, Normanton, and York, it ran right through to Gateshead, arriving there at 2.35 p.m., having covered the 303 miles in 9 hours 32 minutes. Even though these times obviously included stops for the changing of engines (presumably at Rugby, Derby, Normanton, and York) an average of almost 32 m.p.h. for the entire journey then constituted an amazing and absolutely unparallelled feat.

There were plenty of high jinks in Gateshead that day, and at the celebration dinner given later in Newcastle, across the River Tyne, George Hudson stated that it was now only a matter of a few years before bridges could be thrown across both the Tyne and the Tweed, thereby enabling railway communication to be extended right up to the border at Berwick. This forecast proved accurate enough, although by the time the through route was brought into effective operation the 'Railway King' had been toppled from his throne and compelled to 'abdicate'; but for the moment, Hudson's position seemed impregnable, and he positively revelled in both his supreme authority and the enthusiastic, almost hysterical, applause which greeted every public appearance he made.

18. George Hudson

Within two months of the initial meeting of the directors, the first general meeting of shareholders of the new Midland Railway Company was held at Derby on Tuesday, July 16, 1844. This function was so well attended that it had to be held in the large engine house opposite Derby station. It was a thoroughly lively affair with George Hudson presiding in his capacity of Chairman of the Board of Directors. He was in exceptionally good form as he addressed the densely packed gathering and he stated that the accounts of the three constituent companies had been kept separated down to June 30th, just as though no merger had occurred, and the profits accruing from that period would be distributed on a corresponding basis. Therefore, the final dividends for the three constituent companies would be as follows:

North Midland   £100 shares   £2 2s 0d
Midland Counties   £100 shares   £2 2s 6d
Birmingham & Derby Junction original shares £1 6s 6d

Compared with the corresponding period for last year, outgoings had decreased by £9,000, total receipts had increased by £21,000, and excluding the last balance in hand net profits had risen by £33,000. Total receipts for the now consolidated line amounted to rather more than £10,000 per week. Hudson also hinted broadly at the severity of the competition which shareholders must expect to face in the near future, and expressed his firm conviction that all such challenges must be, and indeed would be, successfully opposed, these remarks being greeted with a tumultuous burst of applause from his wildly enthusiastic audience.

Having got Midland policy off to such a lively start, Hudson promptly tackled the developing threat to his supremacy by urging the execution of some technical improvements aimed at accelerating Midland main line through services to and from the North. Thus, in September 1844 the Midland board sanctioned the construction of the avoiding curve immediately north of Derby station. Now, a few miles east of Derby the local pit owners were also reviving their earlier project for a line down the Erewash Valley, their original line having been sacrificed by the Liverpool Party when ensuring the success of the Midland Counties Bill in 1836. In its latest form the Erewash Valley scheme presented two major possibilities. Firstly, it might well fall into hostile hands; secondly, if it were acquired by the Midland Railway, the line could be extended northward along the valley to join the existing Midland main line near Clay Cross, thus providing an even more effective cut-off for fast traffic between London and the north. Consequently, the report made by Mr Swanwick just before Christmas 1844 caused the Midland board to arrange the lease of the Erewash Valley scheme as from the following February, an Act being subsequently granted by Parliament on July 4, 1845. By this time, though, there were many schemes now threatening the security of the southern half of Hudson's 'empire', and not only had he already pitched the Midland Railway into the heart of the fray, he was even counter-attacking with proposals for an elaborate series of branch lines designed to cut the ground from beneath his competitors' feet.

Of all the competitive schemes which flowered during the 'Railway Mania', none menaced Hudson's personal ambitions more seriously than the London & York, which threatened to occupy the long strip of territory to the east of Hudson's trunk lines. Following the appearance of the London & York's advertisement in *The Times* on August 22, 1844, Locke armed himself with the plans prepared earlier by Gibbs and Walker and promptly began the final survey of what soon became the *new East Coast Route*, as we know it today. From Locke's viewpoint, the major problem was whether the line should follow Walker's route through the Fens, or else pursue Gibbs' more westerly track through the towns of Doncaster, Gainsborough and Peterborough. Locke subsequently reported in favour of the latter, generally speaking, but, in September 1844, he, too, suddenly relinquished his post, being succeeded three days later by William Cubitt, who immediately pressed forward with the arrangements for the presentation of the London & York Bill to Parliament during the 1845 session. Furthermore, the supplementary scheme for linking the West Riding to the main line was crystallized. It now became apparent that the intention was to ship railway trucks laden with South Yorkshire coal down the Dun Navigation as far as Doncaster, where they would be transferred direct to the railway without disturbing the load. At a rate of ¾d per ton per mile, it was claimed that coal from both Yorkshire and County Durham would be marketed at King's Cross at 21s per ton, compared with the prevailing price of 29s to 30s. Incidentally, the Midland board had already suggested a ¾d rate to the London & Birmingham people who had rejected the idea as 'unprofitable'.

Hudson promptly countered this threat to his interests by calling a Special General Meeting of Midland shareholders at Derby on October 8th. Consideration centred upon the proposed appeal to be presented to Parliament during the session of 1845 for the Midland Company, or some other companies connected with them, to construct the following lines:
(1) A railway from the Midland Railway at Nottingham to Newark and Lincoln.
(2) A railway from the Midland Railway at Swinton by Doncaster, Bawtry, and Gainsborough to Lincoln, thence passing near Boston, Spalding, and Wisbech to join the Eastern Counties railway at March.
(3) A railway from the Midland Railway at Syston, by way of Oakham and Stamford to Peterborough.
(4) To consider the raising of capital for the above-mentioned schemes, and also the amalgamation of the Sheffield & Rotherham Railway with the Midland Railway.
Of course, the first two of these countermeasures were revivals of schemes originally proposed by the boards of the Midland Counties and the North Midland Companies, respectively, but if any further proof of Hudson's intentions were still needed it was provided by the resolution adopted at the meeting of Midland directors on November 5th, this being to the effect that the projected line from Cambridge to Lincoln appeared to supercede the necessity of the Midland Railway undertaking a line in that direction. It was also resolved that the Midland should also support the Cambridge & Lincoln Company, and that Derby should adhere to the line originally projected, through Lincolnshire, between Lincoln and March. Hudson's schemes also included a branch leaving the Midland extension in the vicinity of Lincoln and running across country to join the former York & North Midland main line at South Milford.

Because of the tremendous number of Bills (224) deposited for the 1845 Parliamentary Session, those which survived Standing Orders were organized in groups corresponding to the number of committees. Under this system George Hudson's schemes, and those of his rivals, were arranged as follows:

Group T: Syston & Peterborough.
  U: Great Grimsby & Sheffield Junction.
  V: Nottingham, Newark & Lincoln.
  W: Wakefield, Pontefract & Goole.
  X: London & York, Direct Northern, Cambridge & Lincoln, Sheffield & Lincoln, Eastern Counties Extension, M.R. Extension Swinton to March, Y.&N.M.R. Extension.

In groups 'T' and 'V' both the Syston & Peterborough and the Nottingham, Newark & Lincoln were successful, each measure receiving Royal Assent on June 30, 1845; but with group 'X' it was a very different story. Perhaps for the first time Hudson fully comprehended the determination of both the City people and influential Parliamentary circles to secure a 'direct line' between London and York. This plan became more obvious when twenty-five days were spent in the hearing of the case for the London & York, thereby leaving little time for hearing the others. Despite these tactics, George Hudson derived considerable benefit from the hearing of the Cambridge & Lincoln, before that scheme was reduced to a project after taking up nineteen precious days. The York, Newcastle & Berwick Bill representing the northern arm of Hudson's 'empire', was also successful, but only after a very fierce struggle. On June 30th, Mr Hilyard, Q.C., called for a summary rejection of the Lincoln & York Bill alleging violation of, and non-compliance with Parliamentary Standing Orders. Notwithstanding these claims, the ferocious struggle concluded with the preamble of the London & York Bill found proven by the Commons on July 23, 1845. With the Direct Northern also long since disposed of by the 'Group X' committee, Hudson now found himself outclassed by very much more powerful interests, and the Eastern Counties, the Midland, and the York & North Midland schemes had not yet been heard. Thus, a mere two days after the London & York triumph, he stated that on this basis an appeal would be made to the House of Commons against the verdict of the 'Group X' committee; this announcement was greeted by a 'hurricane of applause' from his audience at Derby. On the following day, Mr Charles Austin, Q.C., presented written protests on behalf of the three companies, but the committee declined to receive the protests and suggested they should be presented to the full House.

Not to be outdone, George Hudson now concentrated upon gaining control of a line that would give him direct access to the metropolis and would render the London & York scheme completely superfluous, as well as attacking it from either side should it ultimately prove successful. To this end he procured the chairmanship of the Eastern Counties on October 13th; then, at a densely packed shareholders' meeting on October 30th, the Shoreditch directors were authorized to approach Parliament during the following session (1846) with a Bill aimed at promoting an extension of the Eastern Counties northward from Cambridge through Lincoln and Doncaster to a junction with both the Leeds & Selby and the York & North Midland lines at South Milford. To lend additional weight to this scheme, Hudson stated that the Cambridge & Lincoln Party, whose scheme had been reduced to a project by the 'Group X' committee, were now prepared to exchange their own scrip for Eastern Counties Extension Stock on the basis of £20 worth of that stock for £50 worth of the London & York shares to which they had previously subscribed. Hudson's final point was that within a year or two the Eastern Counties would become a ten per cent line. At this, the more easily impressed of the Eastern Counties shareholders 'went mad with joy'. However, the London & York Party counter-attacked the same day by proposing the re-introduction into the House of their scheme for a branch to Wakefield, plus an extension to Leeds. The intention was unmistakably clear, as Hudson saw.

Yet another difficulty overshadowed Hudson's supremacy when the 'Railway Mania' reached its climax in October 1845. By this time Parliament had sanctioned no fewer than 1,428 railway schemes backed by capital estimated at £700,000,000. The following month, November, suddenly produced a reaction and there began a frantic rush to unload scrip, but despite the confusion the London & York Party stayed firm. Hudson kept a cool head, too, and November 19th brought an important meeting at Cambridge to review the question of railway communication in relation to the university towns. Allegedly on behalf of the Eastern Counties Company, George Hudson made

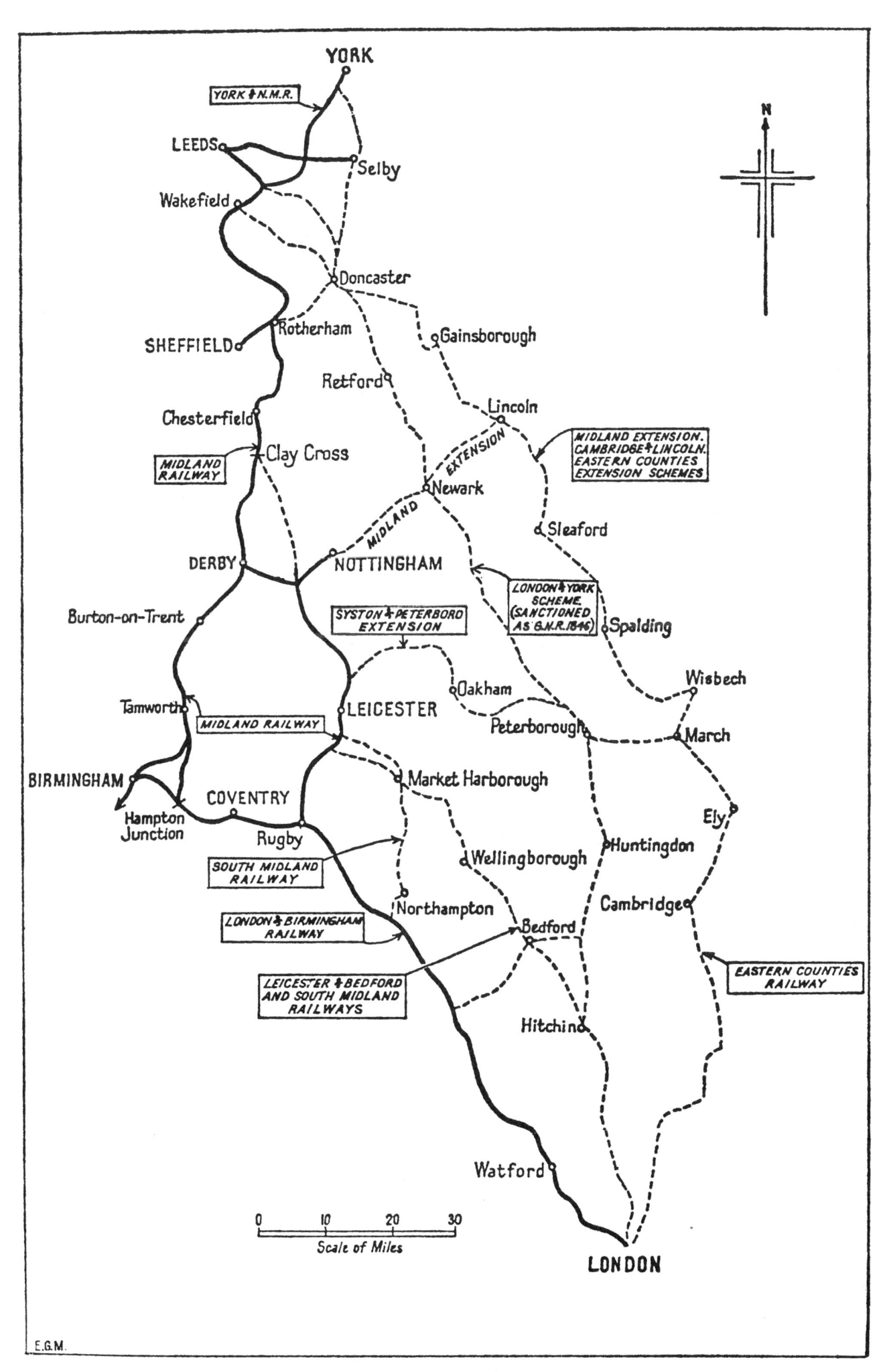

19. George Hudson versus the London and York party, 1845-6

a personal appearance and insisted that Cambridge should be placed upon a main route to the North and, with the approval of the meeting, recommended a merger of the Eastern Counties (of which he happened to be Chairman, of course) and the London & York. To further this scheme, on December 3rd he offered amalgamation and the allotment of £2,000,000 worth of Eastern Counties Extension Stock to the London & York scripholders, but his proposals were rejected a fortnight later on December 16th. On December 18th, however, the Cambridge & Lincoln party acquiesed and were swept into the Hudson net. This now left the Direct Northern and the London & York parties independent of Hudson's activities. Subsequently they also amalgamated, although retaining the title London & York, and their Bill eventually received Royal Assent under the title of 'Great Northern Railway'.

In his attempts to overthrow the London & York party, Hudson is often quoted as having employed 'twelve counsel power at a daily cost to the Midland exchequer of £3,000'. It was actually five counsel power whose joint efforts unearthed evidence suggesting that either non-existent or otherwise untraceable people had 'signed' for at least £29,000 worth of London & York shares. A further £445,000 worth had been signed for by men of virtually no means whatever, who had been paid small sums to lend their names to the 'York scheme'. Upon this 'revelation' the House of Lords ordered an investigation to be made, but despite this the London & York Bill was forced through the House and received Royal Assent on June 26, 1846. Such a development virtually halved George Hudson's 'empire' since the southern part of his East Coast Route, that is from Rugby Junction to York, was rendered virtually redundant. It was now but a matter of time before the 'Railway Napoleon' found himself enmeshed in a self-created web of conflicting interests from which escape would surely prove impossible.

The fantastic speculative boom suddenly collapsed at the end of 1845, an important part in the pricking of the bubble being played by *The Times*, which also published a special supplement listing the railway schemes then on hand. There were some 620 new projects totalling £563,000,000, a further 643 companies still needed to register their prospectuses, whilst Bills representing £11,000,000 worth of schemes had already been deposited in readiness for the Parliamentary Session of 1846. Following the initiative of Lord Dalhousie (then President of the Board of Trade), and Sir Robert Peel in the House of Commons, the Commons' committee recommended that the various schemes should be grouped by a Classification Committee, and this body would then decide which of the new alliances clashed with Bills still outstanding from the Session of 1845. Then followed a Government announcement that the Board of Trade offices would be closed and no further plans accepted after the dead line of noon on November 30, 1845. This news precipitated a frantic rush of almost unbelievable proportions, the plans being conveyed by anything on wheels, and many a dark and dirty deed was perpetrated by the representatives of the rival factions. Then, as if that were not enough, the Press celebrated New Year's Day 1846 with a sly reference to the 'recent mania'. Thousands were completely ruined, and, as so often happens in such instances, the middle classes took the brunt of the blow—some took their lives. Despite the developments of 1845, 1846 proved to be an equally hectic year, and for those who survived the crash the struggle continued with unabated fury.

Of the many elaborate countermeasures which Hudson took against the London & York party, his Syston & Peterborough branch was one with a most lively history. In the autumn of 1844 it was intended that part of the route should cut through part of Stapleford Park, Lord Harborough's estate near Saxby. Now, it happened that the noble lord enjoyed a considerable interest in the Oakham Canal opened at the height of the Napoleonic Wars, and fearing this must inevitably suffer with the completion of the new line he made it clear that the railway people would be most unwelcome and would be refused permission to conduct any surveying operations upon his land.

Trouble first appeared on November 13, 1844, when a party of seven surveyors ignored this warning and attempted to approach their objective from the canal bank. They were instantly stopped by one of Lord Harborough's retainers, whereupon a surveyor's assistant produced a pistol and threatened to shoot. His bluff was called immediately, and the party was promptly 'captured' and taken by cart to the local magistrate's house at Cold Overton Hall, where upon arrival surveyors and instruments were tipped out in a most unceremonious manner. Some of the 'prisoners' are even supposed to have been lodged in Leicester gaol.

The next move in Lord Harborough's private war was launched at 9 a.m. on November 14th. About forty of the estate employees assembled at Saxby Bridge ready to 'welcome' the railway people who drove out by chaises from Oakham and Melton. A lengthy parley about procedure was held on the bridge itself between the Midland Company's solicitors, Lord Harborough's steward and solicitor, and the Clerk of the Oakham Canal. Midland reinforcements, comprising a gang of navvies and several prizefighters from Nottingham, now arrived, but Lord Harborough's employees fenced off the path by drawing up a line of heavy drays and carts close to the edge of the canal.

The engagement opened when the surveyors tried to force the barrier, but they were driven off. Both sides received further reinforcements, and then about half a dozen of the local constabulary appeared and declared their intention of arresting the first man to commit an assault. At this, both sides laid down their shillelaghs and began pushing each other instead, Lord Harborough's men making a most successful stand on the Melton side of the bridge.

The whole of these proceedings attracted quite a few spectators, who roared with laughter at the farcical situation presented by the opposing parties hurtling over each other's heads, crashing through the hedge into the ditch beyond, which soon became filled. During this rumpus the surveyors managed to snatch their measurements, but Lord Harborough's men grabbed the chain, which was snapped in several places. Eventually, the railway party called for a truce, and it was agreed that actions should be brought against several men of each party, the cases being heard by the magistrates at Melton Petty Sessions on November 19th.

Despite the truce, the surveyors made a fresh bid at 7 a.m. on November 16th. While about a dozen men attempted to force their way through the barrier, ten times that number climbed the railings bordering the estate and began taking measurements, a relatively easy task since the defenders were widely scattered over the length and breadth of an 800-acre park. Eventually, Lord Harborough's men confronted the intruders, and thus began a 'battle', in which the local lock-keeper knocked his adversaries 'head over heels' at every blow. So great was the din that it could be heard in villages a good couple of miles away. Later, at Melton, three navvies were bound over for three months, and others received similar treatment at Stamford. The main cases subsequently came up at the Leicester Assizes on March 26, 1845, the defendants being fined 1s each and imprisoned for three months in Ward No. 1, which would cause minimum personal hardship.

Originally, it had been intended that the Syston & Peterborough line should run beneath the Cuckoo Plantation, Stapleford Park, but after the works had begun part of the tunnel caved in, and some sixty trees were destroyed. The cause of this tragedy was the determined attempt to prevent the railway men from taking the correct measurements in the first instance. Such obstinacy also resulted in two other commotions during November 1845 and, in the case brought by the Midland Company against Lord Harborough, more than one hundred of his staff were held at Nottingham in July 1846. After a trial lasting five hours, the jury returned a verdict of 'not guilty'.

Notwithstanding the earlier opposition, the Syston & Peterborough Bill was eventually sanctioned on June 30, 1845. Meanwhile, an agreement had already been reached, on April 19th, for the Midland Railway Company to purchase the Oakham Canal, for which purpose an Act was subsequently granted on July 27, 1846. This occurred about a month after the company had obtained yet another Act for the diversion of the Syston & Peterborough line at Saxby (June 18, 1846) at an estimated cost of £85,000. The first section of this new line, that is between Syston and Melton Mowbray, was opened on September 1, 1846. Next followed the outermost section between Stamford and Peterborough, on October 2nd, this being temporarily worked by Hudson's locomotives from his Eastern Counties line. Finally, the centre section between Melton and Stamford was brought into use for coal trains on March 20, 1848, and for passengers on May 1st. The Syston & Peterborough's 'twin' extension between Nottingham and Lincoln had previously been opened as early as August 3, 1846, but in this instance the inaugural celebrations were marred by a man being killed by the bursting of one of the cannons. Furthermore, at Gonalstone Crossing 'the road subsided, and an engine was upset in the ditch and the fireman killed'.

20. Enlarged Nottingham station (Midland Railway), 1848

21. The Midland terminus at Lincoln, 1846

Under George Hudson's inspired direction the Midland system was expanding in all directions. Nothing was left to chance, and in 1846 even the tiny Leicester & Swannington line was absorbed. As recently as 1845 'King' Hudson's position at Derby and Leicester had seemed impregnable, but by 1846 extremely powerful interests were preparing to invade his empire, as we shall now see.

In his self-appointed crusade against the London & York party, George Hudson had found himself embroiled in yet another hectic struggle which had broken out in the vicinity of Leicester in the summer of 1845. On July 25th, two days after the Commons had expressed its approval of the London & York Bill, a meeting of the Midland board held at Derby had been 'attended' by a deputation from each of the two schemes announced in the *Railway Times* on May 24th.

Of these, the Leicester & Bedford was nominally independent and professed to link two huge rival undertakings (the Midland, and the London & York), but the provisional committee included men with very strong leanings toward the latter. The chairman was William Astell, M.P. for Bedfordshire; the chief engineer was William Cubitt, F.R.S.; and the assistant engineers were Joseph Cubitt and Joseph Gibbs. Their line was to commence at Leicester, to proceed by or near Market Harborough, Rothwell, Kettering and Wellingborough to Bedford, and it was 'to supply the wants of a very rich and thickly populated district of country lying between Leicester and Bedford, and to afford a much shorter and direct communication between the first-mentioned place and London'. The amount of capital required was fixed at £1,000,000 in 50,000 shares of £20 each, a deposit of 25s being payable on each share.

The South Midland scheme, alternatively known as the Northampton & Leicester Railway, was the joint product of the Midland Railway Company on one hand and purely local interests on the other. It was to begin at either a junction with the London & Birmingham main line between Roade and Blisworth, or at the Northampton station of the branch to Peterborough, 'and proceed by Market Harborough to the Midland Railway near the town of Leicester with a short branch to the Leicester & Swannington Railway, effecting a saving of nearly seven miles between London and Nottingham, Derby, Sheffield, Leeds and the North—and will considerably lessen the distance London to York enabling existing companies more successfully to compete for that traffic which must otherwise be diverted to the eastern lines'. The South Midland route, the statement continued, would avoid the London & Birmingham tunnels at Kilsby and Weedon, as well as the long delays at Rugby Junction (often three hours in the early part of 1844), which delays would tend to increase with traffic derived from the Trent Valley line and the branch from Oxford. Between Leicester and London the South Midland route would be three miles shorter than the Leicester & Bedford; furthermore, it would justify the carriage of much larger quantities of coal from Clay Cross to London, a service which had begun via Rugby a little earlier that year. The Superintending Engineer for the South Midland scheme would be Robert Stephenson, and the route would be surveyed by Charles Liddell, who was similarly employed in connection with the new Syston & Peterborough line.

In the middle of August 1845 an arrangement was reached between the Midland and the South Midland companies whereby the latter scheme was modified to include an extension either from or near Market Harborough to Bedford; the capital was to be divided on the following basis:

To the South Midland Railway 45,000 shares of
£20 each   £900,000
To the Midland Railway Company 40,000 shares
of £20 each   £800,000
                                    Total £1,700,000

Each party was to contribute 2,500 shares for the benefit of the landowners between Market Harborough and Bedford. Twelve directors were to be nominated on the basis of six by each company, the six nominated by the Midland Railway being Messrs Hudson, Ellis, Barwell, Hutchinson, Waddingham, and Sir Oswald Moseley.

Upon the completion of complementary negotiations, John Ellis reported to Derby that the Directors of the London & Birmingham company desired to provide every facility for improving their communication with the Midland Railway—that they intended to provide separate booking offices and departure platforms at Euston Station—and had expressed their willingness to convey such further trains as might be desired between London and Rugby independently of the London & Birmingham trains. Such, then, was the reaction of the Derby/Euston Square alliance in face of the pressure already being exerted by the London & York party.

The original Leicester & Bedford scheme foundered in the late autumn of 1845 with the collapse of the Railway Mania, but it was revived and provisionally re-registered in the spring of 1846, by which time the London & York Bill was being presented to the Lords. The new Leicester & Bedford chairman was Wynn Ellis, M.P. for Leicester, although William Astell was still a member of the committee of management. This time the Leicester & Bedford Bill passed the Commons (May 1846), whereas the South Midland Bill was rejected as a direct result of Robert Stephenson's *faux pas* in stating that his party intended to hand over their London traffic to the London & Birmingham at Bedford for completion of the run to the capital by way of Bletchley. At that same time, South Midland capital stood at £2,000,000, of which the Midland company had subscribed some £600,000, and the enlarged scheme then embraced lines to Northampton, Bedford, and Huntingdon.

On July 13th a public meeting held by the Leicester & Bedford party was addressed by Mr Linsell of Bedford, who stated their intention to challenge the Midland monopoly of the Leicester traffic, to charge fares barely half the statutory maximum set out in the Midland Act, and to obviate the notorious delays at Rugby. They also intended to link up with the Leicester & Swannington line and thereby establish a cheap outlet for Leicestershire coal. Already, the Midland was trying to frustrate this plan and even contemplated charging a statutory six-mile rate for an actual distance of one mile wherein coal from the Leicester & Swannington would cross the Midland system. Next, the South Midland people changed their parliamentary tactics most successfully in stating that they had always really intended extending their line to a junction with the newly sanctioned Great Northern line at Hitchin, thereby providing a greatly improved route between Leicester and London. Thus, in August 1846 the Lords rejected the Leicester & Bedford Bill, but as that party had been proposing to commence their works the Great Northern now saw its opportunity to offer to provide one half of the necessary capital for a renewed application to Parliament in 1847.

George Hudson's position at Leicester was undoubtedly weakened by the ability of his arch enemy, the newly sanctioned Great Northern Railway, to drive hard into the Midland flank by supporting the Leicester & Bedford. Then, on July 25th, Hudson's proposal to purchase the South Midland scheme for £110,000 was flatly rejected by 'a subscriber writing from London'. In a bid to regain the initiative, a deputation from the Midland Board held a meeting in the Swan Hotel, Bedford, on September 4th, at which they tried to smooth over the gaffe arising from Robert Stephenson's evidence of their intention for the South Midland line to terminate at Bedford instead of continuing to Hitchin. However, following the revival of that very point by Mr Whitbread, a very influential landowner who had previously supported the Leicester & Bedford project, the meeting degenerated into a slanging match and ended in chaos. But a further meeting was held at Market Harborough only a month later, and there George Hudson successfully convinced the local folk that his latest plan to purchase the Leicester & Bedford Company and build the South Midland line was in everyone's best interests.

Whatever the views of the local inhabitants, the Leicester & Bedford party returned to the fray in the autumn of 1846 by dissolving their original company and re-registering their scheme under the new name of Leicester & Bedford Company (1846) with virtually the same objects of the earlier concern, plus an extension from Bedford to Hitchin to join the Great Northern line. Shares in the Leicester & Bedford were reorganized at 150,000 of £10 each, of which 75,000 were to be taken up by the Great Northern company, which would advance ten per cent of the nominal value and then subscribe the deeds for £750,000 Scrip holders in the 1845 scheme would be able to elect either one new £10 share in lieu of the old £20 shares, or a return of 6s on each of those 1845 shares, that sum being the proportionate amount remaining after the payment of the expenses of the old 1845 company.

George Hudson's next move came in October 1846, when he invited both Captain Laws of the Great Northern company and Mr Whitbread (the principal representative of local interests) to Derby for a conference. There it was resolved that the South Midland scheme should be withdrawn and the Midland company should purchase the Leicester & Bedford concern, the shareholders therein receiving 22s worth of Midland stock for each of their L. & B. shares. Thereafter, the Midland company should pay all expenses and then build the line within two years —on the clear understanding that the Great Northern should offer no opposition in Parliament.

Hudson's Leicester & Hitchin Bill was thus presented to the House on Monday, May 10, 1847, evidence being heard by Group 17 of the Commons committee. This hearing was opened by Mr Talbot, Q.C., who examined the Midland company's first witness, Mr William Whitbread, owner of 15,000 acres in Bedfordshire. Witness began by explaining that 26,000 tons of garden produce left the county annually, much of it being sent by road to London. Other produce was sent twenty miles by road to Wolverton, then by the London & North Western Railway to the cotton and woollen areas of the North. Thus, a direct line to Leicester would greatly improve the whole situation, and also improve the delivery of coal to the district.

A later witness was Charles Liddell, who had taken an active part in making the surveys for the Syston & Peterborough line. Liddell described himself as an assistant to Robert Stephenson, and went on to explain how this year's line, although closely similar to last year's scheme, would effect a junction with the Great Northern Railway at Hitchin instead of Bedford, the total distance from Leicester to Hitchin being 62 miles 7 furlongs, or 108 miles 4 furlongs 9 chains, inclusive of the branches. The line would include four tunnels, namely at Wellingborough (693 yards), Southill (650 yards), Oxenden (154 yards), and Kilmarsh (385 yards)—'the width of them all is the same, 25 feet. The steepest gradient upon the main line is 1 in 100'.

In sanctioning the Leicester & Hitchin line on July 9, 1847 (11 & 12 Vict., cxxxv), the legislature required Midland trains to terminate at Hitchin; they were not to cross the Great Northern Railway for the purpose of linking up with the Eastern Counties line which was also trying to reach Hitchin at that time. This condition is particularly interesting because it demonstrates Parliament's determination to contain Hudson's personal ambitions, and to thwart his bid to establish an all-Hudson route to London. This proved to be his last major attempt to consolidate his position south of Leicester, yet the Leicester & Hitchin scheme was permitted to lapse because, with the collapse of the Railway Mania and the onset of the slump, Midland finances showed very clear signs of having over-reached themselves. Already, the Liverpool Party was raising awkward, persistent, and searching questions that probed deeper and deeper into Hudson's shaky edifice.

Following the amalgamation of 1844, Midland services between London and Leeds were anything but fast during the first eighteen months of the company's existence. Between Euston Square and Rugby Junction, London & Birmingham trains ran to considerably slower schedules than George Carr Glyn's principal expresses to Birmingham. Once upon the Midland line proper, though, George Hudson's trains covered the 49½ miles from Rugby to Derby in 1 hour 40 minutes—an average speed of 29.7 m.p.h., inclusive of the stop at Leicester. In the up direction, trains were allowed an extra five minutes— that is an average of 28.8 m.p.h. North of Derby, 2 hours 30 minutes were allowed for the 72¾ miles to Leeds (Hunslet)— 29.1 m.p.h.—a much better performance, since provision was made for five intermediate stops at the following points, where the principal trains in either direction were met by road coaches. In this way there were properly organized connecting services between the railway stations and important outlying centres as yet without railway communication.

Ambergate	—	Matlock
Chesterfield	—	Mansfield
Eckington	—	Lincoln and Boston
Masborough	—	Retford and Lincoln
Swinton	—	Doncaster

Obviously, such arrangements were only temporary, and with the completion of competing lines during the next few years (particularly the Great Northern and the M.S.&L.), these road services soon disappeared, but for a year or two yet they furnished some lively entertainment for all and sundry; the coaches offered plenty of scope for the young blades to display their powers of horsemanship and showmanship.

Hudson's complete monopoly of railway communication between London and the North-East is reflected in the schedule of the East Coast mail train which, in September 1845, stood as follows:

London & Birmingham
    Euston Square—Rugby   82½ miles (gross)   9.00 p.m.—11.40 p.m.
Midland
    Rugby—Normanton   195½ miles (gross)   11.45 p.m.— 4.15 a.m.
York & North Midland
    Normanton—York   219½ miles (gross)   4.25 a.m.— 5.20 a.m.
Great North of England
    York—Gateshead   303½ miles (gross)   5.40 a.m.— 8.45 a.m.
By coach
    Gateshead—Edinburgh   424¾ miles (gross)   9.00 a.m.— 9.33 p.m.

Thus, the 303½ miles between London and Gateshead took 11 hours 45 minutes (i.e. an average of 25.8 m.p.h.), and the remaining 121¾ miles to Edinburgh gave an average 9.6 m.p.h., the total journey time between London and Edinburgh was 24 hours 33 minutes, an average of 17.3 m.p.h. throughout.

At that time the West Coast Route was even slower, since the 238½ miles between Euston Square and Lancaster took 9 hours 49 minutes by rail (24.2 m.p.h.), and the remaining 159 miles by road to Edinburgh a further 17 hours 24 minutes (9.1 m.p.h.). Thus, the total mileage of 397½ miles was covered in 27 hours 43 minutes—an average of 14.3 m.p.h. Of course, it must be remembered that at this early stage the Midland was still using the very small locomotives inherited from the constituent companies the previous year. Even so, there was a marked difference in the performance of the sturdy machines built by Kitson and Stephenson for the North Midland compared with the tiny Bury types bequeathed by the Midland Counties. Again, the London & Birmingham was also handicapped by the small Bury machines which were completely unsuited to the rapidly expanding traffic they were called upon to handle. However, the conclusion of the budget debate at 1 a.m. on Saturday, February 19, 1848, provided George Hudson with a glorious opportunity to display his powers to the full. Within a few hours details of the budget proposals were printed in *The Times*, copies of which were rushed northward by a special express running to the following schedule:

Euston Square		dep. 5.35 a.m.	Average speed
Rugby Junction	(82½ miles)	arr. 7.15 a.m.	45 m.p.h.
Rugby Junction		dep. 7.29 a.m.	
Leicester	(20m. 5ch.)	pass 7.52 a.m.	52.5 m.p.h.
Loughborough	(32m. 38ch.)	pass 8.05 a.m.	
Derby, South Junction	(49m. 2ch.)	arr. 8.25 a.m.	
		dep. 8.27 a.m.	
Chesterfield	(72m. 6ch.)	pass 8.54 a.m.	
Masborough	(88m. 48ch.)	pass 9.10 a.m.	56 m.p.h.
Normanton	(112m. 49ch.)	arr. 9.35 a.m.	
(Altofts Junction)		dep. 9.37 a.m.	

The gap between the rail heads at Gateshead and Newcastle was covered at full gallop in eight minutes, and that between Tweedmouth and Berwick in one minute less. Glasgow was ultimately reached at 3.57 p.m., so that the gross journey time of 10 hours 22 minutes for the total distance of 470¾ miles gives an average of 45.4 m.p.h.—a stupendous performance. The stamina of the couriers is reflected in the fact that they began the return journey at 5 p.m.

Although these figures represent a startling improvement upon those for 1845, the Budget Express was essentially a showpiece. In all probability the train was hauled between Rugby and

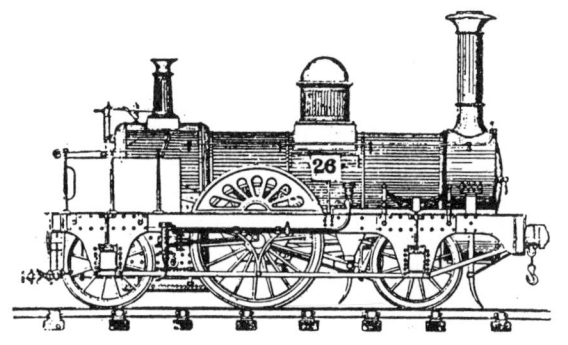

22. Midland Railway 2.2.2 No. 26 supplied by E. B. Wilson, 1847

Derby by one of the then new Sharp '60 class' 2.2.2s, and taken on from Derby to Normanton by a Wilson *Jenny Lind* 2.2.2, as those types then represented the last word in locomotive power on the Midland Railway, not forgetting either that almost £500,000 had just been spent in re-laying thirty-six miles of the old Midland Counties main line, together with other large-scale works. However, the standard passenger schedules between Derby and Leeds were also reduced to 1 hour 55 minutes in each direction. With the opening of the new Wellington station at Leeds in 1849, the Midland abandoned Hunslet Lane for passenger traffic, but five minutes were added in respect of the extra mile on the approach to the new terminus, so that the journey time between Derby and Leeds now became two hours exactly.

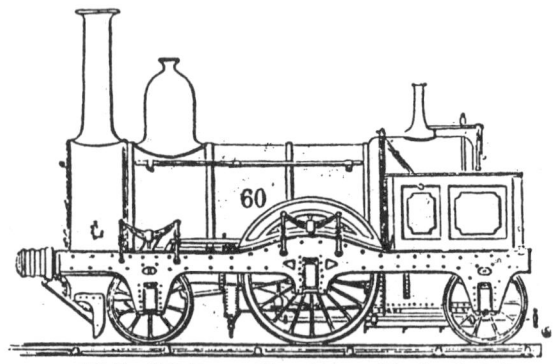

23. Midland Railway—Sharp's 2.2.2. No. 60 of 1848

These early successes were due in no small measure to the thoroughly effective support which Hudson and the Midland Board received from the Locomotive Department at Derby. Immediately after the conclusion of the initial board meeting held at the Derby station offices on May 24, 1844, a Locomotive Committee consisting of Beale, Hutchinson, and Murgatroyd was appointed 'to examine, and report to the board, which of the three Locomotive Superintendents should be retained by this Company'. The three candidates for the post were, of course, J. Kearsley from the Midland Counties, Thomas Kirtley from the North Midland, and Kirtley's younger brother, Matthew, from the Birmingham & Derby Junction. After an interval of three weeks, Samuel Beale reported to the board, on June 13th, that 'the committee has resolved to recommend that Mr Matthew Kirtley be appointed Superintendent of the Locomotive and Carriage Department at a salary of £250 per annum'. The terrific success achieved at the outset by young Kirtley is reflected in the fact that within three months his salary was increased to £400, the increase being backdated to the date of his appointment. Thereafter, he went from strength to strength. By the spring of 1846 he was receiving £700 per annum, and by 1859 no less than £1,200. For a young man of thirty-three, £700 was then a very substantial salary—a good £3,500 (tax paid) by modern standards.

Matthew Kirtley was born at Tanfield, County Durham, on February 6, 1813. As a youth he saw the opening of the pioneer Stockton and Darlington Railway, and having also seen the opening of the Liverpool & Manchester line, young Matthew soon became a fireman on the neighbouring tiny, though highly important Warrington & Newton Railway. From Lancashire he migrated eastward into Yorkshire to become a driver on the Leeds & Selby. Thereafter, his movements are rather obscure, but he is credited with having driven the first London & Birmingham train to enter Euston Square. Very shortly after that, in 1839, he was appointed Locomotive Foreman to the new Birmingham & Derby Junction Railway Company whose locomotive shops were located close to the junction with the London & Birmingham at Hampton-in-Arden. Toward the climax of the competition with the Midland Counties Railway, and following the completion of their main line from Whitacre Junction to Birmingham in the early months of 1842, the B.&D.J. locomotive plant was transferred to 'Brumm' that June. Having been appointed Locomotive Superintendent the previous year, Kirtley went, too, and there he remained until the Midland Railway merger occurred in 1844. Although he was responsible for only twelve passenger 2.2.2s and several goods engines, his administrative, technical, and practical abilities were of such a high order that he was soon noticed by George Hudson, then busily engaged with the two-handed task of stabilizing North Midland finances and besieging Derby.

Upon taking up his new appointment at the age of thirty-one, Kirtley assumed sole responsibility for the Midland Company's locomotives and rolling stock, which dual function he exercised until his premature death in 1873 at the early age of sixty. Nevertheless, during his term of office at Derby, Kirtley's progressive ideas did much to bring the Midland Railway to the forefront, particularly during the eighteen-fifties when the Company initiated a determined drive toward London which finally culminated in the construction of the London Extension to St Pancras during the middle 'sixties.

Comparatively few reliable details of the earliest engines running on the Midland Railway in 1844 have survived, particularly the war years, as so many of the original records have been destroyed, but it can be stated with fair certainty that the Midland Railway began its long and colourful career with about ninety-five machines inherited from the three constituent concerns. Additions to that initial stock were made rapidly enough as other lines were absorbed through Hudson's constant attempts to outwit and outflank his rivals, particularly during 1845 and 1846. Consequently, Kirtley rapidly acquired at Derby a veritable hotch-potch of widely assorted types which proved a serious liability whenever the question of breakdowns occurred, as it did fairly often during those early days. Not only were the engines immobilized, but there would inevitably be extensive and expensive delays because of time taken either to obtain spare parts for minor repairs or, in more serious cases, for engines to be towed away to the maker's works.

Kirtley instantly realized the importance of standardization, the first step towards which he took by urging the Midland board to place future orders for new engines with carefully selected firms. In the meantime, as greater and greater demands for increased locomotive power fell upon his department, he took every opportunity to dispose of the older and smaller machines. Even so, some of these survived the Midland amalgamation by ten or fifteen years. As early as June 1844, a 'coupled engine' was sold for £1,200, this being followed in September by the sale of the undermentioned items to another Hudson protégé, the Newcastle & Darlington Junction:

			£
1 coupled engine			600
4 12 in. cylinder engines and tenders	@	£500 each	2,000
8 Midland Counties 1st class carriages	@	£170 each	1,360
4 North Midland composites	@	£150 each	600
18 North Midland 2nd class unclosed carriages	@	£120 each	2,160
		Total	£6,720

In the same month four Midland Counties second-class carriages went to the Leicester & Swannington, and on November 5th two more engines, six composites, four second-class, and four third-class carriages were sold to the Stockton & Hartlepool Company for £2,720—terms 'cash in three months'—not forgetting the nine assorted carriages purchased for £940 by the Balochney Railway Company. Only three weeks after that, the Midland board directed that the two locomotives *Bee* and *Hercules* (i.e. old Midland Counties numbers 1 and 2) were to be sold for 'the best price obtainable'. Upon being resold to her makers, the Butterley Company, *Bee* fetched £150, a somewhat sad reflection, perhaps, upon her departed youth.

Steps taken to obtain new machines during 1845 included an order placed with Kitson's of Leeds in September 1844 for two new engines identical to the Stephenson long-boilered o.6.0, No. 74, delivered to the North Midland shortly before the merger. Four new passenger engines were ordered that October, followed by four more large goods engines in February 1845, this number being increased in March to twelve—six by Kitson, and six by Rothwell. Various other firms at this stage received orders for a further fourteen passenger engines, making a total of thirty-two machines.

In reporting to the Midland board on December 2, 1845, Kirtley showed that the Company's locomotive stock then comprised:

Passenger
20 with 14in. x 18in. cylinders 5½ft. x 6in. wheels.
25 with 13in. x 18in. cylinders 5½ft. x 6in. wheels.
20 with 12in. x 18in. cylinders 5½ft. x 6in. wheels.
2 with 15in. x 22in. cylinders 5½ft. x 6in. wheels.

Goods

```
13 with 14in. x 18in. cylinders   5 ft. wheels.
 6 with 14in. x 20in. cylinders   4½ft. wheels.
 4 with 13in. x 18in. cylinders   5 ft. wheels.
 4 with 15in. x 24in. cylinders   4¾ft. wheels.
```

Kirtley's summary thus furnishes a total of ninety-four machines, of which forty-seven passenger and twenty-two goods engines were in daily work, exclusive of extras, and five laid up for repairs. At Birmingham, Leeds and Rugby there was a general shortage of engine power, and he drew attention to the fact that the fourteen passenger and twelve goods engines then still on order would meet only current requirements. He also recommended the building of a second roundhouse at Derby capable of accommodating sixteen engines, 'as several locomotives are already standing out of doors at night—and will cause great damage and inconvenience in severe weather'.

As mentioned previously, Hudson's counter-measures to his opponents' schemes reached their climax in 1846, by which time many of the smaller locomotives acquired through the numerous mergers showed very clear signs of being either very well worn or too weak to cope with their daily tasks. As the infant Midland Company assumed greater and greater commitments during 1845 and 1846, it became increasingly evident that many new machines would soon be needed, and a very prompt start was made during the first week of January 1846 with the placing of orders for nearly fifty engines:

Longridge	8 for delivery 1846	(@ £2,025 each)
Longridge	5 for delivery 1847	
Stephenson	5 for delivery 1847	(@ £2,000 each)
Stephenson	20 for delivery 1848	
Hawthorn	5 for delivery 1847	(@ £1,850 each)
Kitson	5 for delivery 1847	(@ £1,900 each)
Total	48	

However, as Stephenson's were unable to deliver more than ten engines between February and July 1848, their order was reduced to ten in February 1846, five machines being added to each of the orders placed with Hawthorn's and Kitson's—at an immediate saving to the Midland exchequer of £750 and £500 respectively. In their amended form, then, these contracts were worth £93,285. Kitson's also provided engines Nos. 70 and 71 with new fireboxes in the spring of 1846, No. 70 being sold to the Eastern Counties Railway a year later. Incidentally, these engines were most probably the old B.&D.J.R. goods 0.4.2s *Kingsbury* and *Willington*, reputedly built by Thompson & Cole. Following the disposal of two more old engines by midsummer (1846), ten new machines arrived during the next six months, so that by the close of the year the locomotive stock stood at 122 engines of which ninety-nine were in good order (with eighty-eight in steam daily) and seven laid up for sale.

A further 'weeding out' occurred during 1847, commencing with the agreed disposal of *Liverpool*, an ex-Leicester & Swannington Bury four-wheeler; but she must have been an unpopular machine because she was subsequently re-offered for sale, this time to the Eastern Counties, in March, when she was again rejected. No. 100 brought £750 in mid-February, and the ex-Sheffield & Rotherham 2.2.2, *Southampton*, commanded no less than £1,000 a month later. Another Leicester & Swannington 0.4.0, *Goliath*, produced £1,200 in July. After these developments, Kirtley was instructed to obtain a six-wheeled passenger engine with 6 ft. driving wheels and 22 in. x 15 in. cylinders—price with tender, £2,350—and this appears to be the origin of the new Stephenson 2.2.2, No. 1, which in 1848 replaced the original Midland machine which then assumed the number 100 left vacant by the sale referred to above.

New machines ordered in 1847 included the following engines ordered on September 22nd:

Kitson (Crampton type)	6 @ £2,150 each	
Kitson (Goods class)	6 @ £2,100 each	
Wilson	6 @ £2,350 each	
Sharp Bros.	6 @ £2,340 each	
Total	24	£53,640

These orders placed during 1846 and 1847 by the Midland Railway alone show conclusively that during the 'Railway Mania' locomotive construction was already very big business indeed.

With the collapse of the boom, 1848 showed definite signs of the impending slump, and thus the Midland locomotive stock tended to stabilize at the 260 mark. There was then a daily average of 145 engines in steam—i.e. seventy-five passenger, forty-eight freight, and twenty-two on shunting and pilot duties, with thirty-six available for disposal. Towards the close of the year, Kirtley stated that he needed forty extra modern engines for working the traffic efficiently, but due to a very serious drop in receipts the Midland board decided to postpone any immediate action in that direction, particularly in view of the partial opening of both the M.S.L.R. and the G.N.R. These precautionary measures proved very well justified; indeed, the constant hammering kept up by the 'Liverpool Party' caused the dramatic collapse of Hudson's regime in the spring of 1849. Consequently, when the committee of investigation reported back to the shareholders the following August, the locomotive stock was still unchanged at the figure of 260, of which 219 were described as being in good working condition, eleven were in need of major repairs, fifteen in need of rebuilding, and the remainder in need of routine minor repairs.

In retrospect, then, under Hudson's enlightened, if autocratic administration Midland locomotive stock had expanded at a furious pace, as the accompanying figures show:

Locomotive stock at 31.12.45	94
31.12.46	113
31.12.47	122
31.12.48	260
31.12.49	260

During the whole of Kirtley's lifetime, Midland engines were painted a deep emerald green (a most popular colour during early Victorian times), the famous 'Derby Red' being adopted by his successor, S. W. Johnson, during the early eighties. In distinct contrast, Midland passenger rolling stock was finished in the wonderful 'Midland Lake' livery from the very outset, following George Hudson's personal directive in 1844 that the new company's carriages were to be painted 'claret'.

The year 1848 foreshadowed the end of the initial phase in Midland history. The opening of the last section of the Syston & Peterborough line for passenger traffic on May 1st was quickly followed by the death of George Stephenson at Tapton House, Chesterfield, on August 12th. His passing at the early age of sixty-seven was undoubtedly a severe loss to George Hudson, and also the many boards under Hudson's control—particularly the Midland, then rapidly approaching a disastrous upheaval. Indeed, Hudson paid extremely generous and sincere tribute to his late friend at the Annual General Meeting of Midland shareholders held at Derby just after Stephenson's death. Then, turning to Midland affairs, Hudson reported that the first half of the year had produced some difficulties, but as the gross receipts were well up compared with the corresponding period for the previous year (1847), a dividend of six per cent was declared. At this point Hudson also denied a rumour that he was about to leave the Midland Railway. At the following ordinary meeting of shareholders (held that August in the Derby locomotive shed), it was disclosed that despite a rise of more than £47,000 in goods traffic receipts for the half-year, the partial opening of both the G.N.R. and the M.S.L.R. had caused a serious reduction in passenger receipts. It was also observed that the falling-off had been pretty general throughout the Midland system and the meeting ended with the expression of the hope that the future would bring about a trade revival and thus improve the situation. However, the 'Liverpool Party', which had influenced Midland Counties and Midland policies for so long, took a very much tougher line. At their own meeting on October 28th they severely criticized the conduct of the Midland board, which then promised a full explanation and that a report of its recent affairs would be duly published.

The storm broke with full force at the shareholders' half-yearly meeting on February 15, 1849, when it was claimed by the representatives of the 'Liverpool Party' that the accounts were lacking in fullness. After a prolonged tussle George Hudson eventually conceded that an item for £36,000 in respect of Parliamentary expenses, formerly posted against 'capital', should now be charged to 'revenue', if the proprietors so desired. The meeting subsequently terminated with a vote of confidence in the Midland directors being carried, again 'amid tumultuous applause'. Even so, Hudson's 'reign' at Derby lasted just nine more weeks, and at a packed extraordinary general meeting John Ellis read the chairman's letter of resignation. A resolution was then moved by Mr Wylie of Liverpool for the appointment of a committee of investigation to enquire into the management and the affairs of the Midland Railway Company, with full powers to report to the shareholders at an adjourned meeting.

CHAPTER 5

THE BIRMINGHAM AND BRISTOL LINE

At the close of 1844 the railway political scene in Britain was one of seething turmoil. Throughout the kingdom many of the earlier and smaller companies were rushing headlong towards the creation of much larger corporations by amalgamation. The newly-formed Midland Railway was then the largest company operating under single management. At Derby, George Hudson and the Midland directorate had already set in motion the first of an elaborate series of schemes expressly designed to thwart the many rival projects already threatening the company's existence on all sides. By far the most ambitious, the most highly publicized, and most menacing was Denison's Parliamentary-backed scheme for a direct line between London and York. Less obvious, perhaps, but equally deadly was the most determined thrust into the heart of narrow-gauge territory then being attempted by the broad-gauge Great Western company and its dependent allies. In this campaign Birmingham was nominally the main objective, and to this end the Great Western people had lately been seeking to persuade the Birmingham & Gloucester board to adopt the broad gauge. Though many miles north of Birmingham, not even Hudson's citadels at Derby and York were completely safe from the broad gauge threat, and with popular national attention riveted upon Hudson's fiery schemes for protecting his eastern flank throughout its entire length, the leasing of the Birmingham & Bristol line for the Midland company at the beginning of 1845 was a major achievement. On one hand, Derby gained a new main line just over ninety miles long; on the other, the frontier of the broad gauge empire was firmly pinned down at two points, at Cheltenham and Gloucester. This highly successful coup produced yet another resounding victory for narrow-gauge interests everywhere, and credit for it belonged exclusively to Hudson's most capable deputy, John Ellis, whose astuteness, business acumen and speed of operation far outclassed that of his Great Western opponents. Indeed, Ellis's bid for the West of England line was made only a few days after the unification of the former Bristol & Gloucester and the Birmingham & Gloucester companies in January 1845, and under Midland ownership the narrow gauge was subsequently pushed southward to Bristol, then the heart of broad gauge activities.

Twenty years had passed since the first serious attempt had been made to establish a through railway connection between Bristol, Gloucester and Birmingham. At a well supported meeting held at the White Lion Hotel, Bristol, in 1824, a deposit of £2 per share had been ordered, but although the route had been partly surveyed, the whole scheme collapsed within only a few months. It says much for the integrity of all concerned that of every twenty shillings subscribed, no less than 17s 6d was returned—only 2s 6d in the £ being retained to cover administrative costs and legal expenses.

Four years later, on June 19, 1828, Parliament sanctioned the construction of two horse-drawn tramways in the Bristol area to provide effective outlets for the numerous collieries of the South Gloucestershire coalfield scattered around the parish of Westerleigh, near Yate. Of those two tramways, the Bristol & Gloucestershire was about nine miles long, running southwards from Coalpit Heath to Shortwood, near which point it swung away towards the south-west, tunnelling through Staple Hill, and then dropping right down the side of the Avon Valley to Bristol and the Floating Harbour.

The complementary line, the Avon & Gloucestershire, diverged from the Bristol & Gloucestershire near Shortwood, and wound its way steadily southwards some five and a half miles before terminating at a wharf on the north bank of the River Avon opposite Keynsham. Whereas ownership of the Bristol & Gloucestershire was held in the early days by a local Bristol party, it later passed into the hands of, firstly, the Bristol & Gloucester and then the Midland companies. In marked contrast, control of the Avon & Gloucestershire was from the outset vested largely in the shareholders of the Kennet & Avon Canal Company, which was absorbed in its turn by the Great Western Railway in July 1851. Thereafter, the canal was allowed to decay since its very existence clashed with the interests of the railway company. The collieries were also gradually abandoned, and by 1865 Paddington had obtained powers to close the smaller line. Today, a century later, the wheel seems to have turned full circle, and most energetic efforts are now being made to restore and revive interest in sections of the old waterway.

Opened for traffic in July 1832 (c.f. the Leicester & Swannington line) the Avon & Gloucestershire tramway secured access to the collieries close to Yate over the northern arm of the Bristol & Gloucestershire, for which purpose rails had been already laid between Coalpit Heath and Shortwood, both tramways being laid to the common gauge of 4 ft. 8 in. Between Shortwood and Bristol, though, the remaining Bristol & Gloucestershire works were still very far from ready; indeed, they were only completed after Parliament sanctioned a year's extension beyond the construction period originally laid down in the company's Act. Finally, the line was opened on August 6, 1835.

In 1835 England was in the throes of its first railway boom, and, as previously explained, many schemes were already well in hand for establishing railway communication between the major towns and cities throughout the kingdom. At Bristol a local party was hard at work campaigning for an extension of the Bristol & Gloucestershire line to the county town, some thirty miles to the north-east. Then, beyond that centre, the Birmingham & Gloucester Railway would carry the communication fifty miles on toward Birmingham, where it was planned to link up with the two national trunk lines already under construction (the London & Birmingham, and the Grand Junction), and George Stephenson's chain of railways striding southward from York and the West Riding. The Birmingham & Gloucester Railway was sanctioned in 1836, but the Bristol & Gloucestershire Extension Bill went down in the following year, thanks largely to the opposition of a rival party based upon Gloucester. Thereafter, these two parties collaborated to re-organize the whole project, and under the new title of the Bristol and Gloucester Railway their new measure was successfully steered through the House in 1839. By now capital was far from easy to come by and, with economy well to the fore, the Legislature sanctioned a twenty-two-and-a-quarter-mile extension of the old Bristol & Gloucestershire line from Westerleigh to Standish where a junction was to be effected with the Cheltenham & Great Western Union Railway, also sanctioned in 1836. To reach Gloucester proper, Bristol & Gloucester trains were required to run about seven and a half miles beyond Standish Junction over the C.&G.W.U. tracks, mixed gauge being authorized by Parliament for this purpose.

The Birmingham & Gloucester Railway Company owed a tremendous debt to the indefatigable efforts of several members of the Society of Friends, among them Charles and Joseph Sturge. Incidentally, the company's affairs were administered by two committees, a decidedly Victorian arrangement which meant that company meetings were held at Birmingham and at Gloucester on an alternate basis. As early as 1832, when the Stephenson lines had already proved highly successful, bold plans were already maturing for linking London with Birmingham, and 'Brum' with the Liverpool & Manchester line near Warrington. Obviously railways were widely regarded as a highly satisfactory form of investment, but the Birmingham & Gloucester party found difficulty in attracting capital and, with only limited funds to draw upon, a young man named Isambard Kingdom Brunel was engaged to survey the cheapest possible route. Bearing this well in mind, and also the distinct possibility of a railway being projected from Oxford towards Birmingham, Brunel's route lay well to the east of the one finally chosen, and it steered well clear of the Lickey. Due to financial and administrative difficulties the scheme was temporarily suspended, and Brunel left. He then entered the service of the Great Western company[1] who were preparing to link London with Bristol. Money now became a major difficulty, and Brunel was succeeded on the Birmingham & Gloucester by Captain William Scarth Moorsom whose remuneration was directly linked to the results he achieved.

Moorsom surveyed two possible routes—the one we have today, and the other lying further north and west of that line, but directly serving the intermediate towns where the cost of land was much dearer. In the interests of economy the choice

[1] March 1833.

came down in favour of the existing route, but this aroused strong criticism from three main sources. To begin with, both Brunel and the Stephensons deplored the use of a route incorporating the formidable Lickey Bank which was regarded as a sad mistake—as indeed it was. Then, huge roars of protest issued from the inhabitants of Cheltenham and Worcester when it was generally realized that those centres would only be skirted and not directly served by the main railway line. When Moorsom's scheme was modified to include Cheltenham—at an additional cost of £200,000—Worcester had to be content with the prospect of a branch line. Between Cheltenham and Gloucester the main line would follow largely the route of an old tramway dating back to 1809 which had cost about £50,000 to build. By now, however, the Cheltenham & Great Western Union scheme had appeared on the local scene, and it was proposed that the old tramway be purchased for £35,000 by the two new railway undertakings acting on a joint basis, so that much of the old route could be utilized and relaid to their mutual advantage.

The Birmingham & Gloucester Railway Bill was presented to Parliament in 1836 and, having encountered little really serious opposition, received Royal Assent on April 22nd. Extremely interesting provisions were inserted in the schedule of this Act whereby Birmingham & Gloucester trains were enabled to use the Curzon Street terminus of the London & Birmingham Railway, then under construction. Furthermore, section 21 of the Act extended this arrangement to permit entry 'to any future terminus of that company in or near Birmingham'. In exactly this way Midland trains from Bristol, Gloucester and Cheltenham were to secure access to the L.&N.W.R. station at New Street practically twenty years later.

Reaction followed the boom conditions of 1835-36, and capital became ever harder to attract than before. Small wonder that at the half-yearly general meeting of shareholders held at the Bell Hotel, Gloucester, on February 6, 1838, it was resolved that the least expensive section of the line—i.e. between Cheltenham and Droitwich—should be completed by June 1839, thus providing the earliest possible return upon capital outlay. Intense dissatisfaction was also expressed regarding the way in which the Cheltenham & Great Western Union people had completely failed to initiate construction of the Cheltenham & Gloucester section on the joint cost basis stipulated in their Act. Other developments at this period included the preparation of contracts for about 500 tons of ironwork needed for the bridge across the River Avon at Eckington about seven miles above Tewkesbury, and, shortly afterwards, in April 1838, the staking out of the northernmost stretch of the company's main line was in progress between Balsall Heath and Camp Hill.

24. Defford Bridge, near Eckington
(Birmingham & Gloucester Railway)

The next half-yearly general meeting was held in Dee's Royal Hotel, Birmingham, on August 7th. Here, the directors' report provides an interesting insight into the company's progress at that time. All the land needed for both the main line between Birmingham and Cheltenham, and the Tewkesbury branch had now been purchased, and the company's executive had most successfully resisted extortionate demands. In fact, the land needed for these works had been obtained at prices well within the estimates prepared in 1837. Construction work was equally satisfactory; about half the line, including some of the heaviest sections, had been let and work was already proceeding apace. The contracts let to date had included the bridges and all other works with the exception of the permanent way. Contracts for that aspect of the work were also being let, following the placing of earlier orders for rails and timber. In all cases the contract prices had proved well within the engineer's estimates.

Unlike the works of many other contemporary lines, the various contracts for the Birmingham & Gloucester Railway were far from spectacular and tended to attract rather less public interest than usual. Yet, appearances can be very deceptive; the directors had deliberately split the whole of their works into a series of relatively small contracts which assured speedy and satisfactory progress without the ultimate cost of the works getting out of hand as was happening with much larger projects elsewhere. Against this marked advantage, however, much extra work was transferred to the shoulders of the company's executive officers.

At the Cheltenham end of the line matters were now proceeding much more satisfactorily. The Cheltenham & Great Western Union Company was actively purchasing the land between Cheltenham and Gloucester for the joint benefit of both parties, and by the autumn the construction gangs were hard at work. All this obviated invoking the clauses within the amending Birmingham & Gloucester Act whereby that company obtained powers to construct that section for its own benefit should the C.&G.W.U. party fail to purchase the land and to build the line within the short time specified in the B.&G. Act. The works for the Gloucester and Cheltenham section proved extremely light, so that by mid-November they were well on the way towards completion. Whereas at Lansdown, Cheltenham work had scarcely begun, work 'on the depot at Tewkesbury' further north, was far advanced. Captain Moorsom had now assumed responsibility for the permanent way, and under his direction experiments with longitudinal timbers had already begun at Swindon, great care being taken to avoid the faults previously experienced by the Great Western company.

Amid so much constructional activity there was one serious snag—the artificially depressed state of the company's shares upon the stock markets. Things were so bad that on January 24, 1839, a special general meeting of shareholders was called at Birmingham to review the company's financial position. Despite criticisms from all sides, the directors held their ground and at length received a decisive vote of confidence. Even so, matters still failed to improve, the main trouble being that having already subscribed £40 per £100 share (at a market loss of sixty-five per cent) shareholders were very unwilling to subscribe anything further. Also, the original Act of 1836 prohibited the borrowing of money until two-thirds of the capital had been paid up. To overcome this difficulty, a Bill was presented to Parliament on April 17, 1839, seeking powers to borrow money against the security of the works so far completed. This immediately produced yet another outcry, and John Hill, the town clerk of Worcester, was hurriedly packed off to London on the evening of Tuesday, April 16th, with specific instructions to relentlessly oppose the Bill until the railway company agreed to give an undertaking to complete the Abbotts[1] Wood branch before the main line. But, in view of Hill's demands, the Birmingham & Gloucester people withdrew their Bill, and the citizens and officials of Worcester were left with only a hollow victory after all their trouble.[2]

Regardless of the battle raging over financial issues the contractors continued with the works at full speed; by June 1839 the line was 'in a great state of forwardness', particularly in the neighbourhood of Moseley and Highgate, and even more so at the Tewkesbury and Cheltenham end. At Gloucester tenders were already being invited for 'building an Engine House and Workshops, and also for building Offices and other Erections for the Railway Station at Rigby, in the parish of Stoke Prior, near Bromsgrove'. Extra tenders were being put out for 'Ballasting, also Fitting and Laying of the Permanent Way between Tibberton (near Worcester) and Aschurch (near Tewkesbury) amounting to about fourteen miles in length of double way'. The Tewkesbury branch was also making very rapid progress at this stage, and the station (finished in the gothic architectural style) 'reflects great credit on the contractor, Mr F. P. Holder'. A contemporary description of the station also mentions that 'the front elevation is 38 feet wide, and at the back is a raised platform 133 feet by 12 feet 6 inches covered by a substantial

[1] Contemporary spelling.
[2] Worcester continued to be served by horse drawn road omnibus running to and from Birmingham & Gloucester Station at Spetchley. (Midland trains reach Worcester direct upon partial opening of O., W., & W. Railway, October 5, 1850.)

roof with glass lights on each side. The roof measures 166 feet long by 32 feet wide'.

Little more than a week after the special general meeting held in Birmingham to consider the question of the shares, the half-yearly general meeting was held at the Bell Hotel, Gloucester, on February 2, 1839. This presented a certain Mr John Tart with the opportunity of drawing attention to the matter of ten locomotives allegedly ordered from Norris of Philadelphia in the USA for service on the Birmingham & Gloucester line. In reply Captain Moorsom explained that one such machine was to be tried upon the Lickey Inclined Plane by way of experiment, and at the manufacturer's own risk and expense. Subject to these conditions, a provisional order would possibly be placed with Norris for ten or a dozen machines.

The introduction of the Norris type engine into this country was actually initiated by Norris's agent in Europe, William Gwynn, who approached both the Gloucester and the Birmingham committees during November 1838 with the proposal that Norris should provide two distinctly separate types of locomotive for trials, either in the UK or the USA. The smaller type, weighing eight tons empty, and costing $7,500 (£1,500 sterling) inclusive of tender, was to be capable of hauling 100 tons (including the weight of the engine and tender) at a sustained speed of 20 m.p.h. along a rising gradient of 1 in 300. The larger machine, weighing twelve tons and costing $8,500 (£1,750 sterling) without tender, would haul seventy-five tons (including its own weight) up a plane two miles long and inclined 1 in 38, at a speed of 10-15 m.p.h., this performance being 'a regular every day duty'. Here, the reference to the Lickey is unmistakably clear. Gwynn's proposal also stipulated that, upon these tests proving successful, the Birmingham & Gloucester Company should bind itself to Norris for the purchase of six more machines of the smaller type, and two more of the larger, ten engines in all, at a total cost of $78,000 (£15,750 sterling).

Under the terms of an agreement signed during November 1838, the first of the smaller Norris machines, the *England*, was shipped aboard the American vessel *Susquehanna* at Philadelphia on February 19, 1839. Exactly a month later news of her arrival was relayed to the Birmingham & Gloucester people by the Liverpool shipping agents and, following reassembly, *England* was put through her trials on the Grand Junction Railway at the request of Moorsom's board.

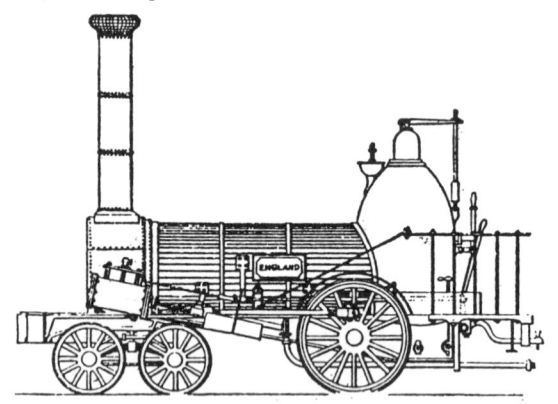

25. Norris 4.2.0. locomotive *England* imported from the U.S.A. via Liverpool in March 1839

England aroused widespread attention, particularly in the Press, and she is described as having '4 feet diameter wheels with 10½ in. cylinders enclosed in copper cases to prevent radiation'. The stroke was 18 in., and the outside cylinders facilitated a straight driving axle. She is also claimed to have been the first bogie locomotive employed on an English main line. An eye-witness account records that 'the engine is got up in a most superior style, and is finished even to the minutest particular in a very beautiful and workmanlike manner, every part having been executed with perfect accuracy by means of self-acting machinery', a description which typifies the traditional thoroughness of American planning and attention to detail. The boiler is also described as containing 78 tubes compared with the 100 to 140 tubes then in general use within the United Kingdom. The fuel consumption was reputedly very small, and the working pressure 70 lb. p.s.i. *England* is credited with having made fourteen return runs between Birmingham and Warrington hauling a gross load of 100 tons, and covering the eighty miles each way at 20 m.p.h. On one occasion she even brought 126 tons up an inclined plane into Birmingham without assistance.

However, following Moorsom's report that the loads employed during the trials had been 'irregular', the engineer was sent northward to ensure that the full loads were actually carried; otherwise the trials were to be suspended. By June Moorsom further reported that, notwithstanding its many excellent qualities, at the boiler pressure of 50-55 lb. originally stipulated, the *England* had technically failed to comply fully with the terms of the agreement drawn up the previous November. The Birmingham & Gloucester Board now informed Norris of 'their intention to decline the said engine', and this brought Gwynn hastening back to the scene to smooth matters out. At length, in August 1839, the Board resolved to proceed with the purchase of *England*, but to rescind the contract for the other six of this smaller type. Gwynn seems to have been a very hard-working salesman; in stressing his conviction that the larger engines would prove completely satisfactory, he succeeded in persuading the British people to take all seven of those smaller locos. Still, this success was only achieved after much really hard bargaining whereby the price was beaten right down to £1,525 each, delivered at Wapping, Liverpool, and with freight and duty paid.

The first of the 12-tonners, the *Victoria*, apparently reached Liverpool at the close of July 1839, but it was not until the following November that Gwynn agreed to accept £1,200. Of this sum, £1,000 was paid at once, but the balance of £200 was witheld pending the full delivery of the two smaller machines which had just reached Liverpool aboard the *Susquehanna*. At length, the *Victoria* was placed on the Lickey Incline on June 17, 1840, that is exactly a week before the opening of the first section of the line between Cheltenham and Bromsgrove. On Monday, July 13th, the *Victoria* was joined by the *Philadelphia*. With Gwynn's assistance she had been fitted up by Capt Moorsom with 'a proper sand box to the engine, and a water tub for wetting the rails'. Engine and tender weighed 19 tons,[1] and upon test she hauled a gross load of 75 tons up the two-mile bank, finally breasting the summit at 10 m.p.h.; with a 36-ton train (55 tons gross), the final speed was 15 m.p.h. As 36 tons well exceeded the normal weight of trains, the arrival on the scene of a third heavy engine that August left Moorsom quite confident that the company's trains would be enabled to safely ascend the bank at 15 m.p.h. under normal working conditions.

These heavier American engines came into regular service with the opening of the extension from Bromsgrove to Cofton Farm in September 1840. As banking engines, they assisted all types of trains up the Lickey Incline (2 m. 4 ch. at 1 in 37.7), the climb taking approximately ten or twelve minutes, according to the load. Once over the summit, it was the fireman's responsibility to uncouple his banking engine from the train engine which was then required to shut off steam and slacken speed, thus allowing the banking engine to draw at least thirty yards ahead and turn into a siding specially provided for the purpose. With split-second timing, the points were now reset to enable the train to continue northward along the main line. With all this safely accomplished, the banking engine emerged from the siding, crossed over to the 'east line', and commenced its descent on the return run to Bromsgrove—running tender first presumably.

Turning momentarily to the southbound trains approaching from Birmingham, and preparing to descend the Lickey Bank—engine drivers were required to shut off steam half a mile short of the summit, and to stop directly opposite a white post erected immediately north of the summit. At night or during fog, the halting point was marked by a white light mounted on top of the post itself. On the final approach, the driver was required to whistle once as a signal for the duty brakesman to be ready to join the train. Having halted, three whistles were used to instruct guards to ensure that all brakes were correctly applied. At this point, the senior brakesman climbed aboard the middle coach and there assumed complete control of the whole train. Under his direction, the second brakesman and the guards stationed themselves at various points along the train. The whole of this procedure was executed very smartly indeed, and took only a few moments to complete. Then, with everything quite ready for the descent to begin, the first brakesman gave the starting signal by means of a solitary, shrill blast on a hand-held whistle, whereupon the engine driver applied just sufficient steam

---
[1] Tenders of 12 ton Norris locos were of British manufacture.

to get the train moving. Next, two blasts on the brakesman's whistle instructed the driver to shut off steam completely, and to continue coasting downhill. Three blasts called for the gradual, yet more forcible application of *all* brakes throughout the length of the train, including the handbrakes fitted to the tender and operated by the fireman. Under these conditions passenger trains were to descend the Lickey as near as possible to 20 m.p.h., and in no case were they to exceed that speed. In slippery weather the maximum speed for the descent was reduced to 16 m.p.h., an upper limit of 10 m.p.h. being imposed upon 'waggon trains'.

The heavy American banking engines were an unqualified success; yet within a year of settling down to work on the Lickey they managed to evoke Mr Bury's famous challenge to match one of his 'five footers' against the Norris 4.2.0s with their smaller four-foot driving wheels. On the morning of Monday, August 23, 1841, Bury type No. 65 left Curzon Street for Bromsgrove at the head of seven wagons laden with rails and a composite carriage with fifteen people aboard fetching up the rear. The official report on the contest makes the illuminating statement that 'At the Lickey Incline No. 65 could not rise with 4 waggons and 1 carriage.' With one of the wagons detached, she mounted the bank in 840 seconds (8·7 m.p.h.), whereas, with the same load, *Philadelphia* took only 483 seconds (15 m.p.h.). With two wagons and the composite, the respective speeds were 13·9 and 16·4 m.p.h.; with one wagon and the composite, 21·0 and 17·4; and with only the composite speeds of 24·7 and 21·3 m.p.h. were attained. Thus, it was only with the lighter loads that No. 65 proved faster than the *Philadelphia,* which otherwise established a clear margin of supremacy when hauling the heavier trains.

In view of his earlier connections with the Birmingham & Gloucester Railway, Bury may have been just a little resentful of the instant success attained by the American machines. As one of the leading British locomotive authorities of the eighteen-thirties he had previously been granted by the English board (in October 1838) an agency for 'taking immediate steps for procuring ten engines deliverable as early as necessary for the general traffic'—i.e. on the Birmingham & Gloucester main line. Bury acted decisively. Two engines and tenders (at £1,660 each, inclusive) were promptly ordered from Forrester & Co. of Liverpool for delivery at Birmingham by January 31, 1839, or as soon as possible thereafter. Two more were to be obtained from Messrs Summers and Co. of Southampton for delivery at Gloucester by early March 1839. These machines were intended to meet the needs of the 'small traffic' when the extension to Droitwich was opened that summer. These plans were badly upset, however, by the board's financial difficulties which delayed completion of the construction works by about a year. By February 1840 no fewer than ten engines were engaged on the works, of which three were occupied in the construction of the heavy embankment across the Rea Valley, Birmingham, the others being mostly employed between Bredon, Tewkesbury and Cheltenham. Apparently, in addition to his five per cent agency commission, Bury also received a gratuity of £100 from the delighted Birmingham & Gloucester Board.

Subsequently, the Forrester engines were found to be too light for the major works at Moseley cutting and a heavier engine and tender was purchased from Banks of Manchester, delivery being fixed for February 28, 1840; by which time the *Southampton, Leicester* and *Victoria*—already working at Moseley—were in bad need of repair, none of the three having been kept properly cleaned. Three more engines, including the *Spetchley,* were ordered that April from Hicks of Bolton, and a second engine purchased from Banks that July at a cost of £1,200. This loco was supplied with two sets of wheels (4 ft. and 5 ft. in diameter), the larger ones being fitted for traffic service upon the completion of the heavy construction works.

Back now to 1839 because, despite the outstanding progress made lately with the construction works and technical preparations, the company's financial position remained in a parlous state; and under the heading 'Will Railways Pay?' the *Gloucestershire Chronicle* (in January 1840) suggested that the Birmingham & Gloucester Railway might be regarded as a secondary line. Attention to the plight of the company's shares, then at a ruinous discount due to overspeculation, was drawn by a shareholder's letter. Still, comparing the company's potential earnings with those of the twenty-six road coaches then plying daily between Birmingham, Worcester and Cheltenham and carrying a collective total of 250 passengers each way daily, the correspondent declared that carrying 750 each way at an average charge of 9s per head should earn the new company £675 daily, or £4,725 per week, plus a further £250 for goods; this would provide a gross income of £5,000 weekly, or £26,000 per year. The company's capital was £950,000, and assuming construction costs to be £1,000,000, with £100,000 borrowed and £5,000 payable yearly on the loan, and operating costs of fifty per cent, a net profit of £12,500 per annum would provide a fourteen per cent dividend for distribution to the shareholders—a statement which was greeted with widespread approval in the Press, though it was not of much practical financial assistance.

Despite the controversy, the contractors pushed ahead, and, on June 1st a party of directors, travelling in two carriages and four wagons, inspected the works. Leaving Cheltenham at 9 a.m., and halting at Eckington, they reached Spetchley in one hour. Resuming at 10.15, the remainder of the journey to Bromsgrove took a further twenty-six minutes. There, at Bromsgrove, the visitors were met by 'an excellent band provided by Mr Baylis, one of the subcontractors, who also furnished a number of flags, and as the party took the musicians, banners, &c. with them on their return, the train assumed a very gay appearance, and led to the supposition that it was a public opening of the line, which opinion was further strengthened by the fact that five carriages, also accompanied with music and banners, containing shareholders and other parties interested in the great undertaking residing in Tewkesbury, joined the train at Ashchurch. After a brief stay at Bromsgrove the train returned to Cheltenham, and then again performed the journey to and fro.'

The first section of the Birmingham & Gloucester Railway—between Cheltenham and Bromsgrove—was formally opened on Wednesday, June 24, 1840, some fortnight earlier than had been expected. The inaugural train, consisting of two first and two second-class carriages headed by the locomotive *W. S. Moorsom,* started off from Cheltenham in gallant style at 9.10 a.m., 'quickly receding from the astonished gaze of the persons assembled'. From time to time speed was slackened as the train

Birmingham and Gloucester Railway.
NOTICE IS HEREBY GIVEN, that on and after WEDNESDAY NEXT, the 24th of June, the portion of this RAILWAY between Cheltenham and the Station near Bromsgrove, will be OPEN for the conveyance of Passengers, Parcels, Carriages, and Horses.
Until further notice there will be only two Trains each way per day, viz.:—
From Bromsgrove Station............... 10½ A.M. and 7 P.M.
From Cheltenham .... 9 A.M. ... 6 P.M.
No trains will run on Sundays at present.
Arrangements have been made to work Road Coaches between the Station near Bromsgrove and Birmingham, by which a limited number of Passengers can be booked through from Cheltenham to Birmingham; and also, by application at the Swan, Hen and Chickens, Nelson, and Castle Hotel Coach Offices, from Birmingham to Cheltenham. The Coaches for the above Trains will leave Birmingham at 8¼ A.M. and 5 P.M. The Fares between Birmingham and Cheltenham are—First Class, 11s. 6d.; Second, 8s.
It is expected the Line will be further opened to within eleven miles of Birmingham early in July, when additional Trains will be put on and arrangements made to convey Passengers, &c., between Birmingham and Exeter, and all intermediate places, in one day.
Gentlemen's Carriages and Horses must be at the Stations at least a quarter of an hour before the time of departure of the Trains.   By order.
                                    WILLIAM BURGESS,
Dated June 17th, 1840.   Superintendent and Secretary.

26. Birmingham and Gloucester Railway: Opening Notice

was transferred from 'one tram to another', after which a stop of three and a half minutes was made at Ashchurch at 9.26. After a stop at Bredon, 'an excellent pace was maintained—at least 30 m.p.h.' Eckington was reached at 9.45 a.m.—i.e. eleven miles in thirty minutes, inclusive of stops—and there 'passengers flocking to ride upon a train for the very first time in their lives, followed by a stop at Defford, crammed the carriages to capacity. When the train reached Spetchley road coaches were waiting to take up passengers for Worcester, this stop also being used to enable the engine to take on water'. The train pulled into Bromsgrove at 10.50, and there a very smart turn round was achieved. Only five minutes later the train was setting out on the return run. At length, the train pulled into Cheltenham at 12.27—a grand morning's work which did much to raise the company's shares from sixty-two to seventy-five.

At first there were only two trains each weekday between Cheltenham and Bromsgrove, there being no Sunday trains whatever; but from the autumn onward the remainder of the Birmingham & Gloucester line was opened in sections as follows:

September 17, 1840   Bromsgrove   —   Cofton Farm
November 4, 1840   Cheltenham   —   Gloucester
December 17, 1840   Cofton Farm —   Camp Hill
August 17, 1841   Camp Hill   —   Junction with L.&B.R.

This last development established continuous railway communication between York, Hull, Leeds, Sheffield, Derby, Nottingham, Leicester, London, Liverpool, Manchester, Birmingham, Cheltenham, and Gloucester. The English railway system was certainly expanding apace.

After such a lively and promising start, it is sad to have to record that the early days of the Birmingham & Gloucester Railway were marred by several accidents. Indeed, at Cheltenham on June 12, 1840, barely a fortnight before the line was officially opened, a twenty-year-old engineer (driver) named William Thornton was 'getting from the engine to put the chains up, when he slipped and the wheel of the engine passed over his left foot. He was conveyed to Cheltenham Hospital where a compound fracture was diagnosed and amputation found necessary. He is now in a fair way of recovery'.

Later that year, on Tuesday, November 10th, there occurred the tragic Lickey explosion. Under the heading 'Dreadful Railway Accident—Two Lives Lost', Berrow's *Worcester Journal* relates that 'Yesterday evening at ten minutes before six, a locomotive engine, once well known at the Vauxhall station, Grand Junction Railway (i.e. at Birmingham) as Dr Church's engine, while standing over an ashpit at the Bromsgrove station, blew up with a terrific explosion. Thomas Scaife, one of the drivers of this railway, a young man of excellent character and abilities, who was by chance on the engine speaking to the driver, was struck dead on the spot. The foreman of locomotives, James[1] Rutherford died this morning (i.e. Wednesday) from the effects of the scalds which he received at the time of the accident. The stoker and one of the breaksmen on the incline were seriously scalded and several others slightly hurt.'

The inquest on the two victims was held by Mr R. Docker, a County Coroner, at noon on Thursday, November 12th, when 'the Jury proceeded to examine the engine, and afterwards viewed the two bodies. Whereas Rutherford was lying at his house near the station, Scaife's remains were laid out in a room in the Dragoon public house adjoining the station'. The full significance of this report becomes clearer from the evidence when it was stated that Scaife had been hurled twenty-five yards, and bits of his clothing, pieces of flesh, and clots of blood were found sixty yards away. Rutherford was projected through the brass rails, three of which were broken by the force of his body, and thrown a distance of many yards. Through 'standing in a higher place than the two deceased', the fireman, Paul Henshaw, was thrown up into the air, and over the rails. However, he was expected to recover. The force of the explosion hurled the chimney 100 yards, and the top of the furnace was thrown clean over the station, behind which it finally embedded itself in a bank. A screw wrench was propelled to such a height that on falling it passed clean through the station roof, and fell through all obstructions to the ground.

The engine, owned by S. A. Goddard of Birmingham, had been altered and repaired by John Henshaw, who stated that on average the boiler was about 3/8 inch thick, but in the place where it had burst no more than 1/4 inch thick. He had seen a boiler 5/16 inch thick work well and attributed more importance to the quality of the iron and workmanship than the thickness of the metal. Pressures of 60-70 lb. per inch were then in common use in Birmingham and were quite safe. He attributed the explosion to sediment in the boiler and also some plugs left in the boiler by the makers. Only a week before arriving at Bromsgrove he had used twenty-five per cent more pressure than at the time of the explosion.

The next witness, G. D. Bishop, an engineer on the Birmingham & Gloucester Railway, disagreed with Henshaw and attached the whole blame to the boiler maker. All boiler plates were ¼ inch thick, apart from the section that burst, and this had been much thinner.

William Creuze, 'chief engineer of locomotives at Bromsgrove station', completely disagreed with Henshaw and blamed 'the thinness of the boiler plates, and its being destitute of stays which ought to have been at intervals of eight or nine inches'.

After a protracted sitting lasting nearly eight hours, the jurors and witnesses were bound over to appear at the Golden Cross the following evening, when the inquiry was resumed before Mr Docker.

A very important witness at the resumed hearing was Dr William Church, who stated that the engine had been built under his direction about three years previously, the boiler tubes and firebox being specially designed to withstand greater pressure than ordinary boilers. The boiler had been made at Brierley Hill and had been proved 'at 150 lb. per circular inch by means of the pump'. Since the accident he had found the inner plate was not of the thickness ordered, but only half the thickness. After completion, the engine was tried experimentally for several days on the London & Birmingham Railway. Alterations were found necessary, and afterwards it was sent to the Grand Junction station. 'It was first tried experimentally, and subsequently attached to a long train of waggons laden with coke, with which it ascended the inclined plane near Wolverhampton, and came to Birmingham; it was afterwards in consequence of breaking an axle removed from the Grand Junction line. The alterations since made would not effect the security of the boiler.' Be that as it may, the explosion had reduced the engine to about 33 cwt. of scrap metal worth £25-£30.

The inquest was again adjourned, this time until Monday, November 23rd. Eventually, after fifteen hours' investigation, the Coroner's Jury returned the following verdict at 1 a.m.— 'We find that Thomas Scaife came to his death in consequence of the bursting of the boiler of a locomotive engine called *The Surprise*, the property of Samuel Aspinall Goddard, occasioned by the boiler being constructed of iron plates, which in evidence appear of insufficient thickness; and we attach a deodand of £60 upon the engine.'

Following the re-swearing of the jury, a similar verdict was returned in respect of J. Rutherford, but without any deodand.[1]

Rutherford's and Scaife's remains were interred in the local churchyard at Bromsgrove, Scaife's funeral on Sunday, November 15th, being attended by about seventy Oddfellows. Their tombstones depict not Dr Church's engine but the Norris type of locomotive, and in the past this has been dismissed as a technical error on the part of the monumental mason. On the other hand, the *Surprise*, a complete outsider undergoing trials at Bromsgrove, had been reduced to scrap, and in view of Rutherford's tremendous popularity (in the eyes of both his subordinates and the board), it is quite possible that the Norris type was depicted as a reminder to later generations of drivers on the Lickey Bank of his devoted service to the company in its early days. His popularity with the men who 'almost idolized him' is clearly confirmed by the 'immediate whip round' made by all ranks, even the directors, for the support of his widow and three young children.

After such a tragic incident, the larger Norris machines of the *Victoria* class were left in supreme charge of traffic ascending the Lickey Bank. Within six months, though, two more serious accidents occurred on the Lickey. Towards the close of March 1841, the boiler of the banking engine *William Gwynn*[2] blew a plug when descending the bank and badly scalded her American driver named Donahue. Far worse was the case of the *Boston*[2] which also blew a plug at 1 a.m. on April 7th, spraying steam and boiling water over three men on the footplate. Ironically enough, the most seriously injured of the three was William Creuze who had been such an important witness during the inquiry into the death of Rutherford and Scaife the previous November. After lingering twenty-four hours, Creuze died at 6 a.m. on Thursday, April 8th, a deodand of £25 being subsequently placed upon the engine.

As with the inauguration of Hudson's and Stephenson's chain

[1] Reporter's error? (Name inscribed on tombstone is Joseph Rutherford.)

[1] S. A. Goddard's subsequent application for trials to be conducted on Lickey Bank using loco *Eclipse* (during summer of 1841) refused.
[2] Both accidents caused by the fitting of incorrect plugs by British personnel during routine repairs (i.e. negligence of maintenance staff).

of companies that summer, the progressive openings of the Birmingham & Gloucester Railway during the second half of 1840 quickly destroyed the earlier road coach traffic. As recently as 1835 there had been six coaches daily setting out from Birmingham along the Bristol Road, that figure being trebled by the opening of the London & Birmingham Railway in 1838 because the new facilities both shortened the time and cheapened the fares for the journey between London and Worcester. By 1839 the number of coaches had risen to twenty-two, but, by the early months of 1841 their fate had been well and truly sealed by the new 'Gloucester line which brought this highly competitive form of transport right into the heart of their formerly isolated territory. Furthermore, on November 14, 1842, through railway carriages were instituted between Euston Square, Birmingham and Gloucester, the departure times being 9.45 a.m. ex London and 1 p.m. ex Gloucester. The journey time of seven and a half hours embraced the forty minutes allowed for transferring the vehicles between the two systems at Curzon Street station, Birmingham.

Like the rest of the early British railway system, the Birmingham & Gloucester Railway was hit very badly by the slump of 1841-42, quite as badly, in fact, as the three companies based on Derby. With receipts rapidly falling away, operating expenses soared to sixty-two per cent of the gross revenue, causing a great outcry from the shareholders, which, in its turn led to a big shake-up in the constitution of the board of directors.[1] By the summer of 1844 there was a very marked recovery with weekly receipts well up by comparison with those for 1843.

Quite soon after the opening of the Bristol & Gloucestershire tramway in August 1835, the earlier scheme for linking Bristol with the City of Gloucester was revived under the new title of Bristol and Gloucestershire Extension Railway. Unfortunately for the Bristolians, another party based upon Gloucester was also attempting to push a line towards Bristol, and their opposition was sufficient to cause the loss of the Bristol & Gloucestershire Bill in 1837. Thereafter, the two parties amalgamated, and having passed the Commons with a majority of 104 the new Bill received the Royal Assent in 1839 under the amended title of Bristol & Gloucester Railway Company. Broadly speaking, the scheme embraced adapting the old Bristol & Gloucestershire tramway between Bristol and Westerleigh Junction, beyond which a new line twenty-two and a quarter miles long was to lead northwards to a junction at Standish with the Cheltenham & Great Western Union line, this company providing access into Gloucester about seven and a half miles further on. By this route the distance between Bristol and Gloucester totalled thirty-seven and a half miles, and the chief engineering works were to be the tunnels at Staple Hill (511 yards) and Wickwar (1,375 yards).

The new Bristol & Gloucester Railway had been conceived as a narrow gauge line consistent with the old idea of providing through rail communication between Bristol and Birmingham, but by 1840 the company was surrounded by three broad gauge concerns—the Bristol & Exeter, the Cheltenham & Great Western Union and, most powerful of all, the Great Western. By 1843 the position was seriously modified by the fact that the Great Western, already dominating the Bristol & Exeter line, purchased the Cheltenham & Great Western Union outright. The implication of this development was that although by 1843 the Bristol & Gloucester Railway was in an advanced stage of construction, it was completely hemmed in at both ends by the broad gauge tracks of the then expanding Great Western system. Again, at Bristol, the B.&G.R. terminus lay some distance from the Great Western station at Temple Meads. This fact alone could easily provide the Great Western directorate with sufficient excuse for diverting the traffic passing between Cheltenham, Gloucester, Bath, Bristol and Exeter on to the all broad gauge route via Swindon, at the expense of the Bristol & Gloucester direct line. Under the guise of negotiations the Great Western party began piling on the pressure, and in view of the severity of the recent slump the Bristol & Gloucester board yielded. Under the terms of an agreement reached in April 1843 they undertook:

(1) To lay their line to the broad gauge.
(2) To establish a physical connection between the two systems at Bristol.

[1] March 8, 1842—Birmingham Committee examine J. E. McConnell's report. Successful economy measures include the fitting-up of Norris Loco *Philadelphia* with coke and water tanks. Tender removed. Very successful. Coke consumption drops from seventeen to thirteen bags per day.

(3) To subscribe £50,000 to the cost of the South Devon Railway which would push broad gauge tracks towards Plymouth.

The first of these points suited the Great Western plan admirably, since Paddington would be spared the expense of laying a third rail between Standish Junction and Gloucester for the benefit of narrow gauge trains, as laid down by Parliament in the Bristol & Gloucester Act. On the subject of the plant needed for working their line, the Bristol & Gloucester board took a much tougher line, and a contract was subsequently placed with Stodart, Slaughter & Company of Bristol, who undertook to work the locomotives and rolling stock for ten years. This arrangement was put into effect in the summer of 1844, and, once again, Great Western policy was admirably suited by such a scheme since Paddington would be spared even further expense.

The Bristol & Gloucester Railway was officially opened on Saturday, July 6, 1844. The new line made a decidedly shaky start which, in retrospect, seems to have typified the company's brief independent career. Whereas the inaugural train should have left Temple Meads at 10 a.m., proceedings were badly delayed for about two hours due to the non-arrival of 'a special train which had gone to Gloucester to bring down some of the directors of the Birmingham & Gloucester Railway. An excellent band of music which was stationed in the terminus served to occupy the attention of the company . . . Mr Brunel and Mr Saunders, the Secretary to the Great Western, came down by the London eleven o'clock train, and the gentlemen from Gloucester having at length arrived at twenty-six minutes past twelve, the first Railway Train from Bristol to Gloucester started.' About 550 guests ('including many ladies') were carried in twelve first and second-class carriages hauled by two locomotives. At the intermediate stations the train was greeted with banners, flags, cheers and music. Perhaps the most spectacular welcome was provided at Charfield where the train was met by a deputation from Wotton-under-Edge. The sergeant-at-mace and a band was followed by the corporation riding in carriages and four, while behind them came a line of horsemen and townsmen on foot no less than a mile long. In order to gratify his friends, a certain Mr Gardner had fitted up 'a spacious carriage in which his capital team of seven horses, gaily caparisoned, drew upwards of eighty persons to the station'.

Less than a mile from Gloucester the inaugural train came to an abrupt halt when the second of the two locomotives left the track whilst negotiating a sharp curve[1] and embedded itself axle deep in the sand. The first engine was detached and used for carrying Brunel and Major General Pasley (the inspecting officer) to Gloucester for assistance, the guests climbed down from the carriages and completed their journey on foot. At the temporary terminus the company had provided 'an elegant *déjeuner a la fourchette* for all as had the foresight to obtain tickets entitling them to partake of the same'. By now it was three o'clock, and as Messrs Brunel and Pasley were preoccupied for a further two hours with the rerailing of the offending engine, the company fell to at 4 p.m. The spread included 'fowls, tongues, hams, cold joints of lamb, veal, &c., jellies and ices. There was also an abundant supply of wine, including an ample allowance of really good iced champagne. The eatables were furnished by Mr Hayward, confectioner, and the wines by Mr H. R. Trehern, of the King's Head, Gloucester. Thereafter, the next half hour passed very agreeably to the music of

Clash of knife and thrust of fork,
Flow of wine, and flight of cork.'

and, despite the delays experienced at Bristol and near Gloucester, a right royal time seems to have been enjoyed by all. It is very interesting to observe that during the course of the speeches, S. Bowly, the visiting chairman of the Birmingham & Gloucester company, remarked 'that if the right thing had been done originally there would have been one line throughout between Birmingham and Bristol, and there would have been no differences about broad gauges and narrow gauges'. Within six months his words were proved true.

Instead of leaving Gloucester for the return journey at 6 p.m., the inaugural train actually set out at 7.50; once again it

[1] The Bristol & G. and the Birmingham & G. stations at Gloucester were alongside each other; but the respective W/G and N/G lines crossed each other ¼ mile from those stations, the Bris. & Glos. W/G line approaching the crossing by means of a sharp curve. Another W/G loco derailed near this crossing on August 10, 1844.

encountered very jubilant receptions at the intermediate stations, rockets were discharged in a particularly noisy welcome staged at Wickwar. It was 10.15 when the train finally trundled into Bristol. After so many delays to the opening celebrations, the local press was quick to observe that 'The line was opened to the public on Monday (i.e. July 8th) and the trains have since continued to ply with regularity and dispatch.' Only two days later a party of more than 650 teetotallers left Cheltenham on a pleasure trip to Bristol. Again, the train was double headed, but there were no mishaps on this occasion.

During the second half of 1844 the full significance of the break of gauge at Gloucester became apparent, particularly in connection with the transhipment of goods from one system to the other. At length, the completely impossible situation eventually aroused the misgivings of the Legislature, and a Parliamentary Committee was sent to Gloucester to obtain first-hand information; here, they were undoubtedly hoodwinked by the antics of the Birmingham & Gloucester company's goods manager, J. D. Payne. This very astute and energetic official not only demonstrated the difficulties invariably associated with the bulk transhipment of goods at Gloucester, but, for good measure, ordered two fully loaded goods trains to be unloaded and then reloaded. The resulting chaos was simply indescribable, but the visitors seem to have swallowed the bait completely and reported accordingly.

The history of the so-called 'Battle of the Gauges' is a completely self-contained subject, but the outcome of one particularly sharp engagement was determined at Gloucester, and not at Birmingham as the broad gauge party had hoped. Following serious negotiations held in the autumn of 1844, the two Gloucester companies came under one management from January 1, 1845, the agreement being formally ratified on January 14th. Despite this administrative unification, the technical problem of the break of gauge at Gloucester still remained unsolved, and it gave the Great Western party their chance. By January 24th, at a meeting held in Bristol, they were urging an extension of their broad gauge from Gloucester to Birmingham, and as an inducement Paddington also offered £60 worth of Great Western stock for each £100 worth of Birmingham & Gloucester stock then standing at 109. However, the united companies stood out for £65 worth of Great Western stock, causing the meeting to be adjourned for three days. On January 26th two of the Birmingham & Gloucester directors, Messrs Sturge and Gibbons, had occasion to travel up to London via Birmingham and Rugby. Quite by chance, John Ellis, also on his way to London, entered their compartment at Rugby Junction, and very soon all three were engaged in amicable conversation. Ellis thus learned of their suspended negotiations with the Great Western board, and, as George Hudson's deputy, he promptly offered terms on behalf of his own company for their consideration should the talks with the broad gauge party fail, as fail they did. On January 27th Charles Saunders, the Great Western Secretary, stated that his board's offer of £60 stock must stand, and, thus, they now turned towards the Derby camp. Purely on his own initiative, John Ellis committed the Midland Railway Company to the extent of leasing the consolidated Birmingham & Bristol concern at a rent of six per cent per annum on a capital of £1,800,000. Outstanding commitments to the tune of £500,000 would also be met. Whereas Saunders had offered stock, Ellis had offered cash—and won—the formal agreement being authenticated by George Hudson's signature on February 8th. Too late for the session of 1845, a Bill for the complete amalgamation of the united Gloucester companies with the Midland Railway was successfully presented to Parliament during 1846, by which time the Gauge Commission had already presented its report. This document came out strongly in favour of the narrow gauge, although existing broad gauge companies should be allowed to continue their operations unhindered. For the time being, then, the broad gauge thrust towards Birmingham was firmly arrested; and under Midland ownership the united Gloucester companies were paying their way by 1848.

With Derby now absorbing the former Birmingham & Gloucester locomotive stock, the behaviour of those early engines was somewhat erratic. A case in point was provided on April 8, 1845, when one of those machines (hauling the 3.30 p.m. train from Cheltenham to Birmingham) blew up a mile south of Aschurch. At 25 m.p.h. the engine lost three wheels but happily

27. Bristol and Birmingham Railway timetable

the driver and stoker appear to have escaped injury 'by clinging to the drags'. Then, only two months later, on June 26th, the 10.30 a.m. train from Gloucester was approaching Camp Hill when another locomotive suddenly appeared from the direction of Birmingham. In the smash one engine was completely destroyed and the other very seriously damaged; one driver and one fireman sustained serious injuries. Fundamentally, this accident was caused by the down train leaving Birmingham contrary to orders and well before the arrival of the up express. Indeed, all the circumstances surrounding the incident tend to suggest that single line working was in operation at the time.

A much happier development by far was the appearance in 1845 of J. E. McConnell's six-coupled saddle tank *Great Britain*. This machine had been specially built at Bromsgrove Works for banking duties on the Lickey, and with her 3 ft. 10 in. wheels, 18 in. x 26 in. cylinders, and weight of 30 tons she was widely regarded as the very last word in locomotive design and performance. The following year (1846) brought full-scale amalgamation of the now united Birmingham and Bristol lines with the Midland Railway. Although made redundant by that latest merger, McConnell had remained in temporary command at Bromsgrove, but with the incorporation of the London & North Western Railway he left to take charge at Wolverton which had already been selected as the locomotive centre for the new company's southern division.

Following McConnell's departure, control of the former Birmingham & Gloucester engines was rapidly centralized at Derby, whereupon Matthew Kirtley's programme of progressive standardization and replacement of the motley collection of locomotive types produced by the mergers of 1844 was extended as far south as Gloucester. The effects of this programme soon began to appear at Bromsgrove, and in February 1847 two engines already on order from Stephenson's were modified to fit them for work on the Lickey Bank. Only a month after that, whereas the sale of the Birmingham & Gloucester machine *Spetchley* produced £1,000, the engines originally supplied in 1840 had their axles removed. The exact fate of the old Norris engines is rather obscure, but as late as January 1858, 'an old Yankee loco was sold for £300'.

South of Gloucester the broad gauge engines and rolling stock previously managed by the outside firm of Stodart, Slaughter & Co. continued to function under Midland suzerainty. Signs of impending modernization soon appeared, though, and in 1848 Hudson's Derby board promoted a Bill seeking Parliamentary sanction for laying a third rail between Bristol and Standish Junction for the benefit of Midland narrow-gauge trains. From Standish Junction to Gloucester independent narrow-gauge tracks were to be laid alongside the Great Western company's broad-gauge lines. On this issue the Midland application was most successfully opposed in the Lords by the Great Western party under the terms of the agreement drawn up with the Bristol & Gloucester company in 1843. Paddington also suggested a compromise solution by undertaking to add a third rail to their existing broad-gauge lines between Standish Junction and Gloucester for the benefit of Midland trains, but, be that as it may, the offer aroused nothing but suspicion at Derby, particularly on the question of tolls, and so the Midland Bill was withdrawn. The Hudson débâcle of 1849 followed, but with the recovery of the early 'fifties the Midland modernization scheme was revived under Hudson's successor, John Ellis. This time the results were much more successful and a third rail was laid between Bristol and Standish Junction, with separate narrow-gauge lines put down over the remaining seven and a half miles into Gloucester. Moreover, under the provisions of the amalgamation Act of 1846, broad gauge was also retained between Bristol and Standish Junction until 1872.

Although withdrawn in 1848, the earlier Midland Bill had really marked the beginning of the end of the broad-gauge engines and rolling stock then running between Bristol and Gloucester. That same year Matthew Kirtley had also given a pretty broad hint of things to come by designing four convertible locomotives, Midland numbers 66-69. These began work as broad-gauge machines, but all four were subsequently converted for narrow-gauge working by the simple expedient of having their axles shortened; within twenty-four hours the whole batch was back on the road. Earlier, in October 1853, a further pointer had been provided when the Midland Locomotive Committee instructed W. H. Barlow to adapt the Bristol running shed for the accommodation of narrow-gauge engines. Further north, the track layout was reorganized at Gloucester to permit trains from Birmingham to pass on to the narrow-gauge lines leading southward to Standish Junction and Bristol. On June 1, 1854, Midland narrow-gauge trains were extended from Gloucester to Bristol, and thereafter the old broad-gauge equipment was rendered obsolete. At Derby orders were given for some of the older wagons to be broken up, but most of the plant was put up for sale from the autumn onward. These tactics met with varying degrees of success, but, little by little, the various items were eventually disposed of, the last of the old broad-gauge engines being sold to Thomas Brassey in 1857.

Back in 1851 the Birmingham & Bristol line had suffered very badly from the side effects produced by the Great Trade Exhibition which had 'pulled' a tremendous excursion traffic towards London, and it was autumn before conditions had returned to normal. By that time the Midland Railway was facing greatly increased competition from all sides, and the close of the year found Derby formulating plans for completely re-equipping all Midland main lines with locomotives much bigger and far more powerful than any other type used hitherto. In step with this forward looking policy Kirtley was already hard at work designing several new series of 2.2.2 express engines in which he completely abandoned his earlier dimensional standards in favour of much bigger cylinders and far larger diameter driving wheels. The former diameters of 5 ft. 6 in. and 6 ft. were thus increased to 6 ft. 8 in., the old 15 in. x 20 in. cylinders being enlarged to 16 in. x 22 in. Boiler pressures were greatly stepped up, so that the standard working pressure became 140 lb. p.s.i., a very high figure indeed for those days. The Derby Locomotive Works had also been brought into effective use during 1851. This establishment subsequently became world famous, but for the first few years these works were mostly concerned with repairs, even though rebuilds of some earlier, smaller machines were already being turned out during the early 'fifties. Consequently, it was still necessary to obtain completely new types from outside contractors, and for working the principal Midland expresses between Birmingham and Gloucester an order was placed with Sharp Brothers in April 1852 for ten of Kirtley's new 6 ft. 8 in. 'singles' at a cost of £2,160 apiece. Delivery had been planned on the basis of four in October, three in November, and three in December of 1852, but production difficulties prevented delivery of the final batch before the first quarter of 1853. In true Sharp fashion all ten were supplied with highly polished domes mounted upon the first boiler ring behind the chimney, a highly distinctive feature which gave them a particularly lively appearance.

These newcomers had been allocated the Midland capital stock numbers 120-129, and having most successfully completed their steaming trials the whole batch was promptly put to work upon the former Birmingham & Gloucester main line in the spring of 1853. Thereafter they rapidly took charge of the more important services between those two cities, and on June 1, 1854, they began running through to Bristol—following the extension of the narrow gauge beyond Gloucester. On that section they joined forces with Nos. 66-69 which had just been modified for narrow-gauge working; but as Nos. 120-129 were main line express engines, Nos. 66-69 were now relegated to the semi-fast and slower stopping trains. Yet another extremely important event occurring on June 1, 1854, was the inauguration of the London & North Western company's huge station at New Street, Birmingham. Under section 21 of the original Birmingham & Gloucester Railway Act of 1836, the Midland singles of the '120 class' were also diverted to New Street—and from that point the old workings to and from Curzon Street disappeared.

Considered as a class, Nos. 120-129 enjoyed quite a long working life. However, in the autumn of 1870 they found themselves displaced when Neilson's delivered Nos. 820-829 which represented the final batch of the thirty revolutionary 2.4.0s of Kirtley's '800 class' ordered from that firm toward the close of 1869. During the next ten years Nos. 820-829 were responsible for the increasingly heavy Birmingham and Bristol trains, and the earlier Sharp singles (Nos. 120-129) removed from the Bristol main line in 1870 were sent all over the Midland system and relegated to secondary trains, No. 125 being withdrawn in 1872. Thereafter, in 1874, Nos. 120, 121 and 123-128 were removed from the capital stock list and given the suffix 'A', the original capital stock numbers being re-allocated to the newest Derby-built 2.4.0.s of Kirtley's '890 class'. By something of a coincidence, all eight of these new Kirtley main line engines were sent to Birmingham to work the company's western lines. Of the nine diminutive Sharp 'singles' then surviving, number 128A ran until the turn of the 'eighties, having been preceded to the scrap heap in 1879 by the old number 122 which remained on the capital stock list until the very end. Of the whole class the last to go was number 129 which was withdrawn ten years later, in 1889, at the ripe old age of thirty-six.

In this extensive modernization drive the capital stock numbers 66-69 were similarly reallocated to decidedly more modern machines. Here, the first to be affected was No. 66, which number was transferred in 1870 to a new Derby-built 2.4.0. of the '800 class'; but in this instance the new locomotive joined with Nos. 60-65 in hauling main line trains on the Leeds and London links. Four years later numbers 67, 68 and 69 were also reallocated—the recipients being three '890 class' 2.4.0s turned out from Derby Works in 1874. These also went to Leicester where they reinforced the '800 class' 2.4.0s numbers 60-66 of 1870.

Away to the west, the locomotive studs at Birmingham, Gloucester and Bristol were completely modernized between 1870 and 1874. With this done, the daily scene on the West of England main line was completely transformed as, from 1870 onward, a third generation of main line engines began shouldering the ever-mounting responsibilities associated with the expansion of the main line traffic on the Birmingham & Bristol line.

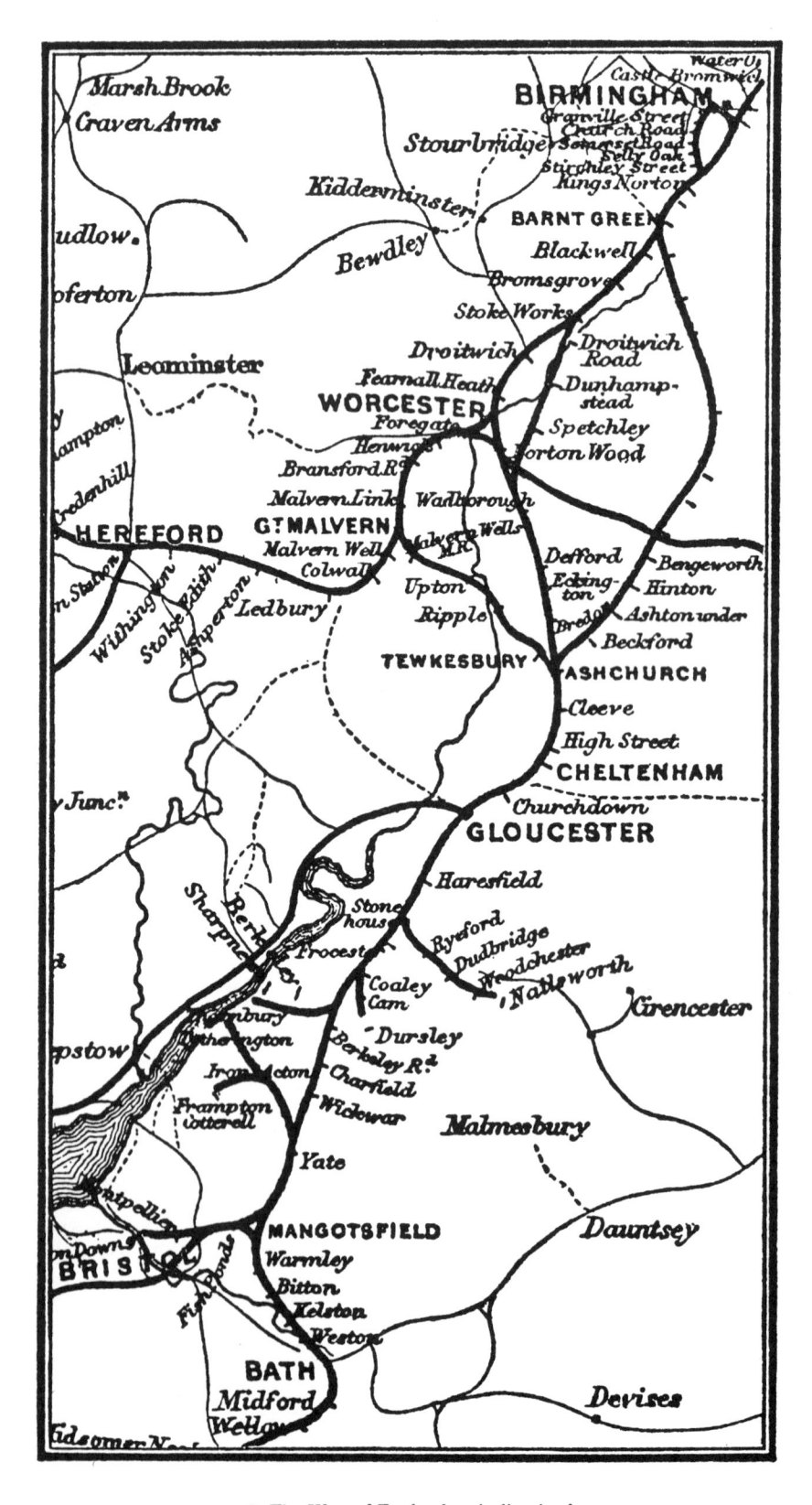

28. The West of England main line in the middle seventies

CHAPTER 6

JOHN ELLIS TO THE RESCUE

At Derby the report prepared by the committee of investigation was presented to the adjourned meeting of shareholders on August 15, 1849. The text of the report revealed that, although somewhat lacking in fulness of detail, the published accounts previously laid before the shareholders on various occasions had actually been in accordance with the company's authentic books. Even so, the committee instantly conceded that a clear differentiation had not always been accurately maintained between the 'capital' and the 'revenue' accounts. For example, since the amalgamation of 1844, no less than thirty-six miles of the old Midland Counties main line, also part of the Sheffield & Rotherham, and thirty-five miles of the former Birmingham & Gloucester line had been relaid with completely new chairs and rails, the cost of which had been charged to 'capital account'. Such a step had given rise to a prolonged discussion, and the accountants had insisted that the expense incurred in a bare renewal of worn-out road should be charged to 'revenue'. On the other hand, substantial improvements should be charged against 'capital'.

The task of answering the committee's most searching questions concerning the fantastic cost (£915,997) of those track relaying operations had fallen to William Henry Barlow, the company's resident engineer. Naturally enough, Barlow replied from the viewpoint of an engineer rather than that of an accountant, and stated that he thought the bulk of the money should be charged to 'capital', because the enlargement of many of the more important stations and the use of heavier engines had demanded the substitution of much heavier rails as opposed to the straightforward replacement of old and worn-out lines by new ones of precisely similar weight. Furthermore, the old rails removed from the main roads had been used for branch lines and sidings, where they became quite as valuable as new ones.

In connection with yet another item in this extremely costly bill, Barlow pointed out that at least 1,000 tons of new rails had been used on the Leeds & Bradford line alone, and a further 3,000 tons had been used in the construction of points, crossings, crossovers, and similar new track work. Permanent way maintenance costs, Barlow claimed, would tend to become cheaper, and as these initial heavy costs would permanently benefit the line he thought that the decision to charge the greater proportion of the cost to 'capital' had been essentially correct in the circumstances. Henceforth, he concluded, the shareholders could reasonably expect to be called upon to support only the cost of the year's working expenses, depreciations, and repairs.

After prolonged and very careful consideration, the committee recommended acceptance of Barlow's explanation without reservation. Further, it also recommended that the proposal to appoint a stipendiary chairman should be rejected, and that the number of directors should be increased to twenty, the object being to secure direction on a much broader and more flexible basis, as compared with Hudson's autocratic regime of the past five years.

According to the accountants, the locomotive stock had depreciated by at least £100,000, and the carriage and wagon stock by some £70,000. This statement caused Robert Stephenson to launch a counter-attack in which he claimed that the permanent way had been greatly strengthened and improved, that the locomotives were bigger and more efficient than hitherto, and that the carriage and wagon stock had greatly increased both in size and value.

The committee's Report was duly adopted by the meeting, but there still remained one important dissentient—our old friend Mr Wylie of Liverpool, who jumped to his feet and launched a bitter tirade against what he termed the incompleteness and the inconclusiveness of the Report. Still, even Wylie was forced to abide by the majority decision, and, with the Report generally adopted, the Midland Railway Company embarked rather shakily upon a new stage in its career. This time, however, it was the dignified, sagacious, and universally respected John Ellis who occupied the chair so hurriedly vacated by the brash and vulgar Hudson. There was absolutely no opportunity for a short breathing space, and already the Midland company found itself confronted by the triple threat arising from the partial openings of the Great Northern, and the Manchester, Sheffield & Lincolnshire lines, coupled with the intensification of the national recession. All over the country railway property was alarmingly depressed, and everywhere the outlook was very, very bleak. Notwithstanding its bold, agressive tactics, the Great Northern company found the going every bit as tough.

Hudson's ignominious collapse in the spring of 1849 had brought chaos to the British political scene, especially when it was discovered that he had manipulated the accounts of his York & North Midland, and York, Newcastle & Berwick companies to such an extent that it was well-nigh impossible to disentangle them. With the outbursts of righteous indignation that followed on each successive revelation, each of the former Hudson companies was left to fend for itself. Such developments left the Midland Railway in an extremely precarious financial position and, as if this were not enough, the Midland lost its former supremacy in the West Riding when Hudson, faced with the onrushing slump, arranged for Great Northern trains to secure direct entry into York via Knottingley, and into Leeds via Methley Junction.

Hudson's downfall left his so-called East Coast route in a completely parlous state. It also provided a golden opportunity for Captain Mark Huish to seize the initiative at Euston Square, where he was General Manager of the London & North Western company. Mark Huish was an extremely capable and completely ruthless schemer, and lost no time in establishing himself as the overlord of the West Coast alliance which now dominated the Anglo-Scottish traffic. To ensure the continued supremacy of the alliance, he strove constantly to restrict the status of the Midland Railway to that of a large provincial line feeding the London & North Western system, and above all to neutralize the Great Northern company, which was then on the point of opening a new trunk line of national importance and thereby establishing a new and more direct East Coast route between London and the Scottish border via Peterborough and York. Thus, during the latter part of 1849 and the opening months of 1850, Huish engineered a series of secret negotiations from which emerged the notorious Octuple Agreement, whereby the supremacy of the London & North Western was assured. Under the terms of this compact, it was Huish who dictated the division of receipts obtained from traffic operating north of York, and thus the Great Northern fared very badly indeed. So, for about five years Huish held sway at Euston Square, until his confederacy was suddenly shattered by the revelations of the illegal 'common purse agreement' contracted with the Midland company. The disclosures were made during the course of evidence heard by Parliament relevant to a Bill presented by the 'Little North Western' company. After the rumpus died away, the Midland board took the opportunity of strengthening their position in relation to the Anglo-Scottish and Anglo-Irish traffic by absorbing the 'Little North Western' line instead.

The fact that in its near bankrupt state the Midland Railway was able to withstand the further financial stresses of 1849 and 1850 was due in no small measure to the company's singular good fortune in possessing John Ellis as its chairman. Here was a man whose personal integrity was completely above suspicion, and who had undoubtedly succeeded in preventing Hudson from manipulating Midland finances in the fashion associated with his other railway interests. John Ellis's task was indeed a formidable one, and at the half-yearly meeting held at Derby on February 27, 1850, he announced that for the six months ending December 31, 1849, gross receipts amounted to £600,000, that is a drop of £20,000 compared with the corresponding period of 1848. Whereas a dividend of £2 10s was then paid, there was now only £100,000 available for dividend purposes, and so only 25s would be paid on this occasion. This sombre news brought Mr Wylie bounding to his feet again to launch a speech that lasted for two hours, in the course of which he championed the cause of 1,200 shareholders from the vicinity of Liverpool. At the height of the 'Mania', their shares had enjoyed a collective market value of £1,623,000, but now they had shrivelled to a mere £524,000. This calamitous state of affairs, Wylie continued, was directly due to the reckless financial policies which, since 1845, had saddled the Midland Company with a tremendous burden of guarantees and leases that had subsequently sapped its strength.

Wylie's forebodings proved only too true, and at the Annual

General Meeting held on August 23rd, the dividend sank even lower to 16s, thus making a total for the year of £2 1s. The announcement met with a very noisy reception indeed, and yet it could scarcely be called unsatisfactory in view of the fact that Midland Consolidated Stock had slumped from its boom-time peak of 160 to an all-time low of only 32/33. But to appease the shareholders the Derby board played heavily upon the news of the arrangements just made with the York & North Midland line for the joint use of the new Wellington Station at Leeds, and also with the Oxford, Worcester and Wolverhampton Company which had consented that Midland trains should have direct access to Worcester, the nearest Midland station then being Spetchley.

Of course, economy was already the watchword at Derby, and this Annual General Meeting provided an excellent opportunity for airing a number of schemes aimed at extricating the Midland Company from its desperate predicament. One suggestion proposed the use of lighter and less expensive engines, but as John Ellis pointed out, much of the company's revenue stemmed from a strangely mixed and very heavy freight traffic, and this alone meant that some twenty locomotives were already unable to cope with their normal daily duties. To provide a further contribution in the avoidance of unnecessary expense, the Parliamentary powers embodied in the Leicester & Hitchin Act of 1847 had also been allowed to lapse that July.

The idea of a major economy drive was no novelty. Indeed, over the past year operational economies had been in force at Derby, and a snap check of 'foreign' companies' wagons passing through that station during October 1849 revealed that quite a few of the 'foreigners' were sporting Midland couplings. Easily the chief offender was the L.N.W.R., no fewer than fourteen wagons belonging to that company being counted at the first check. The Liverpool & Manchester, the Manchester & Birmingham, and the South Staffordshire companies all contributed one apiece. Quite obviously, the South Staffs. people believed in doing a job properly, for in this instance the Midland coupling was found riveted on.

In order to conserve locomotive power, a number of passenger services were reorganized. With effect from November 1, 1849, two 'up' and two 'down' trains were cancelled on the Leeds & Bradford line; and on the short stretch between Sheffield and Rotherham the following alterations resulted in the saving of another locomotive:

Cancelled: 9.30 a.m., 3 p.m., and 3.30 p.m. Sheffield to Rotherham.
10 a.m. and 4 p.m. Rotherham to Sheffield.
N.B. the 3 p.m. was withdrawn due to the cancellation of the 2.10 p.m. from Derby.
Between Rotherham and Sheffield the following trains were retimed:
11 a.m. advanced to 10.30 a.m.; the 8 a.m. and 8.20 a.m. combined to run as one train; and similarly with the 1.45 p.m. and the 2 p.m.

Furthermore, throughout the Midland system passenger guards were required to report on delays affecting their trains at stations, and to submit the reports direct to the Locomotive Committee for detailed scrutiny at weekly intervals.

At Rugby the economies effected that autumn included the dismissal of a driver, a fireman, two fitters, and two cleaners, thus suggesting the withdrawal of a locomotive from the Rugby shed. A resolution made by the Midland board on November 27th to enlarge the turntable at Rugby by four feet was hastily countermanded on December 6th, and Matthew Kirtley was directed 'to give positive instructions for all engines using L.N.W. turntables to carry lights'. At Normanton there was no alternative but to bear the cost of repairing the Midland turntable, and in December 1849 instructions were given for repairing the flooring of three pits within the old roundhouse at Derby, and two within the new. Locomotive 291 was condemned; and Nos. 145 and 146 rebuilt by Wilson's in the spring of 1850.

The year 1850 produced a slight yet detectable change in the economic situation which put fresh heart into the Midland board, and although passenger receipts fell by a further £8,000, income from goods and mineral traffic rose by £32,000, thus justifying a dividend of 25s. Acceleration of the general revival was undoubtedly assisted by the Great Trade Exhibition of 1851. With the arrival of the new year public attention became excited by the preparations then being made in London, and when this wonderful show was opened to all and sundry a huge railway excursion traffic began to converge on the capital from all directions. Once again the Midland was brought into sharp conflict with its arch enemy, the Great Northern, and almost overnight excursionists from the West Riding were revelling in the tremendous clash which brought the return fare between Leeds and London down to 5s per head. Today it seems incredible that trains could possibly pay their way under such conditions; but pay they did, and they ran packed to capacity.

In anticipating the demands of this exhibition traffic, John Ellis had taken the precaution (in December 1850) of ordering no fewer than 100 third-class carriages seating forty people apiece. This contract was put out to competitive tender, the specification calling for the use of India Teak for the bottoms, sides, ends, and top rails; and seasoned English Ash for the remainder of the body framing. Some twelve firms tendered from points as widely separated as Leeds and Manchester, but it was Brown & Marshall of Birmingham who secured the contract. Incidentally, some of the prices quoted in the tenders received at Derby make very interesting reading: e.g. Oak, £88 10s; Teak, £97 10s; Teak and Oak, £90 per vehicle.

From the very outset the Midland Railway had always enjoyed a high reputation for the cleanliness of its carriages, and with the passing of the slump seven more men were engaged for carriage cleaning duties at Leeds, Derby and Nottingham, and all over the system stationmasters received strict instructions 'to attend to the cleanliness of the interiors'. Furthermore, safety precautions also received careful consideration at this period, and it was resolved that 'the side steps of Carriages, Horse Boxes, and Carriage Trucks used in passenger trains be lengthened so as to enable the Guard to communicate with the Driver in case of need; this practice having been approved by the London & North-Western Railway Company'.

Taking the long-term view, though, the exhibition traffic did relatively little to improve Midland finances as a whole, for whereas the bulk of the passenger traffic from all parts of the country was gravitating towards London there was an ominous reduction in traffic on Midland cross-country lines, particularly between Birmingham and Bristol. The position became so bad that in the autumn a further committee was appointed to report upon the state and prospect of Midland finances; and its findings can be summed up by stating that although the company now possessed more than 500 route miles of line it was still a large but essentially provincial concern with its southern outpost (at Rugby Junction) more than eighty miles from London.

It was now imperative that the Midland company should secure direct access to the capital—but this was much easier said than done, for at that moment Midland finances would not bear the cost of building an independent line to the metropolis. Consequently, at the Half-Yearly Meeting held at Derby on February 27, 1852, the directors informed the shareholders that it was of the utmost importance that serious consideration should be given to the possibility of a permanent identification with some company capable of providing a line with terminal facilities in London itself. This subject, they claimed, was of the most urgent and critical importance.

Now, the obvious choice was the London & North Western Railway which[1] had provided Midland Counties passengers with a means of reaching Euston Square following the opening of the Midland Counties line to Rugby Junction in the summer of 1840. Separate platforms had since been provided at Euston where there was still plenty of land available for future expansion. Furthermore, at Euston Square Mark Huish was bent upon consolidating the 'empire' he had created by engineering the Octuple Agreement, and the chance to absorb the Midland Railway by amalgamation was one that was too good to be missed. There now followed a series of interviews between the two boards, but Huish had reckoned without the business acumen of John Ellis who was determined to sign only upon his own terms, and at length Euston's highest bid failed to coincide with the lowest Midland offer by a margin of two and a half per cent. In these unfortuitous circumstances the negotiations were broken off. Yet, these merger proposals did not die out completely at this stage for her other rivals had already spotted that, despite her recent setbacks, Derby was now a power which would soon assume very dangerous proportions. Indeed, throughout 1851 the number of Midland locomotives in steam daily had risen from 169 to 190; and whereas train mileages had increased by more than 300,000, the goods and mineral traffic had increased by more than 250,000 tons. Thus, negotiations with the North Western were reopened on Saturday, August 14, 1852. As such

[1] London & Birmingham Railway merged into L.N.W.R. in 1846.

a merger would obviously menace Great Northern interests, Edmund Denison launched his counter-proposals with great alacrity on Monday, August 16th, notwithstanding the fact that the Midland had 'imprisoned' a Great Northern engine at Nottingham only a fortnight previously. This time, public speculation simply buzzed at the possible outcome of a tremendous merger, but the very idea was subsequently summarily rejected by Parliament then seeking to frustrate all attempts to create large-scale transport monopolies deemed likely to be detrimental to the national interests.

At the time of those important negotiations, the Midland board was also negotiating with various parties interested in reviving the former Leicester & Hitchin scheme. Consequently, in exchange for important concessions in the West Riding, the Great Northern undertook to refrain from opposing any new Leicester & Hitchin Bill which Derby might introduce into the House. Indeed, Denison's party went one step further by withdrawing their proposed branch to Bedford, and even the incident at Nottingham on August 1st was smoothed over and quietly forgotten at board level, although the legal boys were kept very busy for some months yet. Still, such diplomatic exchanges served to advance the Midland cause in numerous ways during the near future, as we shall soon see.

CHAPTER 7

THE LEICESTER AND HITCHIN EXTENSION

During 1851, which was a year of economic recovery, a wave of optimistic expansion surged right across the country, and before long this uplift caused the reappearance of many local schemes which had foundered in the slump. In just this way the important Leicester & Bedford party came to the fore again, and in the spring of 1852 a deputation was sent to Derby 'to wait upon the Midland Board there' and to urge that company to revive its earlier Leicester & Hitchin project in respect of which the Act of 1847 had been relinquished in July 1850. Now a very prominent member of that delegation was Mr William Whitbread, whose family owned about one-eighth of all the land needed for the line, and although the negotiations were conducted in 'a spirit of great liberality', he left John Ellis in absolutely no doubt whatever that, should full-scale Midland support be found at all wanting, the revitalized party would most certainly turn elsewhere for assistance. Now, this was a particularly formidable ultimatum because the Midland and the Great Northern companies were still at loggerheads. Indeed, Denison's board still had their sights trained upon Leicester and the coalfield beyond; at King's Cross, London, the permanent Great Northern terminal facilities were fast approaching completion. Thus, it behove the Midland people to think very, very carefully before rejecting the deputation's demands for fear that the Leicester & Hitchin scheme should fall once again into hostile hands.

Throughout England the economic improvement was already producing far-reaching changes in the railway political scene. Many new alliances were appearing, and on many of the bigger lines traffic was expanding at an extraordinary pace. In this respect the Midland Railway was no exception. Derby's biggest headache of the day was caused by the imperative need to secure an improved outlet to London capable of carrying the company's constantly expanding freight traffic without actually incurring the expense of building an independent line eighty miles long, together with the attendant terminal facilities. The most likely solution seemed to lie in amalgamation with the London & North Western company, and for this purpose a Bill was introduced into the House in time for the 1853 session; but this measure received its death stroke 'in consequence of the appointment of a select committee of the House of Commons which advised the House not to allow any amalgamation this session and which has since reported against the formation of very large companies'. Yet in 1852 alone, no less than 325,000 tons of coal had been loaded on to the London & North Western line at Rugby Junction, a large proportion of this huge Midland tonnage being destined for London and the southern counties, then a rapidly expanding market. Henceforth, Midland goods and mineral traffic increased by such leaps and bounds that eventually, in 1859, the North Western opened a third or up relief line between Watford and Primrose Hill, the new line being extended to Bletchley later the same year. In just this way, the heavy Midland freight trains were prevented from impeding the faster L.N.W. passenger trains on their approach to the capital.

Against all this, Midland through passenger services to and from London remained little changed from what they had been during Hudson's time, with eight weekday and four Sunday trains in each direction. Of the weekday services four were hauled at express speeds by a batch of North Western engines specially allocated for the task, whereas the remainder were attached to North Western semi-fast trains. In most cases, though, the Midland services also connected at Bletchley with L.N.W.R. trains running across country to and from Oxford and Bedford. Thus, the construction of the Leicester & Hitchin line could solve quite a few of these operating difficulties since Midland tracks could be brought southward to within thirty miles of London, with entry to metropolitan terminal facilities being subsequently provided by the Great Northern Railway. Not only would the proposed line relieve the tremendous pressure already being exerted upon the London & North Western facilities south of Rugby, it would also provide a subtle method of containing Great Northern designs upon Leicester and Bedford. Because of this, John Ellis had much less difficulty in persuading the Midland board to revive their scheme for an extension between Leicester and Hitchin. At a special meeting of shareholders held at Derby on June 1, 1853, a show of hands revealed only four dissentients, and further support for the scheme was furnished by proxies sent to Derby by no less than 2,800 other shareholders.

Some twelve months previously a Leicester & Hitchin Extension Committee had been specially convened. It consisted of John Ellis (chairman), William Price (deputy chairman), and Midland directors Sir Isaac Morley and Messrs Hutchinson, Barwell and Paget. Secretary to the Committee was the Company's Secretary, G. N. Browne. The initial meeting of this new body was held at Derby station on July 14, 1852, and there Barwell and Browne were instructed to interview landowners along the proposed line with the dual object of obtaining local assent wherever possible and also to take immediate advantage of any particularly attractive terms which might be offered to them on the spot. This indeed proved to be the case where the line crossed the estates of the Duke of Bedford and the Whitbread family, for in those instances the land was subsequently acquired at its simple agricultural value of about £70 per acre. Incidentally, the precise route for the whole line still remained to be settled. Thus, responsibility for surveying a suitable route and then reporting in detail back to his directors now became the first of many major burdens assumed by Charles Liddell who, it will be recalled, had played such an important part in surveying both the South Midland and the Syston & Peterborough lines at the height of the Railway Mania some six or seven years previously.

As presented to the Leicester & Hitchin Extension Committee on August 18, 1852, Liddell's report was a vitally important document drawing attention to the choice of routes available between Market Harborough and Pytchley, and again between Shefford and Hitchin. Between Harborough and Pytchley the choice lay between the old South Midland route via Desford and the former Leicester & Bedford route via Rothwell. Of the two alternatives, the latter was the shorter by some one and one-eighth miles, thereby implying a potential saving in land purchasing costs amounting to no less than £13,000. However, this advantage would be offset by the cost of constructing a tunnel, numerous cuttings, and other heavy engineering works estimated at an additional £56,000. Even so, the Leicester & Bedford route would cut right through the ironstone beds at a point where the ore lay near the surface—a most serious consideration because there was undoubtedly a golden future for this class of mineral traffic which, relying upon road transport, already amounted to 90,000 tons per annum. On the other hand, modification of the South Midland route would enable the new line to be taken to the west of Kettering, thereby reducing the difference in distance to just about one mile, as well as producing some very considerable improvements in the gradients. Short branches, also on easy gradients, would provide perfectly satisfactory access to the ironstone beds on the hills above Rothwell, the beds having been revealed some twenty-five feet below the surface during the trial borings made along the South Midland route way back in 1845. Taking everything into careful consideration, then, the adoption of the modified South Midland route would probably achieve a total saving of about £28,000. Again, opinion had been somewhat divided as to whether, between Shefford and Hitchin, the new Midland line from Leicester should either join the Great Northern main line at Arlesey or, alternatively, run alongside it for about five miles before affecting a junction at Hitchin. Resulting from his discussions with William Cubitt, the Great Northern engineer, Charles Liddell now advised his Committee that the Midland line should be taken straight across country to a junction just north of Hitchin, and that due to the favourable nature of the locality such a modification should only increase the length of the line by three and a quarter miles, the additional cost not exceeding £10,000 per mile. Further substantial savings could also be effected by selecting Wigston as the point of junction with the existing main line instead of the junction with the Leicester & Burton railway. Construction costs for the new line to Hitchin should average £15,000 to £16,000 per mile, and so the capital outlay for the whole scheme should be £1,000,000.

The immediate acceptance of these proposals enabled Liddell to devote the autumn of 1852 to the preparation of the parliamentary plans to accompany the new Bill into the House early in 1853. Meanwhile, the valuation of the land needed for the new line was also in progress. This highly important task was virtually halved by giving charge of the northern section (from Wigston to the parish of Wellingborough) to Joseph Ellis, the southern portion (from Wellingborough to Hitchin) being entrusted to Henry Trethewy of Silsoe, Bedfordshire.

Thanks largely to the recent rapprochment with the Great Northern, the withdrawal of that company's Bill for a branch between Sandy and Bedford provided the Leicester & Hitchin Bill with a relatively easy passage through the Commons which gave the measure its third reading on May 23, 1853. However, a delay of about six weeks was caused by the deliberations of the select committee which ultimately reported against amalgamation between Derby and Euston. Thereafter, the Lords tackled the backlog of private Bills with really commendable efficiency, and the Leicester & Hitchin Act thus received Royal Assent on August 4th (16 & 17 Vic, c 108.).

In repealing the earlier Midland Railway Acts of 1847 and 1848, the Leicester & Hitchin Act of 1853 now authorized a new project whereby the new line was to extend from a junction with the Midland main line near Wigston to a junction with the Great Northern Railway at Hitchin. At Bedford, the L.N.W.R. branch from Bletchley, and the complementary branch to that company's depot on the south bank of the Ouse, would be crossed on the level; the speed of the trains to be determined by the 'North Western under the regulations stipulated by the Board of Trade. Over the border, in Northamptonshire, the River Nene was to be spanned by a viaduct having a clear span of 350 feet (measured at right-angles to the flow of the river), at a minimum height of nineteen feet across the seven-foot towing path bordering a clear, navigable waterway quite seventy feet broad. Across the River Ise, the bridge was to have a span of ninety feet.

The Leicester & Hitchin Committee went straight into action. At the Victoria Hotel, London, on August 10th, Charles Liddell received formal instructions to prepare plans, specifications, and quantities in readiness for the contracts. A fortnight later, the Company's solicitors began serving land notices to the occupants of lands to be acquired, paying particular regard to entry by the Company's surveyors for boring trial holes and for staking out the line of the new extension. So, by the end of the summer the whole scheme was definitely on the move. Less cheerful, though, was the issue of four per cent Preferential Stock for financing the construction works. Due to a sudden change in the state of the money market, Midland shareholders were reluctant to take up more than a small proportion of the total authorized at the Special General Meeting held in August 1853, and so at the end of the year arrangements were made for the issue of nearly all the remainder to local landowners and other similarly interested parties. Thus satisfied of their ability to successfully finance the construction of their Leicester & Hitchin line, the Midland board promptly addressed itself to the letting of contracts, the value of which had been previously estimated by Charles Liddell at approximately £1,000,000.

The works for the Leicester & Hitchin Extension were split into two main contracts. Of these the first was concerned with the 880-yard long Warden Tunnel, the only one on the new line, which was let to a local man, John Knowles of Shefford. Between Wigston and Hitchin the whole of the remaining works were embodied in one huge contract for which competitive tenders were submitted by about a dozen firms; but it was only upon the receipt of an amended proposal at Derby during the last week of January 1854 that this main contract was subsequently awarded to Thomas Brassey. Thus, by February the whole of the Leicester & Hitchin line was under contract, the date of completion being fixed at October 1856; and in March the Midland Ways and Works Committee followed up by undertaking to provide 1,000 tons of old rails at £7 per ton, with chairs to match at £5 per ton. Following the completion of these essential preliminaries, construction work upon the new Midland extension began that April when Brassey's representative (Horne) was given possession of the Whitbread lands in the parishes of Cardington and Warden. An enduring testimony to the sudden influx into the district of Brassey's men is still to be seen only a couple of miles south of Warden Tunnel in a tiny hamlet named Ireland. The story goes that the lack of a pub was simply remedied by the conversion of an ordinary house for the benefit of the construction gangs engaged upon the railway works only a few yards away. Although those wonderful navvies have long since gone, that beautiful little pub still remains to delight a modern generation.

But a month after the works commenced the extension committee resolved upon the provision of the following stations to serve the new line at: Meppershall, Shefford, Southill, Cardington, Bedford, Great Oakley, Sharnbrook, Irchester, Wellingborough, Isham, Kettering, Rushden, Desborough, 'Harborough, Langton, Kibworth, Glen, and Wigston, a decision which was followed up in June when John Ellis led the committee upon an initial tour of inspection of the works from end to end. During this tour, which lasted three days, the opportunity was taken to make a preliminary selection for the station sites. At Bedford, Ellis and his party were met by the Mayor and representatives of the Corporation who pointed out that the town council were anxious that the Midland station should be built upon the Freeman's Common Land on the north bank of the Great Ouse. However, other powerful local administrative interests were also at work, and these were calling for a joint station with the London & North Western Railway on the south bank at a point close to where the new Midland line would intersect the other company's existing branch from Bletchley. At this stage, Ellis declined to commit himself, and so began the local controversy which raged for the next four or five years, and which was still unresolved when the Leicester & Hitchin line was opened for traffic.

Even if the site of the Midland station at Bedford remained unsettled, at least agreement was reached in July on Mr Whitbread's suggestion that adequate religious instruction should be provided for the men engaged upon the railway works. Three scripture readers were subsequently appointed at 200 guineas per annum, the cost being equally divided between the contractor and the Midland company. Lively as those local skirmishes were, the extension committee's policy was steadily overshadowed by the events of the Crimean War which had broken out the previous March. Also, the construction works soon showed unmistakable signs of becoming both difficult and expensive.

It was also in the summer of 1854 that Brassey, Peto & Betts offered to supply the Midland company with 50,000 logs of Norwegian origin and suitable for cutting sleepers. This offer resulted in a contract being let that July for the supply of some 100,000 sleepers 8 ft. 11 in. long, and with a minimum section of 9½ in. × 4½ in., for delivery and stacking at Great Grimsby by the end of the year. During October, however, a report was received at Derby stating that the logs unloaded so far had proved to be of an inferior standard. Work at the port was abruptly suspended, and on November 14th the cargo of logs was subjected to the personal inspection of John Ellis at the head of a Midland deputation, but the next batch were of much better quality and unloading was promptly resumed. Meanwhile, the astute Ellis seized this wonderful opportunity to place orders in the neighbourhood of a further 75,000 sleepers in anticipation of future requirements.

Back at Derby again, the Leicester & Hitchin Committee was confronted afresh by the problems arising from the Crimean War. By this time the ill-directed and completely neglected British Army had just won immortal fame at the Alma, Balaclava and Inkermann—at a hideous price. Moreover, as if there were no halting the ghastly carnage, the most active preparations were being made for intensifying the revolting siege of Sevastapol. Here, in Britain, an intensive Press campaign exposing the horrors of the wards at Scutari was producing a nation-wide outcry, and with national attention riveted upon the never-ending bungling in the Crimea there was precious little public interest in the efforts of the Midland board, struggling to push their metals across the broad, rolling Northamptonshire uplands. Not only was there an acute shortage of investment capital, but the cost of labour and materials was rising very sharply. The summer of 1854 was punctuated by the loss of many labourers who left the Midland works for the more remunerative harvest fields, and then, in the autumn came the rains, so within six months of the start the tempo of the construction work was slackening off. In order to conserve both labour and capital, arrangements were made for the major cuttings to be reduced in depth. Consequently, the line followed a switchback course that has been cursed by the Locomotive Department at Derby for more than a century.

Even today, the formidable banks at Kibworth, Desborough and Sharnbrook are still no laughing matter, the Sharnbrook Bank with its long climb from the south at 1 in 119 being perhaps the most notorious of them all. Between the ridges of north Bedfordshire and the Northampton uplands proper, rivers and valleys were spanned by very substantial viaducts. In some cases the abutments slid out of alignment during construction, those at Wellingborough and Sharnbrook proving particularly troublesome; at the latter point satisfactory foundations for the piers were only obtained twenty-five feet down, and the river there is a good twenty feet deep. Even after the traffic began in 1857, the provision of inverts that summer proved absolutely essential. South of Sharnbrook the meandering loops of the Great Ouse were spanned another half-a-dozen times before the railway could be brought downhill to the county town of Bedford where the new Midland line was to intersect the London & North Western company's branch from Bletchley by a right-angled level crossing. A so-called economy device, the crossing proved to be a weird and archaic arrangement designed to obviate the cost of building a fly-over, but down through the years it caused tremendous inconvenience, delay and expense. As might be readily supposed, it eventually produced a fatal accident. One misty morning in the spring of 1875, the last vehicle of a 'North Western train setting out late for Bletchley was rammed and splintered into fragments by the engine of a Midland train. However, all this is looking very far ahead of the construction works for the Leicester & Hitchin line during the middle eighteen-fifties.

By the autumn of 1854 operations had been in progress for about six months and the major engineering works for the new line were beginning to take on definite shape across the landscape. Gangs of navvies were to be seen toiling away on the cuttings and embankments, and at Glendon and Desborough the cuttings were occupied by a couple of hundred men. Elsewhere, the bricklayers and the masons were busy with the abutments for the bridges and the viaducts. They were extremely hardworking and likeable men, although a local press report of the day adds the somewhat supercilious comment that 'the conduct and morals of railwaymen have greatly improved during the past few years and scripture readers are employed on different parts of the line. Most of the men are able to read the religious tracts and magazines'. Perhaps it was as well that they could for on the evening of October 17, 1854, 'a young single man locally known as "Peter" suddenly slipped whilst tipping on the Desborough embankment, and the wheel of the truck passed over his leg which has since been skilfully amputated by Mr Carpenter, surgeon of Rothwell'. There is also evidence that chloroform may have been used during that operation.

Further south, in Bedfordshire, extensive preparations were made during the spring of 1855 for throwing a bridge across the Great Ouse at Bedford, and in the nearby meadows immense timbers were stacked for use as piles and similar purposes. Vast quantities of materials were being carted to the low ground between Clapham and Bedford for the construction of an embankment, and whilst a small station was being laid out at Clapham (in sharp contrast to the far more spacious one at Kettering) provision for a new bridge was being made north of Bedford. At Radwell and Sharnbrook brick kilns were in constant operation, and work had already begun on a 'splendid and lofty viaduct over the Great Ouse at Sharnbrook' which, when completed, would have ten semi-circular arches of fifty-foot span apiece, those arches being more than forty feet high, and two of the piers would stand in the river, which is about twenty feet deep at that point. By the early part of August 1855 the first pair of arches had been successfully turned.

From the early part of 1855 onward the progress of the works was punctuated by many more accidents, quite a few of which were fatal. On February 12, 1855, a team of men was undermining a bank in Southill cutting when the bank collapsed upon two of them. One poor chap of twenty-three, named Trust King, was almost completely buried and even though he was extricated within three minutes, he died from his injuries within about an hour. Three weeks later, another death occurred a couple of miles to the north at the Warden Tunnel. At the Deputy Coroner's inquest held on March 8th it was stated that a labourer named Charles Clarke had been loading spoil into some contractor's wagons when the embankment gave way and a large quantity of earth covered him. The earth was got off his head as quickly as possible, but he just spoke and died immediately. Between May and September, 1855, wet weather caused numerous falls of earth in the cuttings at Kibworth, Glendon, Rushton and Kettering which either killed or seriously injured more than half a dozen navvies. One slip was so severe that a difficult and expensive culvert was fractured, and its restoration cost a further £500—a very substantial sum during the nineteenth century.

During 1855 and 1856 there were some particularly serious accidents involving juveniles and young people. On August 21, 1855, fifteen-year-old John Thompson was working in the brickyard at Warden when his hand was trapped by the clay-grinding rollers which crushed his forearm thereby leading to amputation at the middle of his upper arm. Only a week later, on August 29th, a ten-year-old boy, William Hughes, employed at Little Bowden to grease the axles of contractor's wagons, was run down by some earth-laden vehicles, his injuries proving fatal after five days. About a year later, in September 1856, a girl of twelve, having taken a midday meal to her brother employed upon the works at Kettering, was also struck by a moving wagon which, allegedly, rolled right across her thighs. By some miracle no bones were broken, and the young lady seems to have escaped with little more than a nasty shaking; but far less fortunate was another ten-year-old lad at Kettering who was run over whilst greasing wagon axles that November, with the result that one of his legs was subsequently amputated.

Reverting to the actual construction work, the labour difficulties are clearly reflected in the monthly progress reports prepared by Charles Liddell for presentation to the Extension Committee. As late as July 1855 only sixty per cent of the fencing had been completed. Of the 3¾ million cubic yards of earthworks scheduled to be made, barely 1¾ million had been executed, leaving a balance of 2 million still to be tackled. Now, although this progress was far from good, Liddell sincerely believed the works could even yet be finished in good time, if only a substantial effort were to be made at once.

Of the brickwork and masonry, seventy-five per cent of the culverts and forty per cent of the bridges had been built, and he expected that the bulk of the remainder would be completed by the close of the year. Nearly twenty miles of line was then ready for ballasting and this section of the work had already begun at several points, with rails and chairs being delivered in readiness for track laying operations. Elsewhere, the last of the most obstinate landowners had finally yielded, and the contractors were in possession of virtually all the land needed for the completion of the line. Despite Liddell's confidence that the works would be finished on time, the extension committee were already very seriously worried by the labour situation, and they urged Brassey's representative (Horne) to 'get cracking', but Horne pleaded that too much labour had been lost to the harvest fields —a readily understandable situation when, in those far-off days of negligible taxation, work provided both a genuine incentive and a realistic and profitable return upon one's exertions.

Subsequent to the agreement reached in April 1855 for Midland trains to use the Great Northern station at Hitchin, the extension committee received sanction that autumn to remove about 25,000 cubic yards of material from the Great Northern chalk cutting to form the bank on which to build the Midland freight terminus to the north-west of the station. At this time, the committee also adopted their high-level plan for Shefford station.

Reference has already been made to the way the Midland board, during the summer of 1855, had urged Brassey's representative (Horne) to press on faster with the construction work. By the end of the year these fears proved only too well founded, and in his monthly progress report summarizing the work done up to January 1856, Liddell stated that of the 3¾ million cubic yards scheduled to be excavated for the whole of the earthworks, barely two-thirds had been dealt with. Since July 1855, only 720,000 cubic yards had been removed, that is less than 125,000 cubic yards per month. The latest position was that if the works were to be completed on time (i.e. by October 31st) the contractor simply must exceed 130,000 cubic yards monthly. Indeed, the latest figures had only been achieved through the big spurt made by the contractor during November and December following the return of those labourers who had decamped for the harvest fields during the summer and autumn. But despite all these difficulties, Liddell was still optimistic that the improving situation would result in the completion of the works on time. Of the brickwork and the masonry, ninety per cent was already done, and of the bridges and viaducts, seventy per cent. Very little had been done on the permanent way since last July, again due to the labour question, and not more than four miles (i.e. six per cent) had been laid. At Warden the tunnel was finished and the north face partly built, but the fronts could not be completed until the cuttings had been cleared out. The sites for the stations had also been partly cleared, and building would begin when the summer weather came.

Brassey's men began the new year (1856) in fine style, and on January 23rd ballasting operations began near Sharnbrook where Brassey's engine *Trio* was keenly watched by the engineering authorities and local villagers. At Shefford work began in February.

The approach of summer produced still more labour troubles. In May 1856 the extension committee received a letter from the Clerk to the Magistrates for Bletsoe 'complaining of the irregular and riotous conduct of the labourers on the railway works in the neighbourhood, and suggesting the appointment of special constables to preserve order, for which purpose the High Constable of Bedford had offered his co-operation'. Special constables were also sworn in at this time to preserve the peace for the parishes of Sharnbrook, Souldrop, Wymington, Felmersham, and Milton Ernest. Of course, drunkenness was frequently the charge, particularly at the Bletsoe Petty Sessions, the miscreants generally being fined 5s with costs. Other charges were related to poaching; and at Sharnbrook one landlady was even robbed by her lodger of the golden guinea she had set aside for her rent, but a smart piece of detective work resulted in the arrest of the culprit in Bedford within twenty-four hours. Earlier, at Northampton Petty Sessions, a labourer charged by Thomas Brassey in December 1855 with stealing a sleeper worth 9d had received fourteen days hard labour 'as it was his first offence, he had pleaded guilty, and expressed contrition'.

The foregoing represent but a random selection of the incidents occurring during the construction of the line, but they do highlight the difficulties which Brassey and the extension committee so often experienced. In fact, Liddell's report for May 1856 states significantly that the month's quantity of earthwork, ballasting and permanent way works was far below the appropriate rate, and at the latest rate of progress it would be quite impossible for the contractor to finish on time.

At Bedford the scheme for building a joint station was beginning to receive much more detailed consideration. In November 1855 a conference was held there between the engineering and executive officers of both the Midland and the 'North Western companies when it was agreed that a joint station would prove the most suitable arrangement. The negotiations continued for about six months, the leading Midland Railway delegate being W. E. Hutchinson, then a director but later Chairman of the company. In May 1856 he reported having reached the following heads of agreement with the 'North Western party:

1. The joint passenger station was to be built by the L.N.W.R., but the Midland Railway would construct its own coal wharfs.
2. The L.N.W.R. would maintain and work the passenger station, but undertook to afford the Midland Railway permanent access (and also certain rights) into and in the station itself.
3. The Midland Railway was to pay five per cent of the costs, exclusive of land costs, as well as sundry expenses arising from the cost of porters and clerks.
4. The Midland was to have full control of the Leicester & Hitchin lines running through the station.

The only major point left unsettled was the choice of a site for the Midland engine shed, either to the east or the west of the Leicester & Hitchin line. But as the agreement was never ratified by the Midland board, a glorious opportunity to establish a joint station at Bedford was irretrievably lost.

Yet another fatal accident occurred that summer. At Bedford a temporary bridge had been thrown across the River Ouse. At 5 p.m. on August 22nd a long girder intended for the permanent bridge was being swung into position; it was caught by a gust of wind and three men went hurtling down into the river. Two managed to haul themselves on to the bank, but the third, a very well respected young man of twenty-two, was drowned, his body only being recovered after an intensive search lasting half an hour. As the Coroner remarked, this was 'the twenty-second inquest arising from the railway works'.

Despite the setbacks of the past two years, tenders were obtained in June 1856 for the supply of signals, points and crossings, and in terms of modern conditions some of the prices quoted by the successful firms make very interesting reading, e.g.:

Semaphore signals, delivered at Derby	£21 7 6 each
Wire signals, delivered at Derby	£13 7 6 each
Points, delivered at Derby	£4 10 0 each
Three throws, delivered at Derby	£9 10 0 each
Angled or other crossings, delivered at Derby	£3 3 0 each
Acute crossing, delivered at Derby	£3 12 6 each

Just in passing, it is of particular interest to note that the successful bidders were required to accept twenty-five per cent of the payment subsequently due to them in the form of four per cent Preference Stock, such a subtle and searching stipulation typifying Midland diplomacy in the mid-Victorian years.

On August 1, 1856, the Leicester & Hitchin Extension Committee commenced a fresh two-day inspection of the contractor's works, Liddell being then instructed to prepare a detailed report. At that stage no less than 265,000 cubic yards of earth still remained to be excavated, but, as the work done in June amounted to 180,000 cubic yards, he still thought that completion of the work by the end of October would be a relatively easy matter. Ninety per cent of the bridges had been finished, and forty per cent of the ballasting and track laying had been executed. Although work on the stations had begun, considerable delay had been caused by an acute shortage of bricks. Finally, he commended the contractor for having overtaken the arrears. However, when reporting from Wellingborough that September, even the optimistic Liddell was forced to admit that it was now quite impossible for the contractor to finish the works on time, despite the very heavy penalties which could be imposed for non-completion. It was the same old trouble of men leaving in great numbers for the harvest fields. In July the earthworks fell to 168,000 cubic yards, and in August plummeted further to 124,000 cubic yards. Nor were the harvest fields the only attraction, since large numbers of fairs, statutes, and feasts were then being held up and down the country. Indeed, the labour question was so difficult that Horne was quite unable to find sufficient men to tackle the work by day, and so it was absolutely useless for Liddell to insist upon night work to remedy the situation. Prolonged and severe frost early in the year had seriously affected the supply of bricks, and although work had actually commenced on the stations this was also well behind. The delivery of rails had been suspended, many of those already delivered lying useless, due to the non-completion of the earthworks and the ballasting.

With the onset of autumn the situation assumed critical proportions. In his report dated November 5, 1856, covering work done to the end of October, Liddell stated that at the present rate of progress the earthworks and ballasting would take a further ten weeks, and the permanent way six months. However, in the vicinity of Kettering the snorting and the puffing of the steam engine had been heard for the first time. During the last week of October 1856 the ballast trains began running 'from within a short distance of Kettering station to Harrowden gravel pits, whence they return laden with the material for ballast'. The district seems to have been taken by surprise, as a luckless heifer strayed on to the line one dark and foggy evening: 'the train came into contact with it, knocking it quite off the line and killing it on the spot'.

Although the completion date had already expired, an exceptionally small amount of work was done during November 1856, operations being even further retarded by the dislocation arising from Mr Horne's death. Thomas Brassey had sent down his brother-in-law (Mr Harrison) to carry on the works, and with Charles Liddell they spent two days going over the whole line, while Brassey gave directions and made such arrangements as would enable Harrison to complete the works as quickly as possible. Work in one or two of the cuttings was particularly behindhand, and unless the weather was unusually dry it would be very difficult to do any work there during the winter months. Long lengths of ballasting and track-laying were still to be done, retarded by the incomplete cuttings, and the time needed for these works would also depend on the weather. Liddell's calculations showed only too clearly that the line could not be opened in less than three months, that is, not before March 1857.

Perhaps the greatest obstacle to the speedy completion of the line was the particularly difficult section through the hills between Sharnbrook and Irchester. With every available man drafted into the district, work was proceeding night and day. The lofty embankment between Sharnbrook and Radwell was finished just before the close of 1856, but the major cutting between Souldrop and Wymington was a much more troublesome proposition with the stuff taken from the southern end still lying tipped close to the Sharnbrook viaduct. From the opposite end of the cutting the earth was being carried northward to form a spoil bank near Irchester where another large embankment was still scarcely ready. Under these conditions progress was such that by the first week of February (1857) the Leicester & Hitchin Extension Committee deemed it prudent to plan the passenger services on the basis of four trains in each direction on weekdays, and two on Sundays. The committee also made yet another tour of inspection on February 18th, when they expressed complete satisfaction with the appearance of both works and stations. Only one major item was still awaiting completion—the junction with the Great Northern main line at Hitchin. There, right at the southern tip of the new Midland extension, a dispute had arisen between the two companies over the valuation of about half an acre o Great Northern land needed for the actual junction. As late as March 4th the Midland people were still urging Denison's party to install the junction and then to resort to arbitration on the question of the purchase price. These tactics proved most successful, the connection being put in by March 25th, that is about three weeks before the line was brought into regular service, and five months after the time scheduled for completion. The line was actually ready for traffic on April 8th, but as the contractor was still putting the finishing touches on both the engineering works and the stations, the official inspection on behalf of the Board of Trade was deferred until the end of April when Captain Galton, R.E., expressed great satisfaction with Brassey's works, particularly with the design and structure of the buildings throughout. At Sharnbrook the viaduct was tested by the simultaneous passage of four engines and tenders representing a combined weight of

29. The Leicester and Hitchin railway—Kettering station
(Illustrated London News, May 23, 1857)

200 tons. Of course, such praise placed yet one more feather in Liddell's cap.

The Leicester & Hitchin Extension was opened for traffic on a somewhat piecemeal basis, with mineral traffic on Wednesday, April 15th, followed by goods traffic exactly a week later. The line was officially sanctioned on Monday, May 4th, and the formal opening for passenger traffic took place on Thursday, May 7th. This event proved to be a most gay and light-hearted affair, as a local press report by an unknown journalist clearly shows: 'Marked by a red flag, the first train consisting of eighteen carriages left Hitchin at 7.33 a.m., Bedford being passed at 8.15 a.m., and arrived at Leicester at 10.50 a.m.' In taking forty-two minutes for the run to Bedford (L.N.W.R. crossing), intermediate stops were made at Shefford and Southill. A separate train consisting of no less than sixteen first-class and fourteen second-class coaches left Bedford for Leicester at 9.2 a.m. The proceedings were enlivened by the band of the Bedford Militia installed in an open carriage immediately behind the engine, while reputedly, the Mayor of Bedford rode in 'a beautiful coach'. Third-class passengers were catered for by yet another train which left at 9.16 a.m. Both trains were decorated with white flags, and 'both reached Leicester without accident or delay'.

For the townsfolk of Bedford, Thursday, May 7th was a gala day, and upon the Mayor's directive the shops remained locked and shuttered with business definitely put off for the whole day. The local administration rose splendidly to the occasion, and to ensure that nobody was overlooked, schoolchildren were specially catered for. Even seventy children from the local orphanage were treated to a free trip. Since there wasn't a murmur from the ratepayers about the charge on public funds, it seems quite possible that the cost was met by some anonymous benefactor(s), the Whitbread family, perhaps. Anyway, a good time was evidently had by all, and for those who had been employed upon the constructional works 'a special entertainment was prepared, there being plenty to eat and plenty to drink, and all of the very best'. The general public were equally enthusiastic and immense crowds gathered outside the London & North Western station at Bedford (the Midland station not having yet been built) as early as 7 a.m., so that when the first train left two hours later, more than 3,000 tickets had been sold. Contributions to these inaugural celebrations were also made at the other major towns along the line—at both Kettering and Market Harborough the day was similarly treated as a holiday. A train marked by green flags and comprising twenty-nine coaches of all three classes left Kettering at 9 a.m. and Harborough forty minutes later, subsequently reaching Leicester at 11 a.m. There the Midland station had recently been enlarged, and at noon a special luncheon given by John Ellis and his board was attended by the mayoral parties from Leicester and Bedford. Yet another local press report relates that the party of children from Bedford were entertained at the local institute, but the other trippers were left to fend for themselves. Apparently, the opening of the new line had not received a great deal of publicity at the Leicester end, so the local shopkeepers were taken completely by surprise upon the sudden arrival of several thousand excursionists, who snapped up every scrap of food in sight, which they ate with gusto.

On the return trip, the inaugural trains left Leicester at short intervals between 2.30 and 3 p.m., and at Bedford that evening a celebration dinner was given which lasted until almost midnight—John Ellis, Charles Liddell, Robert Stephenson and William Whitbread being prominent members of the lively company attending this historic function. The local press report concludes by relating that although these trains made a combined total of well over one hundred carriages, with six locomotives, and whereas 5,000 tickets were issued for the whole of the celebrations, all of those trips passed off smoothly, and that 'they all reached their destinations without anything occurring to mar the pleasure of the day'. So, upon this very pleasant and homely note, the Leicester & Hitchin Extension got off to a really lively start, the events of that day being *the* topic of conversation in those parts for many a year to come.

Regular passenger traffic on the new Leicester & Hitchin line came into operation on the following day, Friday, May 8th, with a service of four trains in each direction on weekdays, and two on Sundays. Of these, two of the weekday trains and both of the Sunday trains were 'government trains'—that is they called at all stations along the line, and carried third-class passengers between all stations at a penny a mile, as prescribed in the famous Parliamentary Act of 1844. There was also a morning train (not shown in the table) which gave a connection off the down Great Northern Scotch Express (9.15 a.m. ex Kings Cross, 10 a.m. at Hitchin Junction). Leaving Hitchin at 10.15 a.m., the Midland train made stops at Shefford and Southill before reaching Bedford (L.N.W.R.) at 10.50 a.m. In the return direction this train left Bedford at 11 a.m. and, having called at Southill and Shefford, reached Hitchin in forty minutes. Here, an excellent connection was given by the main line Great Northern train, which left only five minutes later and stopped at Hatfield and Holloway, reaching King's Cross at 12.45 p.m. Thus, the Midland train discharged the dual function of providing two extra services between King's Cross and Bedford, together with that of operating a local mid-morning shopping special between Hitchin and Bedford.

Whereas the journey times between Leicester and London by the two routes were closely similar, the bulk of the passenger traffic continued to utilize the Midland main line route via Rugby which for years had enjoyed through bookings and through carriage facilities. Perhaps these long-established arrangements are most clearly reflected in the fact that between Leicester and Rugby there were eight weekday trains in each

1. George Stephenson, Engineer to the N.M.R.

Robert Stephenson, Engineer to the Leicester and Swannington Railway, Loco. Supt. to the N.M.R.

R. Stephenson's Long Boiler Goods Engine for N.M.R., 1842

0.6.0 No. 312 Kirtley Straight-Framed Goods Engine, 1849

M.R. First-class Coupé, 1848

3. 2.2.2 No. 29, built 1865, on Birmingham Link (Series 25 - 39 of 1863-66)

4. Kirtley Curved-Frame Goods Engine, No. 759, built 1870

5. Norris Locomotive at work on Lickey Bank, 1840

6. John Ellis, M.R. Chairman 1849-58

Mr. James Allport, General Manager 1853

7. 2.2.2 No. 28, built at Derby 1864, for Leicester - King's Cross trains

8. Four-wheeled composite No. 538 for Wellingborough slip services

9. Midland Down Local Train (centre) leaving King's Cross (MET) in 1868

10. 4.4.0.T. No. 207 (Series 204 - 209 of 1868), for working local services to Moorgate Street

11. Erection of first Principal for roof of St. Pancras Station, November 1867
(photo of Butterley Timber Staging by works foreman)

12. 0.4.4.T. No. 784 (Series 780 - 799) built for London District Services, 1870

13. 2.4.0 No. 813 (Series 800 - 829 of 1870)

THE CLOSING YEARS

0.6.0.F.T. No. 889A (Series 880 - 889 of 1871)
for working T.&H.J. Line

JOHNSON SUCCEEDS AT DERBY

14. 2.4.0 No. 900 (Series 890 - 909 of 1871)

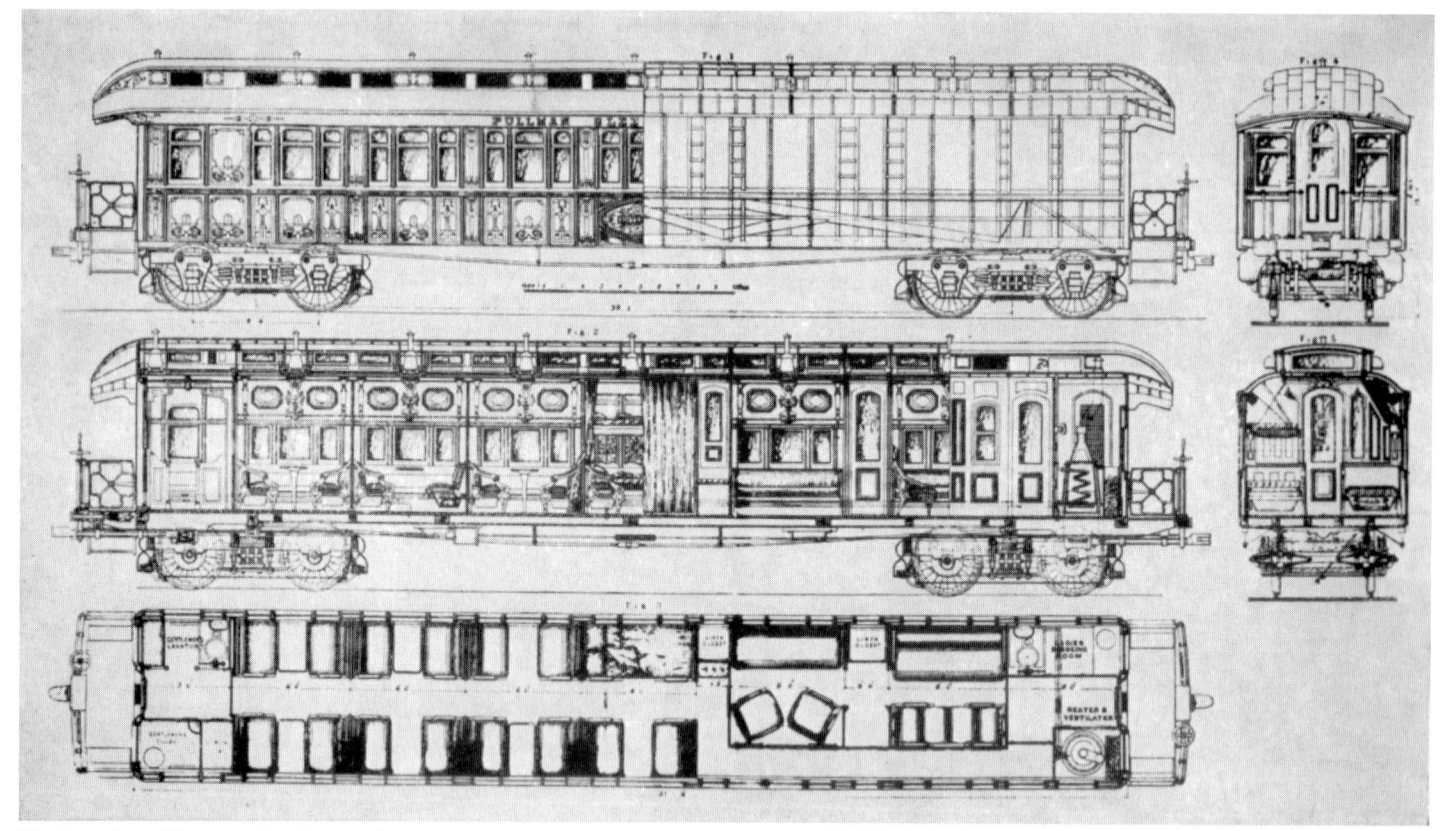

15. American Sleeping Car 'Enterprise' reassembled at Derby, early 1874

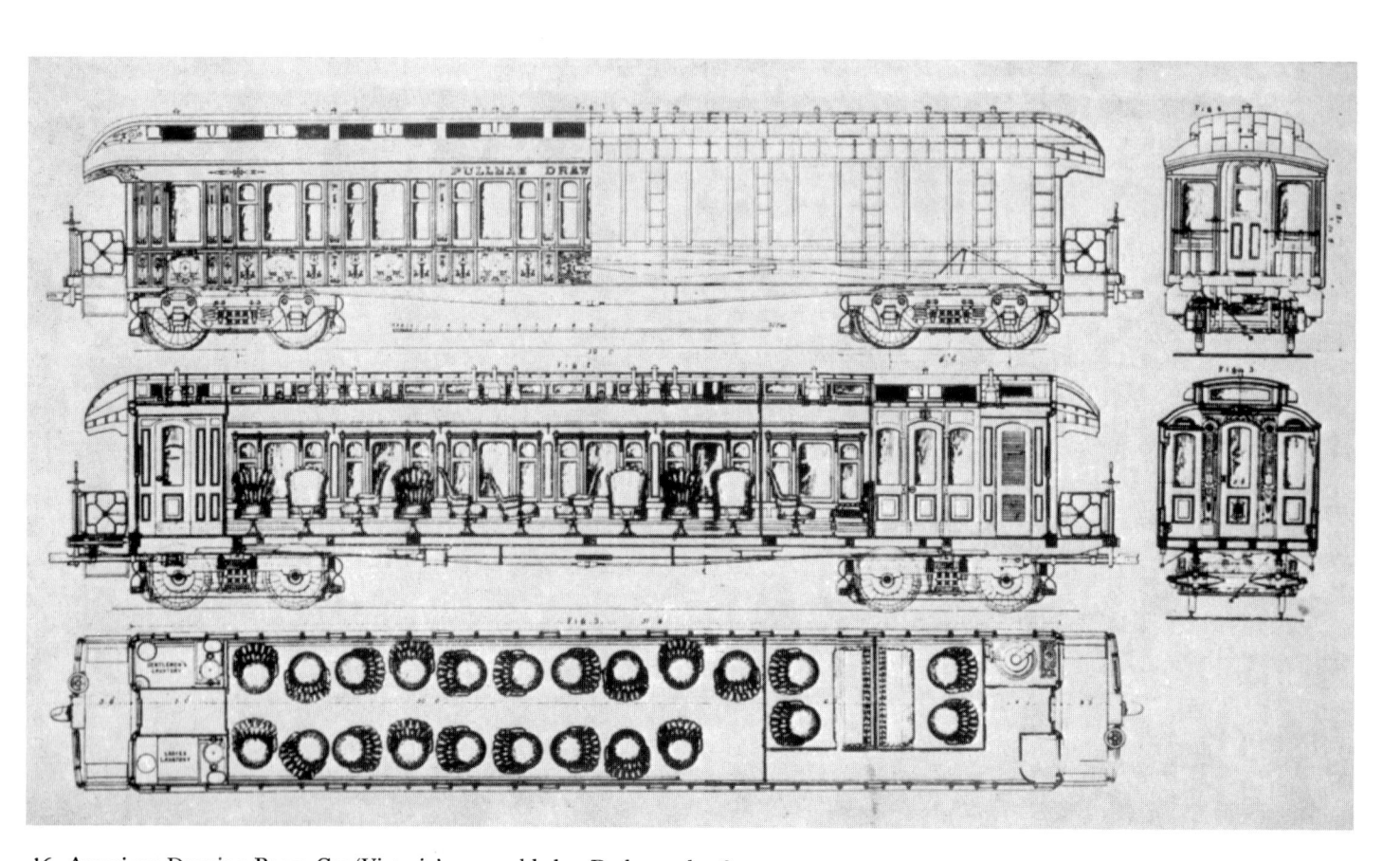

16. American Drawing Room Car 'Victoria' reassembled at Derby, early 1874

direction, whereas between Leicester and Hitchin there were but four. This clearly emphasizes the fact that at the outset the Leicester & Hitchin Extension was primarily intended to act as a relief line for accommodating the ever-expanding Midland goods traffic. Still, because of the heavy tolls levied by the Great Northern Railway in protection of its own mineral traffic from South Yorkshire, Midland coal trains continued to pour on to the North Western main line at Rugby which was already choked by its own traffic originating in Scotland, Ireland, Wales, the North of England and the Black Country. In fact, the Leicester & Hitchin line discharged several functions of a somewhat diplomatic nature, for beside relieving the pressure on the L.N.W.R. south of Rugby, it also met local and Parliamentary demands for a second route between Leicester and London. Thirdly, and just as important, it kept at arm's length Great Northern designs upon Midland preserves at Leicester where the coal traffic now constituted a critically important part of the lifeblood of the Midland system. Of those three functions, it was perhaps the last mentioned which made by far the deepest impression upon the Great Northern people. Indeed, perhaps it was one of the reasons why, less than a fortnight before the new Midland extension was officially opened, the Great Northern board (meeting in secret session) declined to grant permission for John Ellis's trains to run right through to King's Cross, and rigidly insisted that *all* Midland traffic should terminate at Hitchin. Nor would Denison's board agree to the suggestion that Midland through coaches might be hauled from Hitchin to King's Cross by Great Northern engines. Of course, these emphatic refusals were partly due to the fact that at this time Great Northern traffic was also expanding most rapidly (particularly to Sheffield and Manchester); but Denison was also beginning to feel uneasy about committing his company to a progressive arrangement which, little by little, could leave the Midland not merely a tenant but an equal partner in the freehold rights of their main line and terminal facilities at King's Cross which had been completed only during the past five years. As the events of the *next* five years were to show, Denison's misgivings were not without foundation.

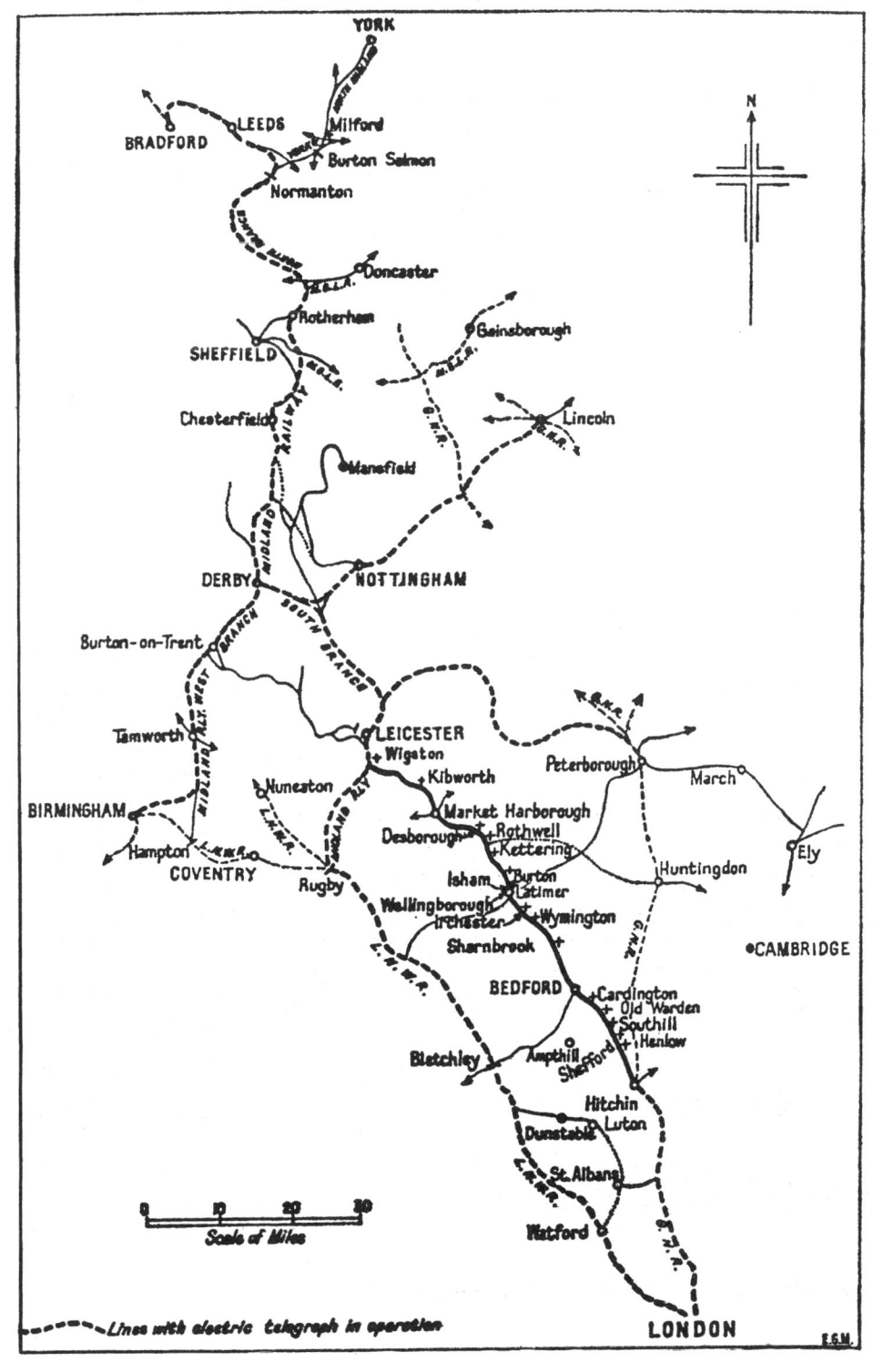

30. The Leicester and Hitchin Branch in 1857

CHAPTER 8

MIDLAND TRAINS AT KING'S CROSS

The opening of the Leicester & Hitchin Extension in May 1857 was undoubtedly an unqualified local success, and yet it could hardly be described as a major triumph for the Midland board since a somewhat uneasy Great Northern directorate had recently ruled that all Midland traffic must terminate at Hitchin. There the Midland terminal facilities laid out by Charles Liddell embraced a small locomotive shed, a hand-operated turntable, and a goods station. Midland passenger trains from Leicester and Bedford ran into the specially lengthened Great Northern station by means of the junction between the two systems some nineteen chains to the north of the station proper. As there were no through booking arrangements, Midland passengers not only changed trains at Hitchin but also obtained fresh tickets from the Midland booking offices newly installed on the Great Northern platforms. As most of the connections were made within a matter of minutes, Hitchin station must have been the scene of much hurrying and scurrying quite incompatible with the popular modern conception of the supposedly leisurely pace of life in the late eighteen-fifties. Admittedly, passenger traffic on the new extension was quite light, being drawn mostly from the intermediate stations, since main line passengers from Leicester and beyond continued to avail themselves of the long-established through facilities via Rugby and Euston Square when travelling to and from the capital. But within a month John Ellis was busily engaged seeking running powers for Midland trains to use the Great Northern main line between Hitchin and King's Cross. To begin with his efforts were unsuccessful, as relations between the two companies were still somewhat strained, due to the dispute arising from the price to be paid for the Great Northern land taken for the junction at Hitchin. Although the matter had already been referred to arbitration in May 1857, six months were to elapse before the purchase price was fixed at £5,000, that is about half what the vendors had demanded. Meanwhile, a Great Northern committee with Denison in the chair had met in secret session at King's Cross on August 4th when it was resolved that the Midland company should be refused running powers between Hitchin and London, and that the Great Northern should convey Midland traffic between those points, even though the Midland might have collecting agents and similar facilities in London. Ellis remained undeterred, and from that time forward even strove to establish a friendly alliance with Denison's board. He also sought to obtain running powers in perpetuity into King's Cross, but Denison decided that virtual joint ownership of their main line between London and Hitchin was highly undesirable, as there were already signs that in the years to come the capacity of the Great Northern line would be strained to the utmost.

Notwithstanding these objections, Ellis persevered and on December 2, 1857, the heads of an agreement between the two companies was reached whereby the Midland would receive running powers into King's Cross, and that through services were to begin whenever the Midland company might elect. For the use of the passenger station at King's Cross the Midland would pay £1,500 per annum, and would be allowed the privilege of booking its own passengers and parcels by its own clerks. Receipts from passenger fares were to be divided on the basis of mileage proportion, the Midland retaining one-third for working expenses. The Midland would also be allowed to fix the times of arrival and departure for their trains at King's Cross, subject to the general convenience of the Great Northern. Also, Midland passenger carriages and guards were to be accommodated at King's Cross on similar terms, but the Great Northern undertook to build at their own cost separate goods and mineral premises as well as engine sheds for the occupation of the Midland company. However, any coal drops needed would have to be installed by the Midland, and upon the Midland quitting these would be taken over by the Great Northern. Although allowed to deduct one-third as working expenses, the Midland was to pay the Great Northern 6d per ton on goods and 2d per ton on minerals other than coal as a modified terminal for the use of station accommodation in London. For coal traffic the Midland was to pay 1s 9d per ton. Furthermore, Derby undertook to abstain from injuring G.N.R. and M.S.L.R. interests and from invading the territories of those companies, but this clause was not to prevent the Midland company from making a line of its own into London after notice had been duly given. The above agreement was to be for a minimum period of seven years, and the Midland company undertook to pay a minimum annual sum of £20,000 in respect of traffic passing between Hitchin and London, the first payment becoming due on January 1, 1859.

Thereafter, Midland passenger trains began running through from Hitchin Junction to King's Cross with effect from Monday, February 1, 1858, the status of the company being instantly elevated to that of a 'London line'. Freight trains followed eight months later, since some time had necessarily to elapse before the Great Northern could provide suitable terminal facilities at King's Cross for the use of its new tenant, and for which purpose Denison's board sanctioned the cost of the following works:

	£	£
Engine shed, sidings, turntable, and the removal of earthworks		10,482
Goods shed	4,273	
Sidings	2,570	
Potato sheds	8,171	
		15,014
Smiths and Carpenters, and new premises		4,000
		£29,496

These works were sanctioned without demur, and work began at once. The engine shed, for sixteen Midland engines, was brought into use at the beginning of 1859, the accommodation being increased to house twenty-four machines four years later. Other alterations put in hand in January 1858 included the special modification of the down platform at King's Cross passenger station for the benefit of the new Midland services, at a further cost of £1,300.

Only a week after Midland passenger trains began running through to King's Cross (on February 1, 1858), the Great Northern board decided that with so many extra trains about to use their main line, it would be prudent to provide special breakdown facilities. Accordingly, a travelling crane and a special accident van were stationed at Hitchin, the latter vehicle being derived from the modification of an old covered goods van at a cost of £90, with £265 being voted to defray the cost of the crane. This proved to be a very wise step as the services of the unit were frequently called upon during the next ten years that John Ellis's trains occupied the Great Northern main line between Hitchin and London.

At this stage, the London & Hitchin Extension Committee resolved that at Bedford their permanent station would be built upon the north bank of the Great Ouse. Notwithstanding the finality of that decision, the Vestry of St Mary's at Bedford continued their campaign for a joint station on the south bank; but the Midland men remained firm, and this was followed by the construction of the nucleus of the present station known as Midland Road. That station was brought into use on February 1, 1859, and thereafter Leicester & Hitchin trains abandoned the somewhat prolonged temporary arrangement (in force since May 1857) whereby they had either backed into or out of the London & North Western terminus by means of the sharp curve which joined the Midland line near the bridge subsequently erected to carry the Ampthill Road across the Midland tracks. Incidentally, the new arrangement met with the warmest approval of both Colonel Yolland and the Railway Department of the Board of Trade.

Further south, the Great Northern main line between Hitchin and King's Cross consisted of only one pair of tracks straddled by a long succession of tunnels. Already, those two lines were only just capable of coping with the traffic of the two companies, and there was no margin whatever for dealing with the chaos which accidents must surely produce. From the very outset, there was a spirit of intense rivalry between the two concerns at operational staff level. Perhaps the first really serious case of this kind emerged in the early autumn of 1859. For various reasons, Midland trains on the new extension were often late, and on the evening of Thursday, September 8th, the 7.45 p.m. Midland train from Leicester was delayed for more than half an hour by a bad connection off the North Eastern Railway at Normanton. Still running nearly thirty minutes late, the Midland train began slowing down from 40 m.p.h. on the approach to the junction at Hitchin, three blasts being correctly given as it passed the distant signal. Having lowered the signals for this train, the Great Northern signalman on duty in the junction box had his attention called by the whistle of the 9.15 p.m. Great Northern Scotch Express (itself running ten minutes late) as it made a very lively start from Hitchin station, some 400 yards away. The signalman now attempted to give his own train priority at the junction by countermanding the signals just given to the Midland driver. But he was too late! Travelling at about 10 m.p.h., the Great Northern locomotive struck the Midland machine (now passing through the junction at 5 m.p.h.) almost buffer to buffer. The Midland crew jumped at the very last moment and escaped injury; of their fourteen passengers, only one received a shaking, and the damage to their engine was relatively slight. But in the Great Northern train the third coach mounted the second and thirty-five passengers were injured, the more serious cases being carried to the hotels situated close to the station. Now although this accident was primarily caused by the error of the Great Northern signalman, this proved to be the first of a considerable number of mishaps which subsequently occurred as the two companies fed more and more traffic on to the one pair of tracks south of Hitchin during the next few years.

Traffic expanded at such a pace that by 1861 Derby was paying no less than £32,000 to the Great Northern exchequer as compared with the minimum of £20,000 laid down in the agreement drawn up at the close of 1857. At King's Cross the facilities rented by the Midland company were already inadequate and Derby began casting around for a suitable site in the district on which to build a separate Midland goods station. The most promising spot for the new depot proved to be a triangular piece of semi-waste land lying behind Agar Town in the parish of St Pancras, about three-quarters of a mile to the north-west of King's Cross, bounded by the North London Railway, the Great Northern Railway, and the Regent's Canal. As early as February 1859 the Midland board had set up a special Agar Town Committee consisting of Samuel Beale (Chairman), William Price (Deputy Chairman), and Sir Joseph Paxton (Chairman of the Midland Traffic Committee). In barely six months, Samuel Beale successfully negotiated the purchase from the Ecclesiastical Commissioners the leasehold estate and interest of some twenty-seven acres of ground at a cost of £8,500. In view of modern property trends, it is most interesting to see that in June 1860 a further six acres and three roods cost no less than £32,000, that leasehold purchase being followed by the acquisition of some wharf ground and premises adjacent to both the Regent's Canal and King's Road in Agar Town. Such were the origins of the *original* Midland goods station in St Pancras, and in all the Midland exchequer had paid more than £50,000 to obtain a satisfactory footing in that locality.

Following these initial acquisitions in Agar Town, the Midland Railway (Station in St Pancras) Bill was presented to Parliament late in February 1860. As chairman of the company, Samuel Beale, M.P., explained that all over the Midland system the volume of passenger traffic had remained virtually unchanged since 1848, whereas the company's goods traffic had virtually trebled and, until the opening of the Leicester & Hitchin line, the Midland Railway had been completely dependent upon the London & North Western main line south of Rugby, and that company's facilities at Camden Town, for securing entry to the metropolis. Samuel Beale also emphasized the absolute necessity for his company to obtain access to the coal drops at the Great Northern company's King's Cross goods station, the Regent Canal giving access to many parts of London, and the North London Railway providing access to the Docks. Access to the canal was particularly important, otherwise both the coal and the Burton-on-Trent ale traffic would otherwise have to be abandoned for lack of proper storage facilities, even though the Midland company had spent £60,000 in providing improved facilities at Burton which both the Great Northern and the London & North Western companies were now enjoying. Following the tremendous growth in the brewing industry, the Great Northern company had recently concluded an agreement with both the North London and the London & Blackwall companies for the through carriage of Burton ale to the East and West India Docks, and the Midland company had lately received an offer from the London & Blackwall company of storage facilities for about 10,000 barrels at premises adjoining the Royal Mint Street Station. However, Beale thought it essential that the premises should be at the actual waterside, and so the Midland board had entrusted him with the task of purchasing land secretly to foil the land speculators.

Beale was followed by the company's general manager, James Allport, who confirmed his Chairman's evidence and stated that the comparative figures for the past seven years were:

	Goods Traffic (tons)	Mineral Traffic (tons)
1852	104,000	98,000
1859	218,000	321,000

Due to the toll of 1s 9d a ton paid to the Great Northern company, about 290,000 tons of coal were then being sent annually to London via the London & North Western route, compared with a mere 30,000 tons via Hitchin and King's Cross. The Great Northern board had already proposed some coal drops on the high ground near the North London Railway, where the extensive excavations and the heavy retaining walls associated with the scheme were estimated to cost £15,000 to £20,000.

Such weighty evidence went far towards establishing an overwhelming case for the Midland Bill which subsequently received the Royal Assent, but as early as April 1861 the board was already giving most careful and detailed consideration to the plans for their new St Pancras Goods Station.

Derby policy was one of non-stop aggressive expansion. As late as May 1860, Samuel Beale formally asked Denison's board to provide still more accommodation at King's Cross, but the Great Northern people declined, particularly as there was now every prospect of the Midland company building its own depot at Agar Town, and also because the Great Northern needed every scrap of accommodation available at King's Cross for handling its own ever-expanding traffic. Moreover, friction was developing between the companies on two other points. Firstly, there was the highly competitive coal traffic derived from Nottinghamshire and Yorkshire. Secondly, a new threat to Great Northern interests appeared in November 1861 with the proposal 'for a new line from the King's Cross station of the Metropolitan Railway to a point on the Midland Railway at Hitchin'. However, this most interesting project was nipped very smartly in the bud at the Standing Orders stage by the fierce opposition raised by Denison and other pro-Great Northern interests. Of course, at this stage the constructional works at King's Cross for the new Metropolitan Railway were already quite well advanced.

Due to the heavy Great Northern tolls, most of the Midland coal traffic for London proceeded via Rugby, and in May 1858 the Midland board signed an agreement with the Clay Cross Company whereby a minimum quantity of 30,000 tons was to be sent up annually to depots located on the North London line at Highbury and Kingsland, the new rate being that formerly charged to the North Western depot at Camden. If less than 30,000 tons were sent, the charge would be the existing rate to Camden plus 6d per ton for the last few miles beyond that point. For coal carried to the Clay Cross Company's depot on the Blackwall Railway the rate for the next fourteen years would be 6d per ton above the rate to Camden. If, however, other companies such as the Great Eastern reduced their rates, then the Midland coalition would follow suit. Conditions in the coal trade thereafter became so competitive that only six months later similar facilities were extended to all other firms on the Midland system which were then sending coal to depots on the North London line. Elsewhere, competition between the Midland and the Great Northern companies intensified to such a pitch that at the turn of the year the Midland reduced their charges for carrying coal to Hitchin by 1s 6d per ton, and pro rata for shorter distances. Even though a bare ten per cent of the Midland's coal traffic followed the Hitchin route into London, coal drops were built at King's Cross for use by the Midland company, some 3,000 tons being handled there during February 1859 —that figure increasing steadily to 4,000 tons during the following September, and to 6,000 tons per month by October 1861.

Another source of intense rivalry between the Great Northern and the Midland companies was the traffic running between London, Nottingham, Sheffield and the West Riding. Early in April 1860 the Great Northern board directed that the third-class carriages originating from competitive points en route should be attached to their 12.20 p.m. train from Bradford to King's Cross. The Midland instantly went one better by arranging for third-class passengers to be admitted to *all* their trains between Bradford and London, as well as at intermediate points. Naturally, the Great Northern retaliated with interest! Next, the Midland offered Mr Storey, an important carriage manufacturer of Nottingham, a reduction of no less than forty-one per cent in the rate charged for conveying his products between Nottingham and London. Of course, Great Northern reprisals followed immediately!

Midland passenger traffic was also expanding rapidly at this time. Whereas in 1858 there were but four up and four down services between Leicester and King's Cross, within a year there were six. By 1860 a prosperous excursion traffic was making a very important contribution to the Derby exchequer, and, despite a trade recession, the 1861 season produced more than £39,000. Then, in the spring of 1862 even greater efforts were made by the companies possessing terminal facilities in London for handling the colossal excursion traffic that converged upon the capital from all points of the compass in connection with the Great International Exhibition of that year. Both the east coast and the west coast partnerships made very extensive and important arrangements, but the Midland declined an invitation to join in upon a 'pool basis'. Instead, Matthew Kirtley turned out from Derby Works a special batch of six 2-4-0 locomotives specially designed for the London Excursion traffic. In addition to the 6 ft. 2½ in. wheels and the 16½ in. × 24 in. cylinders lately adopted as standard features at Derby, they were fitted with boilers of the then standard goods engine pattern. These six very powerful machines were consecutively numbered 80-85, their numbers being derived from the scrapping of six earlier machines dating back to the Hudson regime. A great number of excursion trains were most successfully run to London that Whitsuntide, and but a week after the Exhibition was opened Derby fixed the following return excursion fares:

	First-class carriages	Covered carriages
Lancaster, Ingleton, Colne, Skipton	15/-	10/-
Keighley, Bradford, Leeds, Normanton, Sheffield	15/-	8/-
Chesterfield, Trent, Derby, Lincoln, Newark, Nottingham	14/-	7/-
Mansfield, Burton, Loughborough, Leicester	12/-	6/-

Compared with the corresponding months for 1861, both June and July of 1862 produced a very substantial increase in both passengers and receipts, viz:

To King's Cross	Increase in number of passengers	Increase in receipts
by ordinary trains	2,794	£3,402
by special trains	29,002	£11,796
Total increase	31,790	£15,198

The climax of the 1862 season was reached in August when the amazing total of 64,066 passengers were carried by Midland specials into King's Cross. Thereafter, the traffic fell steadily until the season concluded at the end of October. Incidentally, the brand new Midland 0-6-0, No. 479 was shown at the exhibition.

During the first two months of the exhibition, Midland specials were accommodated on the Great Northern sidings at King's Cross; but the traffic became so heavy that, in preservation of its own interests, the Great Northern found it imperative to request the Midland people to vacate the facilities they leased there. On June 20, 1862, Seymour Clarke, the General Manager of the Great Northern, wrote to James Allport, his opposite number at Derby, stating that having visited the new Midland goods station at St Pancras (then approaching completion) and having noticed that the works providing access from the Great Northern main line to the new depot were also complete, he called upon the Midland company to vacate the Great Northern premises forthwith.

At the next meeting of the Midland Traffic Committee (held at Derby on July 1st) James Allport stated that he had already arranged for the company's coal traffic to be removed from the precincts of King's Cross that very day, although their other traffic could not yet be accommodated at the new St Pancras goods station. Consequently, the Ways and Works Committee would be urged to arrange for the completion of the coal drops and the station yard as quickly as possible. But even as Allport was speaking, the Great Northern was going into action. In two instances at least, passengers entering Midland trains at King's Cross were compelled to do so from ballast level, a particularly difficult and dangerous feat for ladies dressed in the costume of the day. Next, the Great Northern people erected a platform a mere two planks broad, and this was to serve as an intermediate step between the ground and the carriage footboards. Midland coal traffic was also removed from the two sidings it occupied at King's Cross. This, then typified the treatment which caused the Midland board to complain to the world at large of being evicted in the night. Nor was that all, for during the next fortnight Midland excursion trains were constantly subjected to very prolonged delays south of Hitchin, with the result that by the middle of July, Allport was calling upon Seymour Clarke to uphold the terms of the existing agreement between the two companies.

To be quite fair, not all the blame rested with the Midland. Indeed, competition between the two concerns was so fierce that from many angles July 1, 1862, proved to be a turning point in the prolonged struggle. To begin with, the Great Northern undertook to convey members of a Working Men's Institute from Leeds to London and back for a mere 5s per head. This was a very artful dodge, for the ordinary public could easily become members by paying as little as 1d each for a week's ticket to the Institute, and so virtually anybody could take advantage of the scheme. Allport retaliated immediately. As from July 7th the Midland reduced its excursion fares between Leeds and London to 5s a head, covered carriages being provided a week later on July 15th. Reverting to July 1st, the Great Northern delivered a third, and even more aggressive blow with the announcement of its arrangements for a private society to run an excursion from Nottingham to London at a return fare of only 1s 9d for children and 3s 3d for their teachers. Hostilities were only halted in August when the profits from the hitherto competitive excursion traffic were divided equally between the two companies.

Quite apart from the competitive element, the summer of 1862 produced a tremendous spate of technical problems that proved one long headache for the Great Northern traffic authorities at King's Cross, and the flood of excursion trains operated south of Hitchin by both companies caused the already difficult situation to degenerate into a chaotic nightmare. It became necessary for the Great Northern to institute a system of traffic operational priorities and under these conditions Midland trains soon formed a seemingly never-ending queue on the newly installed four track section north of Holloway while the Great Northern traffic took precedence over them as they edged steadily forward through the tunnels and into the terminus.

The events of that hectic summer compelled the Midland board to review in the minutest detail the whole question of improving and consolidating their means of approach to the metropolis, and even at this stage they clearly foresaw that the time was now rapidly approaching when they would have to consider seriously the possibility of building a completely independent line of their own from some point on their existing Leicester & Hitchin extension to a completely separate London terminus. The cost of building such a line would be colossal, and so before finally committing themselves to such a course it was essential to determine whether the existing facilities could be adequately improved at a more economical figure. One possible solution would be the complete quadrupling of the Great Northern main line between London and Hitchin; therefore, Samuel Beale and James Allport continued to negotiate with their opposite numbers, Edmund Denison and Seymour Clarke, for a grant of running powers in perpetuity between Hitchin Junction and King's Cross. Needless to say, their efforts were largely unsuccessful, as the Great Northern men feared that concurrence would virtually confer upon the Midland a joint ownership of the freehold interest and once installed in this way the Midland could never be ejected should the need arise. Consequently, Denison countered the Midland application with an offer to quadruple the Great Northern main line between London and Hitchin, on condition that Derby would guarantee to increase its minimum payment of tolls from £20,000 to £60,000 per annum. However, as no less than £193,000 was also being paid annually for the use of the 'North Western line south of Rugby, the Midland board resolved that a far more economical long-term solution would be the construction of an independent Midland extension to a completely separate London terminus. Events soon proved this to be very far-sighted and wise.

During the highly successful season of 1862, the Midland excursion traffic on the Leicester & Hitchin line was marred by two serious accidents which occurred in very quick succession. At about 6.30 p.m. on August 10th, the 2.25 p.m. cattle train ex Leicester was kept standing on the main line immediately north of Hitchin Junction by another Midland goods train which was also halted on the up line while the engine brought some brick and coal wagons from the Midland yard at Hitchin and attached them to the front of the train. Most unfortunately for all concerned, a Midland excursion train, returning to London from the Bedford Regatta, came dashing up the mile-long gradient of 1 in 132 on the final approach to Hitchin Junction. An injector which had proved defective shortly after leaving King's Cross at 9.40 that morning was still giving trouble and, thus occupied, the driver passed the distant signal at about 25 m.p.h. About 150 yards from the home signal, the excursion train (slowing down for the junction proper) struck the rear of the stationary cattle train at about 6-8 m.p.h. Two cattle trucks were overturned; and sixty of the 500 excursionists were injured.

Only a week later, on Thursday, August 28th, a far more serious accident occurred at Market Harborough. As traffic proved unexpectedly heavy, a Midland excursion train, due to leave King's Cross at 7.30 p.m., was run in two portions, each carrying more than 500 passengers. The first part (for Burton) left at 7.41 p.m., being followed by the second (for Leicester) after an interval of barely five minutes. In accordance with Midland practice at that time, the progress of the second portion was not telegraphed down the line, the only indication of its existence being a white light exhibited on the rear of the first. Both trains were very heavy (twenty-five and twenty-four coaches, respectively), and although the first scheduled stop was Desborough, Driver Greenwood stopped at Bedford for eleven minutes to take on water before tackling the difficult Sharnbrook Bank with such a load. Upon leaving Bedford at 9.32 p.m., this train was immediately followed in by the second portion, which also spent eleven minutes in taking on water, leaving at 9.48 p.m. Crossing the Northamptonshire uplands made exceptionally heavy demands upon the locomotives and so the Burton train made another stop for water at Market Harborough at 10.52 p.m. By sheer bad luck the train was standing on a curve in the blacked-out station when the second portion was heard approaching. Driver Greenwood made a most determined effort to get his train on the move, but the jolt produced by a sudden start snapped a coupling in the middle of the train. Within seconds the second portion struck the rear of the first at about 5-6 m.p.h. There were panic-stricken shrieks in the darkness, then the scene was suddenly illuminated by fire, the last two carriages and the van of the Burton train being 'greatly crushed'; the engine of the Leicester train being 'also derailed and much damaged'. Within thirty minutes a special train from Leicester brought four doctors to the scene, and it was found that one passenger had been killed outright, another man's arms were crushed and had to be amputated (most probably without any anaesthetic, not even alcohol), twenty-eight were seriously injured, and of the 131 less seriously or even slightly injured, forty-five reached Leicester at five the next morning. An inquest was held at Market Harborough Town Hall on Friday the 29th, being adjourned until the following Thursday, September 4th. After retiring for only twenty-five minutes, the coroner's jury blamed the driver of the second train of 'culpable negligence', but also stated that the company was highly censurable in providing insufficient brake power. Well over £2,800 was paid in compensation. In the years to come the question of brake power came up on many more occasions.

During the eighteen-sixties, the Great Northern main line between Hitchin and London was severely hampered in two respects. As previously mentioned, it consisted of but one pair of lines which after 1858 were called upon to carry the freight and passenger traffic of two major companies. From the outset this was an exceptionally difficult task, which was further complicated by the frequent need to shunt heavy goods and mineral trains out of the path of faster passenger trains, there being no facing loops in those days. This state of affairs contributed to numerous accidents on that stretch of line between 1858 and 1868, and whenever congestion developed the Midland people found that the Great Northern operating staff invariably gave precedence to their own trains. A typical example of this occurred when an up Great Northern coal train fouled the main line during shunting operations at (New) Barnet on December 30, 1862. There it was struck at 25 m.p.h. by the 10 a.m. Great Northern express from York, lately travelling at 55 m.p.h. but successfully slowed down by the prompt action of the local signalman. Although the engine and tender were both derailed, a brake van and four wagons smashed to pieces and a footbridge swept away, only four persons were slightly hurt. In the ensuing dislocation to traffic, the Midland fared very badly indeed.

On Friday, October 7, 1864, the 2.20 p.m. ex-Peterborough Great Northern pick up goods was inadvertently shunted across the down main line at Welwyn just as the 7 p.m. Midland express to Bedford and Leicester came dashing across Welwyn Viaduct at 40 m.p.h., and running eleven minutes late. Once again, disaster was averted by the prompt action of a local signalman, but in the ensuing collision the Midland engine was badly damaged, six goods wagons were smashed, and fourteen people injured, one seriously. Single line working was introduced after two and a half hours.

A somewhat similar accident occurred near Colney Hatch station (now New Southgate) at about 7.15 p.m. on August 30, 1865. A Great Northern up coal train of twenty-nine wagons made a stop there to pick up another truck. As a Midland excursion returning from Derby and Nottingham to King's Cross was almost due, the Great Northern driver was instructed to back his train into the nearby up siding as quickly as possible, but he had only just started when a draw-bar broke. Despite the stationmaster's prompt instructions the local signalman was unable to halt the Midland train of twenty coaches and three brake vans, which could be 'heard approaching at very great speed'. Although the Midland driver 'whistled for brakes' and threw his engine into reverse, his train collided with the coal train (still fouling the main line) at about 10 m.p.h. Many coal wagons were thrown across the down line, three or four being smashed to pieces; the Midland engine was thrown on to its side, overturning several coaches in the process, and although the Midland crew managed to jump clear, a dozen passengers were seriously injured. Something of a minor panic seems to have occurred, with the uninjured leaping clear of the wreckage while those less fortunate lay helplessly watching them making good their escape. Within thirty minutes the Great Northern Superintendent and the Medical Officer to both companies at King's Cross arrived on the scene. Seven of the more serious cases were carried to a nearby hotel, the others being taken on to the Great Northern Hotel at King's Cross. Traffic on the main line was halted for some hours and the wreckage cleared away next morning with the arrival of breakdown gangs from London, Hatfield and Hitchin; it would seem that the crane and van were brought down from Hitchin, too. At the ensuing enquiry, the Midland driver was uncertain whether the accident was attributable to his personal error of judgment or the slippery state of the rails—but there can be little doubt that mere handbrakes fitted to tender and guards' vans were quite inadequate for dealing with such an emergency. In fact, throughout the 1860's trains continued to become heavier and faster, and the question of continuous brakes came to the fore time and time again.

In the summer of 1866, by which time the construction of the Midland extension from Bedford to St Pancras was getting into its stride, there was yet another bad collision south of Hitchin, indeed one of the most destructive in British railway history. Shortly before 11.30 p.m. on the night of Saturday, June 9th, a Great Northern down empty-goods train stalled in the middle of Welwyn North Tunnel (1,066 yards) when a boiler tube collapsed; the locomotive was barely a year old. The guard of this train neglected to give warning to the signalman in the rear, and even advocated that the train should be backed along the falling gradient of 1 in 200 until it was clear of the tunnel, but this the driver rightly refused to do. While the Great Northern train was still obscured by smoke and steam, it was struck in the rear by a Midland goods train travelling at 20-25 m.p.h., the driver was thrown against the firebox door and pinned there by coals from the tender. Freeing himself and his fireman within a few minutes, he then heard a southbound Great Northern goods train approaching at speed. Both men scrambled for their lives over the wreckage. Debris from thirty-eight empty Great Northern coal trucks and twenty-seven Midland vehicles extended from rail level to the crown of the arch at a point very close to a ventilation shaft, and this huge pile of rubbish was struck by the third train which was made up of a locomotive and thirty-three vehicles, the engine being thrown against the up side of the tunnel. The guard of the first Great Northern train was found crushed in the wreckage of his van. With him was a guard from the Metropolitan Railway, a friend of the dead man, who was having a free ride to Peterborough. He died from head injuries on Monday morning. About 4 a.m. on Sunday, June 10th, while the wreckage was being cleared, some burning naptha dropped from one of the men's lamps and ignited a truckload of furniture packed in shavings, and scattered in the tunnel by the force of the collision. The fire raged throughout the rest of the night and at dawn on Sunday morning, when the Great Northern's Chief Engineer reached the south end of the tunnel, flames were leaping from the airshaft, and the thick, choking smoke and the blasts of intense heat were accompanied by intermittent explosions from the tunnel mouth. Due to the impossible conditions, the breakdown gang moved to the north end of the tunnel and succeeded in detaching and drawing clear some of the rearmost Great Northern vans. It was not until six o'clock on Sunday evening that the 450 men now on the scene succeeded in forcing their way into the southern end of the tunnel, and soon afterwards sufficient wreckage was dragged clear to enable the Marquis of Salisbury's fire engine (on loan from Hatfield) to be manoeuvred to the seat of the fire. Later, when two heavy cranes were able to clear some of the heavier debris, it was found that the tunnel brickwork had sustained only superficial damage. Even so, goods traffic through the tunnel was not resumed until Monday, June 11th, passenger traffic being deferred until Tuesday the 12th. Great Northern traffic was diverted on to the Great Eastern line via Hitchin, Royston, Cambridge and the Hertford branch.

Only a mile or two to the south, a relatively minor collision occurred at 4.45 p.m. on November 5, 1867, at Welwyn Junction. This was yet another example of an up Great Northern goods train being shunted accidentally on to the down main line, where it was struck by the 3.51 p.m. Great Northern passenger train from London, travelling at about 40 m.p.h. The crew of the goods engine were able to jump clear, but those of the passenger loco were badly knocked about, having stayed at their posts. In the dislocation that followed, it was the Midland passenger services that suffered, since the company's goods traffic had been transferred two months previously to their new London Extension.

In this catalogue of accidents during the Midland's tenancy of the Great Northern main line between Hitchin Junction and King's Cross, two factors constantly recur—the tremendous volume of traffic carried by just one pair of tracks, and the complete lack of continuous brakes.

The question of greatly improved braking power assumed critical importance during the eighteen-sixties as bigger and more powerful locomotives were built for hauling heavier and faster trains on virtually all the major British lines, and in this respect the Midland Railway was certainly no exception. From 1852 onward the majority of the old main line 2.2.2s remaining from Hudson's regime were progressively replaced by about seventy handsome 'singles' of which more than sixty were turned out in batches at Derby Works between 1853 and 1866. Although all the engines had 6 ft. 8 in. driving wheels, there were some detailed differences between the batches—e.g. frames, cylinders and boilers. For the moment, though, we are immediately concerned with thirty-nine machines turned out in two clearly defined series for hauling the company's main line trains between London and the West Riding.

Firstly, there were Nos. 1-24 built at Derby during 1859-61 with 16 in. × 22 in. cylinders. Of these, Nos. 1-10 were stationed at Derby, and Nos. 11-20 at Leeds, and these twenty engines handled the lion's share of the fast trains between Rugby, Derby and Leeds, a task which they discharged most successfully for about ten years until they were displaced by the arrival of Kirtley's 800 class 2.4.0s in 1870. Following Kirtley's death in 1873, the No. 1 class was mostly broken up shortly after Johnson took over at Derby.

The most powerful and possibly the most handsome of Kirtley's 'singles' were those of the 25-39 series. These had 16½ in. × 22 in. cylinders and could be readily distinguished from the former series by their frames (of several types) and their general proportions. They weren't numbered in anything like order of construction but acquired their numbers as old warriors of the previous generation went to the breaker's yard between 1863 and 1866.

Due to their increased power, the 25 class singles spent their early years on the Leicester-Hitchin-King's Cross run, and very early on they won a reputation with the main line drivers for racing like greyhounds down the Sharnbrook Bank. In fact, something like a minor public scare was precipitated when a letter from Charles Dickens appeared in *The Times* on January 29, 1867, stating that on the 26th the 9.35 a.m. Midland express from Leicester to London had lurched in a most alarming manner for many miles of the journey. This promptly caused James Howard to defend Midland speeds in his letter published on January 30th, although, on the same day, a naval captain stated that on the 28th he had travelled by the 9.10 a.m. from London to Leicester, and during the return journey (3.35 p.m. ex Leicester) the lurching was so violent that, after timing the train at 57 m.p.h. over one stretch of the line, he had left it upon reaching Bedford. 'A shareholder' who had left Leicester by the 1.35 p.m. on January 26th referred to 'a descent of miles down an incline at 60 m.p.h., and this was apparently a constant practice'. 'Another traveller' pointed out that on January 26th the 9.35 a.m. had averaged 40 m.p.h. all the way between Leicester and Hitchin, and 50 m.p.h. from Hitchin to King's Cross. A further comment from another reader produced the information that in August 1866 the 9.35 a.m. from Leicester covered 40 miles in 45 min. 58 sec. (52.5 m.p.h.), and that 'express trains have daily traversed the line for some years past without the slightest accident'. Bearing in mind the major banks across the Northamptonshire uplands at Kibworth, Desborough and Sharnbrook (the latter on the north-Bedfordshire borders), such a performance was little short of miraculous. It also serves to dispel the popular misconception of travel in the eighteen-sixties being a leisurely affair.

Whatever the pros and cons, though, James Allport seems to have taken the hint, and in his report to the Midland Traffic Committee at Derby in February 1867 he referred to his recent meeting with the Locomotive Superintendent (Matthew Kirtley) and the arrangements subsequently made by them 'to allow more running time between Leicester and Hitchin during the Summer Season'. However, for that section of the Leicester & Hitchin line between Bedford and Hitchin the writing was on

31. Midland train hauled by Kirtley 'Single' approaching Leicester

the wall, for in the autumn of 1867 the London Extension between Bedford and St Pancras was opened for main line goods traffic. With the passenger traffic it was a far different story because, due to the financial stresses of 1866 and 1867, a crash programme was put in hand whereby the construction of the passenger station was to be delayed, even temporarily abandoned if necessary. As events proved, it was found possible to bring the huge station into use in the autumn of 1868, whereupon main line trains were turned on to the London Extension at Bedford Junction. South of Bedford, the old main line to Hitchin sank into obscurity.

CHAPTER 9

THE LONDON EXTENSION
(PARLIAMENTARY CAMPAIGN)

Following the collapse in the autumn of 1862 of the protracted and fruitless negotiations with the wily Great Northern party, the Midland board reviewed their position at a full meeting held at Derby on October 14th. Without further ado it was formally resolved that all steps should be taken immediately 'for the necessary surveys to be made and plans to be prepared for a line of railway from some point on the Leicester & Hitchin Railway at or south of the town of Bedford to London, and the necessary Parliamentary notices to be given'.

That this was a most carefully conceived decision is clearly illustrated by the acquisitions made on behalf of the company almost a year earlier, in December 1861, when land had been purchased 'south of the Regent's Canal in St Pancras, Middlesex, and south of the Regent's Canal and east of Cambridge Street'. A third site 'fronting the New Road in St Pancras' had also been obtained from the Skinners Company so, even at this early stage, the Midland board obviously intended to drive a line southward from their newly sanctioned goods station in Agar Town toward the New Road where the works for the Metropolitan Railway were already very well advanced. However, in June 1862 (when the struggle between the Midland and the Great Northern companies south of Hitchin was reaching its climax), the Fleet Sewer burst and a mile of the newly completed Metropolitan works between Farringdon Street and King's Cross was flooded and seriously damaged. By a tremendous effort, though, the damaged works were completely rebuilt by the end of the year, by which time the Midland board was actively planning a junction with the Metropolitan system whereby Midland freight trains would eventually secure access to the L.C.D.R.

The board's decision to project the London extension marks a major turning point in the history of the Midland Railway, and a further link with the past was also severed that autumn with the death of John Ellis on October 26, 1862. Perhaps the full significance of his unswerving devotion to the elevation of the company from a near bankrupt provincial concern to the highly enviable mid-Victorian status of a vigorous and prosperous 'London line' only becomes apparent in the completely sincere and extremely moving tribute recorded by his old colleagues in the minutes of the board meeting held at Derby on November 5, 1862, when it was resolved

'That the Board cannot enter upon the consideration of the Business of the day until they have placed upon record the expression of their unfeigned regret at the loss of their valued and lamented colleague Mr Ellis.

'A Director of the Midland Railway from its formation, he was called upon to preside over it as Chairman at the moment of its greatest difficulty; his extensive knowledge of business, large experience and correct judgment combined with strict integrity and manly bearing very soon won for himself the confidence of the Board and of the Shareholders and have contributed in a very great degree to the present high position and prosperity of the Company.

'While the Directors feel that collectively they have lost an able counsellor each individual member mourns his loss as a kind and warm-hearted friend and can deeply sympathize with his bereaved family under the heavy affliction which they have been called upon to sustain; they trust it will be some consolation to them to be assured of the affectionate respect in which he was held by all those who knew him and of the deep regret felt at his loss.'

So ended a wonderful era in the development of the Midland Railway, but at the close of his long and honourable life John Ellis had the crowning satisfaction of realizing that the task of pushing Midland tracks southward into London would be safely fulfilled by the competent hands of his surviving friends, now reduced to a mere handful of those who had been present, with him, at the amalgamation of 1844.

The new Midland line was scheduled to leave the existing Leicester & Hitchin extension in the vicinity of Bedford and then travel southward through Luton, St Albans, Mill Hill and Hendon. This would not be an easy route to follow for the engineers' choice was severely restricted by the fact that the easier approaches to the capital had long since been occupied by the Euston Square and King's Cross parties. Furthermore, Luton, St Albans and Mill Hill had already been appropriated by the Great Northern company. From Elstree the last dozen miles into London presented the most serious problems of all, of which one of the most awkward was undoubtedly the location of suitable sites to provide the terminal facilities capable of handling the colossal traffic which the new line would surely produce. Now, although the new Midland coal depot, sandwiched on the waste ground between Agar Town and the North London Railway, had already been brought into use that summer, the highly prohibitive Great Northern toll of 1s 9d per ton levied on Midland coals south of Hitchin meant that a good eighty per cent of this traffic still poured on to the North Western system at Rugby. Behind the slums of Agar Town, the St Pancras Goods Station was still very far from ready so, pending its completion, Midland goods trains continued to use the warehouses and terminal facilities provided at King's Cross by the Great Northern people in 1858. To cope with the colossal traffic which would be diverted to their new London line during the next five years the Derby board was already hatching plans for enlarging and reorganizing their new London goods station as part of their overall scheme to secure a completely independent route to the metropolis.

One of the greatest problems facing the London Extension Committee at the close of 1862 was the location of a site on which to build their London terminus. At Agar Town the ground adjoining the still half-finished goods station was completely unsuitable for two main reasons. Firstly, it lay more than half a mile from the Euston Road and, secondly, the conveyance of passengers and their luggage between Agar Town and the Euston Road would be thrown into a state of complete chaos by the colossal bulk of goods being carted to and from the goods station next door. Indeed, if the Midland company was to compete effectively with the long-established opposition at both Euston Square and King's Cross, it was imperative that their new passenger station should have its front upon the Euston Road proper.

By a most remarkable coincidence a wonderful opportunity presented itself when the eastern part of Lord Somers' estate at Somers Town came into the market. This was the ideal site for the passenger station, provided, of course, that it could be acquired upon suitable terms. But in order to reach the site the new Midland line would have to be extended southward from the goods station, clean through the slums of Agar Town, then either over or beneath the Regent's Canal, the old burial ground adjoining the old St Pancras church, the river Fleet and the old Pancras Road, a total distance of sixty chains. Both the technical difficulties and the cost of a scheme of this magnitude would obviously prove enormous, but the site now offered at Somers Town was so admirably suited to the board's requirements in every way that negotiations were promptly put in hand and brought to a highly successful conclusion. Negotiations were also opened with the Vestry of St Pancras for the acquisition of Agar Town, as well as the right to carry the new line either across or below the old burial ground lying between the Regent's Canal and the north-eastern edge of Somers Town. But in this instance the discussions were much more protracted, a basis of settlement being reached only when the Midland Railway Company deposited a bond of £15,000, whereby the company was to be indemnified by the Vestry of St Pancras against damage to the local sewers likely to be caused by the railway works. Heavy compensation was also exacted by the Vestry for allowing the new line to negotiate the old churchyard, and from that sum more than £6,500 was set aside for the Ken Wood preservation scheme, the remaining £1,000 needed being obtained from the general rate. Then, from the midst of all these discussions, there emerged the name to be adopted for the Midland passenger terminus—St Pancras—the sixty chain length between the new goods station and the Euston Road being dubbed the Pancras Extension.

The name St Pancras is very ancient and traditionally a corruption of Pancratius, the name of a boy born in Asia Minor about A.D. 290. Apparently, the lad was orphaned before reaching his teens and went to live at his uncle's villa near Rome

Then, in A.D. 303, the notorious Emperor Diocletian launched a wave of terror and persecution against Christians throughout the whole Roman empire, and during the massacres which followed both the boy and his uncle were converted to the Christian faith. Shortly afterwards, the boy allegedly refused to abandon his newly-adopted religion, and was ordered 'to be led out of the city, and to be put to death by the sword on the Aurelian Way'. Thus, Pancratius was martyred at the early age of fourteen, and to the memory of his martyrdom the original church of St Pancras on the banks of the River Fleet was dedicated well over a thousand years ago. But this was by no means the first time this district had felt the impact of Roman influence, as tradition claims that a critically important battle was fought to a finish in this locality some 250 years before the martyrdom of Pancratius. Today, nearly two thousand years later, the only visible reminder of that most bloody engagement is Battlebridge Road adjacent to the north-eastern corner of St Pancras station. In A.D. 61, Boadicea, Queen of the Iceni, rose in rebellion against Roman treachery and misgovernment—and not without just cause! Under her inspired leadership, the British hordes swept out of East Anglia sacking and completely destroying the newly-established Roman settlements at Camulodunum (Colchester), Verulamium (St Albans) and Londinium (London). The Iceni and their allies struck when the Roman legions stationed in Britain were pinned down in Anglesey, at Glevum (Gloucester), and at Lindum (Lincoln). So serious was the rebellion that a detachment of the crack 9th Legion, 2,000 strong, was virtually annihilated as it made a forced march southward across the Fens. Only the commander, Petillus Cerialis, and a handful of cavalry survived. Consequently, the task of crushing the rising fell to the governor, Suetonius Paulinus, who deliberately sacrificed Londinium to the ravaging hordes, thereby giving himself the opportunity of facing 200,000 British tribesmen upon ground of his own choosing with only two heavy legions flanked by lightly armed auxiliary troops, about 10,000 men in all. Tactitus's account of this most decisive struggle in *Annals*, book xiv suggests that whereas the British tribes lost 80,000 in the battle, Roman losses amounted to only 400, that is about four per cent of the original force. Faced with the inevitable indignity and disgrace of the Roman triumph, Boadicea committed suicide.

Of the Roman camp supposed to have existed in the vicinity of Somers Town no evidence has come to light, despite the numerous, methodical and painstaking searches made over the last 200 years. Not even the tremendous excavations for the foundations of St Pancras passenger station yielded anything at all. In 1825, however, the remains of a Roman camp were discovered near Caledonian Road, half a mile to the north, but all traces of this were lost when the property speculators of the day ran riot. Perhaps the most significant thing of all is that the traditional name for the area surrounding the bridge across the River Fleet was Battle Bridge, the modern name of King's Cross having been adopted as recently as 1830 following the death of George IV.

The original church of St Pancras was particularly ancient. As early as A.D. 603 the Saxon king Ethelbert created St Pancras a prebendal manor coinciding, broadly speaking, with the districts later called Agar Town and Somers Town. Some 500 years later, the Norman Domesday survey indicated that in 1087 the St Pancras manor comprised one curacate, that one plough was used, and that twenty-four men paid an annual rent of thirty shillings. It is also possible that the manor was held at one time by the Canons of St Pauls, and that the old church was the mother church of St Pauls. Despite such a wonderful history, it has been described within the last hundred years as a mean, squalid, wooden structure typical of the Middlesex countryside of those times with enlargements made in 1727 and 1792, followed by rebuilding in a pseudo-Norman style in 1847-48. During these operations some Roman bricks and tiles came to light, together with the remains of an altar dating from about A.D. 625. The altar was marked with five crosses, made from tough Kentish Rag and hollowed out to receive the relics of a saint. Adjoining the manor of St Pancras, and also having strong links with St Pauls, was the manor which came into the possession of the Cantlo or Cantilupe family. Many generations later the name became corrupted into Cantler's, Kennistoune, and finally into Kentish Town.

Much more recently, in 1757, the New Road between Paddington and Islington was opened, primarily for military purposes. Yet within a few years a settlement appeared at Battle Bridge, and by 1786 Somers Town was beginning to appear on the marshy ground about half a mile to the west. Until that time, Lord Somers' estate had centred upon the old Brill Farm, but with the development of the estate, the farmhouse was replaced by the Brill Inn, and the large pond outside became a favourite spot with eighteenth-century suicides. A number of houses were erected during the 1780's, designed by a French architect, one Jacob Leroux; the centre of the development was subsequently known as the Polygon. With the outbreak of the French Revolution, a large number of emigrés settled in the district, which later found fame as the home of the costermongers. The purchase of the eastern part of Somers Town by the Midland Railway during the eighteen-sixties caused the demolition of hundreds upon hundreds of dwellings in that desperately congested area to make way for the erection of St Pancras station. With no alternative accommodation provided, the displaced population simply crowded into the western part of Somers Town, creating a terrible legacy of overcrowding to be dealt with by the London County Council in the generations to come.

Immediately behind old St Pancras church sprawled yet another sordid, teeming, festering slum known as Agar Town. Until about 1815 this district consisted of comparatively unimportant meadowland between Pancras Road and Maiden Lane, in the centre of which stood a fine country house with a neat tree-lined drive giving access to Maiden Lane. At the close of the Napoleonic Wars, this estate was acquired by William Agar, a notably successful barrister, who was, by that time, sufficiently influential and powerful to frustrate an attempt by the Regent's Canal Company to carry their new waterway through his estate. Having successfully resisted the collective might of that huge commercial enterprise, William Agar retired to his rural stronghold. Although Agar died in 1825, his land retained its essentially residential atmosphere with its tree-lined drive, its handsome gates, and imposing lodge entrance. In 1840, a drastic change occurred when the Agar estate was sub-let on leases of twenty-one years, attracting swarms of speculative builders—jerry builders at that! Hundreds of tenement dwellings were thrown up, the vast majority nothing more or less than hovels run up by 'brickies and chippies' working in their spare time, weekdays and Sundays alike. From the very outset many of these buildings were occupied before the floorboards had been put down and, very soon, the original tenants began bitterly to regret their lot. Although some of these squalid streets enjoyed imposing names such as Cambridge Street and Salisbury Crescent, their true status was rapidly revealed by repeated outbreaks of disease and epidemics. Cholera became a regular occurrence, and under such appalling conditions Agar Town quickly received the nickname 'Ague Town'. These outbreaks were so persistent and so lethal that it was not unknown for both parents and several of the children in a family to succumb. About ten years later, in 1851, Charles Dickens wrote a graphic description of this district which, under the title of 'An English Connemara', was published in *Household Words*.

'Rows of squalid makeshift houses were erected opposite one another, no attempt was made to build roadways, and when rain fell on the rubbish-strewn ground the latter was churned into a thick paste. Every garden had its nuisance, one containing a dung heap, the next a cinder heap, the third (adjoining the cottage of a coster) had a pile of periwinkle shells, rotten cabbages, and a donkey. The inhabitants displayed a genuine Irish apathy, and as there were no sewers the stench on a rainy morning was overpowering. Whenever there was an outbreak of cholera an Inspector of Nuisances would appear on the scene, but directly the epidemic was over his vigilance was again relaxed and things reverted to their former condition.'

In the eighteen-forties there was neither the Metropolitan Board of Works nor the London County Council to make the late William Agar's successors toe the administrative line; but with the proposed construction of the Pancras Extension from the new Midland goods station to the Euston Road, the Vestry of St Pancras refused to renew the leases, and the whole of this sordid district was demolished in the spring of 1866. By that summer scarcely a trace remained.

In preparing the Parliamentary plans for the Pancras Extension at the close of 1862, William Barlow found himself confronted by a whole series of major engineering problems. Firstly, in Agar Town, the slum terraces were bisected by the Regent's Canal some forty-five chains north of the Euston Road, and the presence of the canal meant that to preserve suitable gradients on the final approach to the passenger station he would have to choose between either a low level or a high level terminus, the general elevation of the line varying from the Euston Road by some twenty feet in either case. The final approach to a high level station could only be made by an inclined embankment enabling the extension to span the major obstacles presented by the Regent's Canal, the old burial ground, and the old Pancras Road. The low level scheme would involve underground works on a colossal scale, and would be further complicated by the very close proximity of the works for the connecting line between the Midland main line and the Metropolitan system which was just about to be opened for traffic. Having given the most careful and detailed consideration to both schemes, Barlow reported in favour of a high level terminus with the station roofed by twin spans of 120 feet apiece rising to 90 feet above the level of the rails. Adoption of the scheme would mean the acquisition and demolition of Agar Town.

Because of the many Bills proposing tremendous extensions to the railway network within the London area, and the social distress caused in so many instances by thrusting these extensions through thickly populated working-class districts where land was cheaper, a special Metropolitan Railway Commission was set up in 1863 (and subsequently reappointed in 1864) to enquire into and report upon the various schemes before the relevant Bills were subjected to full-scale Parliamentary deliberation. In both years the Secretary to the Commission was none other than our old friend Colonel Yolland, R.E., who, during the early part of 1863, reported upon the Midland proposals as follows:

'Midland Railway Extension Bedford to London with a terminus at Euston Road. Length 51 miles 4 chains. Capital £750,000.

'Line 49 miles 5 chains long from Bedford, enters London on the east side of Edgware Road, crosses over the Hampstead Junction Railway and the Finchley Road, then tunnels 1,484 yards under the Hampstead Hill and the Hampstead Road. It then proceeds under the Hampstead Junction Railway and Kentish Town Road at the point of junction with the Highgate Road, through the Camden Town, under the North London Railway, over the Regent's Canal, across a mass of small streets to the Metropolitan Railway in the New Road which it joins by a short branch 31 chains long at the King's Cross Station of the Metropolitan Railway.

'There is no tunnel in the vicinity of London except that at the foot of Hampstead Hill. The ruling gradient is 1 in 129.

'A short junction line 1 mile 6 chains proposed to the L.N.W.R. at St Albans where there is a steep gradient of 1 in 61.

'Another junction 31 chains long is formed with the Hampstead Junction Railway, and another 11 chains long joins the Luton and Dunstable branch of the Great Northern Railway. The proposed terminus at the Euston Road is just outside the Metropolis as defined in 1846.

'The propriety of sanctioning this scheme must rest upon other considerations than those which apply merely to the Metropolitan schemes. I have no doubt that strong evidence may be produced in favour of this large Company to obtain a Terminus in London, but I doubt the propriety of sanctioning the junction with the Metropolitan in its present form.'

The concluding paragraph of Colonel Yolland's report obviously alluded to James Allport's proposal for the Midland branch to leave the main line some two hundred yards north of the New Road (i.e. Euston Road), and cross beneath the Midland terminus on its way to join the Metropolitan Railway. The ruling gradient would be 1 in 40; the branch would cross over both the New Road and the Metropolitan Railway, and then fall very sharply to join that line immediately east of the Metropolitan station at King's Cross. During the eighteen-sixties the New Road fell very sharply towards its eastern end. As we shall see in due course, the Midland branch at St Pancras was fiercely contested by the neighbouring Great Northern Railway Company which had long taken very similar steps to establish their own connections with the Metropolitan Railway at King's Cross.

The Midland Railway (Extension to London) Bill was presented to the Commons Select Committee on Wednesday, March 3, 1863. The opposition to this Midland Bill was formidable; no fewer than seventeen petitions against it had been presented by some very influential bodies of which the more important were the Edgware, Highgate & London Railway; the Metropolitan Board of Works; the Vestry of the parish of St Pancras; the Regent Canal Company; the Grand Junction Canal Company; the Imperial Gas Light and Coke Company; the Metropolitan Railway; the Great Northern Railway; the London & North Western Railway; the North London Railway and the Metropolitan, Tottenham & Hampstead Junction Railway.

In opening the case for the Midland Railway Company, Sir William Alexander, Q.C., informed the Select Committee that at present the promoters did not intend to proceed with the branch to join the Metropolitan Company's underground line or with the junction with the Hampstead Railway. He also objected to the *locus standi* of the Metropolitan, Tottenham & Hampstead Junction Company. Thus, with one stroke, Sir William disposed of two very important elements in the opposition.

The first witness to be called on behalf of the Midland Railway Company was the Earl of Verulam who warmly supported the Bill and stated that there was a very great need for railway communication between London, St Albans, Luton, Bedford and the North. Witness also confirmed that earlier, in 1847, the L.N.W.R. had obtained an Act to build a line from Watford to St Albans, Luton and Dunstable, and there was a somewhat similar scheme for a line between Watford, St Albans, Luton, Dunstable and Leighton. Later still, in 1859, there had been two other schemes to provide railway communication between St Albans and the Midland Railway at Shefford, and from Hitchin to St Albans, but neither Bill had been implemented, even though one succeeded in reaching the Standing Orders Committee stage. In concluding his evidence, the Earl of Verulam stated that Clay Cross coals were delivered to his house at Gorhambury near St Albans at a cost of 28s per ton, having been carted by dealers from depots on the railway line and the canal at Boxmoor at least four miles away.

The next witness for the Midland company was Hastings Russell, Member of Parliament for Bedford. Upon being examined by Mr. Vernon Harcourt, Q.C., he expressed his support for the Bill from the viewpoints of both the county town and the surrounding agricultural district, drawing attention to the fact that Luton was already bigger than Bedford and continuing to expand apace.

Now came the Reverend John Campion who farmed 800 acres at Westoning in the heart of the county. In that district, he said, coal was brought to Toddington from Shefford nine miles away, a full day's work for a man with a horse and cart. In referring to the frequent delays between Hitchin and London, he explained that meat, butter and poultry were almost exclusively sent by road to the London markets, the journey taking twenty hours.

A particularly important witness was James Howard, a large-scale manufacturer of agricultural machinery with large premises at Bedford whose output exceeded 5,000 trucks each year. In replying to Counsel's questions, Howard explained that the distance by road between Bedford and Luton amounted to merely nineteen miles. By rail, though, with breaks at Bletchley and Leighton, it was thirty-four miles, and via Hitchin and Hatfield forty-three. Also, there were invariably delays at that. By road, a return trip between Bedford and Luton took a whole day and third-class goods and agricultural implements were charged at the rate of 16s 8d per ton for the nineteen-mile journey. A steam plough was charged at 14s 2d. Howard, who was in the habit of making two or three return trips by rail weekly between Bedford and London, complained that Midland trains mostly kept good time at Bedford but were constantly baulked by slow Great Northern trains south of Hitchin, and that the delays caused him much loss of temper and inconvenience which had a bad effect upon his London business deals.

During the eighteen-sixties the most important trade in Luton was the straw hat industry. The Luton factories consumed nearly

30,000 tons of coal yearly, domestic consumption accounting for a similar amount, but whereas industrial coal from the Midlands cost about 18s per ton, the domestic coal from the North cost 22s. William Willis, a Luton straw hat manufacturer with warehouses in Manchester and Glasgow, estimated that the opening of the new Midland line would reduce the price of industrial coal by a good 4s per ton, thereby breaking the monopoly of the Great Northern branch from Hatfield, in addition to saving £5,000-£6,000 per year. Subsequent witnesses referred to the loss of the road omnibus services ten, fifteen, and even twenty years ago when the various branch lines were opened in the county.

James Allport's evidence demonstrated the broader significance of the Midland scheme. Questioned by Mr Venables, Q.C., he stated that the Company's route mileage amounted to 700 reaching points as widely scattered as Ingleton, Bristol and Hitchin, and that a new line under the course of construction would later give access to a branch of the M.S.L.R. at New Mills. Eight miles further on that branch joined the Sheffield Company's main line at Guide Bridge, from which point Manchester was but five miles distant. When opened, this new enterprise would provide the shortest route between London and Manchester.

Last year (1862), Allport continued, the Midland Railway had carried almost 5,000,000 tons of coal, and these figures were very rapidly increasing, although in 1861 there was hardly a colliery between Derby and Leeds. Very large quantities were sent to London, and also across the Thames on to the L.S.W.R., even as far afield as Dorset, and just lately an agreement had been reached to deliver coal to the L.B.S.C.R.

In 1862 alone, 818,000 tons were carried from collieries on the Midland system to London, as distinct from the South Yorkshire pits. Of this gross figure, 491,000 tons were sent via Rugby and the L.N.W.R., 117,000 tons via Hitchin and the Great Northern, 110,000 tons via Peterborough and the Great Eastern Railway, and almost 100,000 tons via Nottingham and the Great Northern.

To illustrate the terrific rate of growth in his company's goods and mineral traffic, Allport produced the following figures:

	Goods and Coal Traffic	Coal Traffic only
1857	676,000 tons	492,000 tons
1858	680,000 tons	498,000 tons
1859	784,000 tons	576,000 tons
1860	997,000 tons	760,000 tons
1861	1,105,000 tons	840,000 tons
1862	1,111,000 tons	818,000 tons*

* Slight decrease due to a mild season.

Relevant to the fact that four times as much coal was sent via Rugby compared with that via Hitchin, the Midland manager explained that under the terms of the agreement with the Great Northern company, ordinary goods were carried between Hitchin and London at normal rates, but coal was a very different matter. For the privilege of carrying coal between Hitchin and London, the Midland paid the Great Northern 1s 9d per ton plus 33⅓ per cent of the working expenses (i.e. 10½d), making a total of 2s 7½d for the thirty-two miles. Thus, the cost of transporting coal from Clay Cross was 2s 7½d per ton to Hitchin, and a further 2s 7½d from Hitchin to London where City Dues of 1s 1d made a total of 6s 4d per ton. Consequently, the bulk of the Midland coal traffic continued to be sent via Rugby, and despite the existence of a third (up relief) line between Bletchley and London, coal was often seriously delayed south of Rugby. In fact, in November 1861 there had been a complete stoppage lasting three days. This had been caused not by any increase in Midland traffic but simply by overcrowding on the 'North Western main line.

Allport also pointed out that the agreement signed with the Great Northern for securing running powers between Hitchin and King's Cross did not debar the Midland company from building its own line into London. Under that agreement passenger trains had commenced running through to King's Cross in February 1858, and freight trains the following October. Quite soon the Midland had found the facilities at the Great Northern's King's Cross terminus quite inadequate, and as the Great Northern had declined to buy additional land, the Midland had bought the necessary land itself. Even now, in March 1863, only the new Midland coal depot had been opened so far, and the new goods station was still being built, so that use was still being made of the Great Northern goods warehouse. Again, as the Midland coal drops on the Regent's Canal were still incomplete, it was still necessary to use the Great Northern facilities there. The Midland had no passenger station of its own at present, and so was completely dependent on Great Northern facilities and staff at the King's Cross terminus of that company.

On the subject of tolls, Allport stated that the agreement signed in 1857 had fixed the minimum payable to the Great Northern with effect from January 1, 1858, at £20,000. Tolls had subsequently been paid as follows:

1858 (including rent and toll)	£37,888
1859	£28,075
1860	£32,821
1861	£39,845
1862	£59,161

The last-mentioned tolls of approximately £60,000 paid in 1862 were derived from a gross traffic value of £88,741 compared with £187,453 in tolls paid to the London & North Western Company upon a gross traffic value of £276,194 despatched via Rugby. Allport considered that a very low estimate of the traffic likely to be sent along the new main line (if built) would be about £92,000 gross. Allowing for working expenses of 43-44 per cent (say £42,000), this should give a return of at least £50,000. Of the completely new local traffic to be created between Bedford and London, the General Manager gave a conservative estimate of £75,000 gross yield giving a net profit of £40,000 a year.

Allport now invited the attention of the Select Committee to the traffic operating difficulties between Hitchin and King's Cross. In the up direction the punctuality of Midland trains on arrival at Hitchin Junction was very badly affected by connections from the Scottish traffic at Ingleton and Normanton; and thus it was quite common for the company's trains to be at least thirty or even sixty minutes late at Hitchin. Moreover, the serious nature of such delays was made much more acute by the fact that south of Hitchin there were only two lines, one up and one down for handling the traffic of both companies. These two lines were further restricted by the numerous tunnels, and completely overburdened by the demands placed upon them. The trouble was particularly acute on the final approach to King's Cross, particularly at Holloway, where at the close of 1861, a Midland goods train was delayed for fifty-six minutes. Then, only a little later, in February 1862, another Midland train was delayed forty minutes. Of course, such a situation had produced a tremendous volume of correspondence between the two companies and, on behalf of the Great Northern, Walter Leith had written to Derby expressing regret for the delay and explaining that due to the pressure of traffic, and in order to avoid congestion in the tunnel, the locomotives normally running light from the passenger station to King's Cross engine sheds were being examined and coked at the passenger station instead, a procedure which was very inconvenient to all concerned.

Midland down trains also suffered very severely, Allport continued. In some cases Midland passenger trains due to make their first stop at Bedford were halted by adverse signals between King's Cross and Hitchin, and in any event the timing of trains between competitive points such as London, Nottingham and Leeds meant that the Great Northern trains took precedence at King's Cross so that Midland trains were basically operating under a great handicap without taking into consideration the question of signal checks. In the afternoon, for example, the 5.35 p.m. down express was inevitably delayed by the 5.5 and 5.10 p.m. Great Northern trains from King's Cross, both of which were very heavy and made stops at Hatfield and Stevenage. At length, the Select Committee declined to inspect a huge pile of correspondence between the two companies on this subject, but accepted instead Mr Leith's résumé of the working of Midland trains between London and Hitchin during the months of March to May 1862 and November 1862 to January 1863— i.e. the three months preceding and the three months following the Great Exhibition of 1862—an abbreviated version of the résumé being given herewith.

In 1862 Midland traffic between Hitchin Junction and King's Cross consisted of six passenger and seven goods trains on weekdays, and two passenger trains on Sundays. During weekdays seventy-five per cent of the trains were almost invariably anything up to fifteen or twenty minutes late on reaching Hitchin Junction, due in the main to late connections given off at

SUMMARY OF MIDLAND TRAFFIC BETWEEN HITCHIN
AND KING'S CROSS DURING MARCH, APRIL, MAY,
NOVEMBER AND DECEMBER 1862, AND JANUARY 1863

UP TRAINS	Run in 6 months	Late at Hitchin	Between Hitchin and King's Cross		
			Time made up	Time kept	Time lost
Passenger	938	683	474	184	280
Goods	855	672	622	15	218
Total	1,793	1,355	1,096	199	498

DOWN TRAINS	Run in 6 months	Between King's Cross and Hitchin		
		Time kept	Time lost	Time made up
Passenger	1,093	100	885	108
Goods	593	44	459	90
Total	1,686	144	1,344	198

Leicester by the main line trains from Derby and the North. Generally speaking, Sunday trains kept very much better time. South of Hitchin the bulk of the delays occurred in the late afternoon, particularly on the newly-installed four-track section between Seven Sisters Road (later Finsbury Park) and the north end of the Copenhagen Tunnel just beyond Holloway. Here, the delays usually amounted to about eight or ten minutes in each case.

In the outward direction, there were seven Midland passenger and four goods trains between King's Cross and Hitchin Junction on weekdays, and again two passenger trains on Sundays, of which about eighty-five per cent of the weekday passenger trains suffered five-minute delays south of Hitchin. As with the up traffic, the congestion mainly occurred during the late afternoon. As if all this counted for nought, the already difficult position was aggravated by the Midland excursion trains which poured southward from Leicester from June to October. The situation is perhaps best illustrated by the two serious crashes (previously described) which occurred at Market Harborough and just north of Hitchin Junction that August, right at the height of the excursion season.

From the very outset counsel had established a particularly strong case for the Midland Bill, and so the Select Committee devoted the later stages of its enquiries to engineering matters. Here, William Barlow outlined Midland policy for that season which would concentrate upon communicating with the south side of the Thames at the expense of building the Tottenham & Hampstead Junction line, which project would be deferred for the time being at least.

In the House of Lords one of the most important witnesses for the Midland Company was their general manager, James Allport. His evidence, begun on May 1st, was largely concerned with the company's coal traffic. It was the Midland Railway, he explained, which pioneered the carriage by rail of coal to London. Ten or twelve years previously Midland coal traffic barely amounted to 200,000 tons. Now, in 1863, some 5,000,000 tons were being carried on the whole system annually, and of the 4,500,000 tons delivered yearly within the metropolitan circle embraced by the Coal Duty Act, the Midland Railway was delivering more than 800,000 tons, or about one-fifth of the total. Still further large increases in this coal traffic were anticipated if the company were to secure access to railways on the southern side of the Thames, for at that time Midland coals were already finding their way by very roundabout routes to Brighton, even to Southampton and Dorchester, and more direct access to the south of England would tend to diminish the price and increase consumption. During the last few years, though, the policies of the Midland and the London & North Western companies had become separated, and for full development of the coal traffic the Midland Railway should have an independent outlet to London and points beyond. The recent treaty with France had undoubtedly caused a large increase in the Midland Company's coal and iron traffic, particularly the latter, for where there were originally hardly any ironworks along the whole of the North Midland route, by 1863 there were very extensive ironworks between Derby and Leeds. Furthermore, large quantities of coal were being sent to France from the North Derbyshire and the South Yorkshire pits.

Whereas their Lordships found the case for the Bill proven, the Royal Assent being given on June 22, 1863, the Midland board gave immediate notice to treat to the owners of vacant land in Hampstead and St Pancras, thereby forestalling the erection of buildings and the creation of leases and agreements since the interest on the purchase moneys would be much less than the compensation to be paid for such buildings and the profits on such agreements. Already, on June 3rd, the company's Common Seal had been affixed to a covenant by the Midland Railway Company to the Ecclesiastical Commissioners for England indemnifying Derby against all liabilities in respect of 'certain hereditaments at Agar Town purchased by the Company of them'. Within but six weeks Midland engineers and solicitors were instructed on July 14th 'to take steps to obtain sufficient land for four lines of Railway between the south end of the Hampstead Tunnel and the Goods Station in St Pancras, and also sufficient land for the approaches to the said Goods Station'.

During the second half of 1863 very detailed consideration was given by both the Midland board of directors and the South Construction Committee to the question of the land needed for the remaining forty-five miles between Hampstead and Bedford. That autumn William Barlow and Charles Liddell were instructed to make a closely detailed survey of the precise route to be followed by their new line; and, following the completion of their survey, they prepared a joint report outlining the phasing of the major engineering works that would have to be undertaken. With the presentation of that report to their Chairman (Samuel Beale) in the very first week of 1864, the Midland drive for London entered its most important phase yet.

CHAPTER 10

THE LONDON EXTENSION UNDER CONSTRUCTION

At Derby the Midland board celebrated the New Year (1864) by launching their campaign for the construction of their London Extension. As early as January 5th, Barlow and Liddell presented a joint report which throws the whole project into very sharp relief.

'To Samuel Beale Esq., M.P. January 5, 1864.
Dear Sir,

'We have considered the question of the time required for the execution of the principal works of the line from Bedford to London and have to state that the parts to which the most immediate attention should be directed are:

'1. From the London Goods Station to the Brent, a distance of six miles.

'2. The Elstree Tunnel and the cuttings on each side of it.

'On the first and most important part the Excavation amounts to 800,000 Cube Yards, most of which must be taken out in one direction and half of it through the Tunnel.

'50 millions of Bricks are required for the works and a great part of the Ballast must be brought from a distance of 12 miles after the Tunnel is finished.

'To accomplish these works will require a period of not less than four years.

'On the second part the Elstree Tunnel and Cuttings will occupy about 2½ years, but as there is no gravel Ballast to be obtained between London and the north side of Elstree Tunnel, a distance of 12 miles, they ought to be completed at such time as to allow 15 months for ballasting the line and Stations.

'The other principal works on the Line are the Cutting at Chalton and the Tunnel and Cuttings at Ampthill to complete which the time required, with Economical execution, will not exceed 3½ years.

'The times above stated are exclusive of time required for staking out the Line, obtaining land, and preparing the Contracts.

We are
Yours truly,
(signed) W. H. Barlow
Charles Liddell.'

Within twenty-four hours this report was referred to the newly-convened South Construction Committee consisting of Samuel Beale (Chairman), William Price (Deputy Chairman), and Midland directors Heygate, Lewis and Mercer. Absolutely no time was lost, and following the completion of their initial preparations the team went straight into action at Derby on March 2nd. With the arrangements for the retention of the engineering services of Barlow and Liddell confirmed, immediate attention was given to the appointment of land valuers. In view of his outstanding success in negotiating the purchase of the land taken for the southern half of the Leicester & Hitchin line ten years before, Henry Trethewy of Silsoe was chosen to acquire the land for the northern part of the new line between Bedford and the Herts-Middlesex county boundary at Elstree. Between Elstree and St Pancras the route selected for the remainder of the line incorporated many highly specialized problems, and thus the negotiations were entrusted to Messrs Clutton, who had quite recently negotiated the purchase of the land taken for the St Pancras Goods Station.

Compensation to be paid by the Midland Railway to local land and property owners in the vicinity of London was another most important matter, and during March 1864 payments exceeding £35,000 were made, of which total no less than £20,000 was spent in the acquisition of Harrison's Estate, a large tract of land extending from the Kentish Town Road westward toward the massive embankment of the Hampstead Junction line. This estate was already earmarked for the construction of an extensive Midland goods and coal station, carriage sidings and engine sheds.

On the final twelve-mile stretch between Elstree and London there were many serious difficulties to be overcome. These arose partly from the configuration of the intervening countryside (e.g. the major tunnels at Elstree and Hampstead), but more particularly from the interception of existing engineering works belonging to the prominent vested interests and corporate bodies which had so rigidly opposed the Extension to London Bill during the Parliamentary proceedings of 1863. So, from the very outset, the South Construction Committee resolved that for construction purposes the London Extension should be split into two engineering districts, the point of demarcation being milepost 14½ (measured from London), this being adjacent to the pits from which would eventually be taken the materials for ballasting the whole of the line and the stations between that point and St Pancras. The outer district between Bedford Junction and milepost 14½ was awarded to Charles Liddell, who had so ably assisted Robert Stephenson with Hudson's South Midland project of 1845-46, and then his Leicester & Hitchin scheme of 1847. The inner or London district was given to William Henry Barlow, who also assumed responsibility for the design of the station shed at St Pancras. At this time Barlow was also very busily engaged in shepherding through Parliament the Bill for the replanned St Pancras branch, not forgetting the application also made that May to alter the vertical level of the main line by eight feet for a distance of 3 miles 7½ chains, for the improvement of the gradients through the Belsize Tunnel from 1 in 129 to 1 in 176, the estimated cost being about £70,000.

The survey teams were already in the field, and May 1864 found Barlow's length of the new line staked out from a point near the Camden Road to milepost 14½, and the longitudinal section for that same stretch also taken. Land plans had also been prepared for the length between Camden Road and Cricklewood at five miles, and in following up this development notices had already been served upon landowners as far out as the Hampstead Junction Railway at three and three-quarter miles (i.e. beyond the outer end of the Belsize Tunnel), the remaining notices being in the course of preparation. Samples of clay taken from the outer end of the Belsize Tunnel had already been sent to Messrs Thomson for brickmaking trials, and although the initial tests had proved unsatisfactory, Barlow expressed his confidence that, with the admixture of other materials, the second trial would prove more successful. Yet another important point was the disposal of the residual spoil obtained from the tunnel, the cuttings, and other workings. Barlow had recently opened discussions with Messrs Furness and Ritson (the public contractors then engaged upon the construction of the Thames Embankment), but as these talks had proved fruitless he now suggested that any surplus material should be dumped upon two acres of land which the Midland board was about to re-purchase from the Tottenham & Hampstead Junction Company near Kentish Town.

The construction of the London Extension is invariably associated with Barlow's superbly elegant station at St Pancras; but yet this magnificent structure was really a showpiece placing the seal of success upon his herculean labours. All too often it is overlooked that the hard core of the Midland company's revenue came from its freight receipts, and thus the London Extension was built primarily for the company's goods and coal traffic. Of course, the St Pancras Goods Station was still being built under Crossley's supervision at that stage and with its traffic outlet facing eastward towards the Great Northern Railway. Consequently, the Extension Committee's next stratagem was revealed that June with their directive to Allport, Crossley and Barlow to ascertain exactly how the company's new line from Bedford would approach and enter the goods yard, and for that trio to make all the arrangements necessary for the implementation of their joint decision. Furthermore, such a golden opportunity was seized to enlarge the depot and to completely reorientate the outlet for handling the tremendous volume of traffic that would surely pour down from the Midlands and the North once the new extension came into effective operation and the existing routes abandoned.

In September 1864, Barlow and Liddell presented to the committee a further joint report in which they stated that 'we are of the opinion that the line may be opened from Bedford to the Acton Junction by the early part of the summer of 1867, and from thence to the goods yard at Agar Town within a few months of that time, and to the passenger station in the summer of 1868. To facilitate these arrangements, and to allow for the preparation of the drawings and specifications for letting the contracts between St Albans and Bedford, the three large cuttings, namely at St Albans, Chalton and Ampthill should be opened up by "gulleting", and the shafts of the tunnel should be sunk so that when the contracts are let the work may be carried on with the greatest speed. Purchases should also be made of all the good bricks in the district and contracts made for a supply in the spring of next year so that the embankments may be carried on without stoppage for culverts and bridge building next summer. The land required for the purpose of the above preparatory work would be about 50 acres and the whole expenditure for land and work will not exceed £25,000'.

Acting upon this report, the South Construction Committee resolved that between Bedford and Acton Junction the line should be commenced immediately, that the price of bricks should be limited, that the necessary land plans should be prepared and notices served, and possession obtained to enable the contracts to be let. To foil the land speculators, prompt steps were also taken to acquire at an economic price land sufficient for the eventual provision of four tracks all the way between Bedford and London, although for the present there would only be two sets of rails between Bedford and Hendon, the second pair of tracks to be laid in as the traffic expanded.

Between St Pancras Goods Station and milepost 14½ Barlow's length had already been split into four contracts in a way that enabled the various contractors to tackle the engineering problems on something like an equitable basis. Since there were to be no deviations from the parliamentary line between the goods station and 1 mile 70 chains, he suggested to the committee that the contract for this length should be let by the middle of July, and that the others should be let as soon as possible thereafter. Indeed, as a preliminary to the letting of Contract No. 1, some nine tenders were opened at Derby on July 6th. Although many famous names were represented, including those of Rennie, Waring Brothers, Furness, and Brassey, it was the lowest bid of all that secured the contract for A. W. Ritson. At £164,000 his tender was some £14,000 below that of his nearest rival, and about £90,000 below that of the highest bidder. Subsequently, the whole of the works for the forty-nine-mile length between the St Pancras Goods Station and Bedford were let out in the form of eight contracts upon the following basis:

Contract			Let	Contractor
No. 1.	0m. 60ch. to	1m. 70ch.	Sept. 1864	A. W. Ritson.
2.	1m. 70ch. to	4m. 00ch.	Oct. 1864	J. Firbank.
3.	4m. 00ch. to	6m. 20ch.	Oct. 1865	J. Firbank.
4.	6m. 20ch. to	14m. 40ch.	Dec. 1864	Waring Brothers.
5, 6 & 7.	14m. 40ch. to Bedford		April 1865	Brassey & Ballard.

Ampthill Tunnel (716 yards) formed the subject of a separate contract which was awarded to John Knowles of Shefford, a local man who had built the Warden Tunnel for the Leicester and Hitchin line during the eighteen fifties.

As shown above, the No. 1 contract, let to Ritson in September 1864, was a little over a mile long. Commencing in the yard of the St Pancras Goods Station at a point sixty chains north of the Euston Road, it featured four very important engineering works of which the first was the bridge at seventy chains, by means of which the new extension would thrust its way clean through the North London Company's embankment. In sanctioning this arrangement, Parliament had clearly stipulated that the bridge must be of such proportions that would enable the North London to lay down additional tracks as their traffic expanded, as soon proved the case. At seventy-nine chains a massive bridge would carry St Paul's Road across the four tracks of the Midland main line at its point of junction with the newly-sanctioned St Pancras Branch, and immediately beyond that bridge the four lines were to be carried beneath Lord Camden's estate by twin covered ways 306 yards long at the outer end of which the line would emerge into a deep cutting curving westward toward a heavy bridge beneath the Kentish Town Road at approximately 1 mile 40 chains.

Following the letting of the No. 1 contract, the first sod for the London Extension was turned on Harrison's Estate to the west of the Kentish Town Road. Thereafter, the plain was invaded by the advance guard of Ritson's labour force, temporary offices and workshops sprang up almost overnight, and arrangements were immediately put in hand for the large-scale manufacture of bricks from the clay hacked from the adjoining works. The Midland Company's plans for transforming the open Fleet Ditch into a completely enclosed sewer were now sanctioned by the Metropolitan Board of Works, and so within a matter of weeks order began to emerge from the apparent chaos.

The new year (1865) produced a marked acceleration in the tempo of the work. Although a total of 57,000 cubic yards of 'stuff' had been excavated by February, brickwork and masonry were both well behind, due to the extremely bad weather. To rectify such a serious setback a very sharp spurt was made during March, resulting in the completion of the Fleet Sewer scheme the following month. Furthermore, a start had also been made upon the arches for the bridge beneath the Kentish Town Road, for which purpose the thoroughfare had been specially diverted. In the early summer of 1865, 400 men and twenty-seven horses were to be seen hard at work on the Kentish Town site, yet in June, Barlow was obliged to advise the Extension Committee that in his opinion progress was much too slow, with the result that during July and August additional men and animals were drafted into the works. Despite such measures, output remained virtually unchanged, and in the face of Barlow's prolonged complaints regarding the unsatisfactory progress and quality of the brickwork the contractor's works manager was replaced that September. Thereafter, matters underwent a very marked improvement and by the end of the year 193,000 cubic yards had been excavated, 21,500 cubic yards of brickwork built, and the arches for the road bridge at Kentish Town completed. By that time, a steam locomotive was already working at the western end of the contract, but no record of its identity seems to have survived.

At the southern end of the contract the close of 1865 found a start already made upon the length of the covered way for carrying the St Pancras Branch beneath the North London Railway. However, bad weather, particularly in January 1866, caused a sharp falling off, and once again Barlow was obliged to voice his complaints about the unsatisfactory progress. Only two months later, the South Construction Committee became alarmed by reports of the contractor's shortage of capital, whereupon Barlow recommended an immediate advance of £5,000 to prevent the works from collapsing altogether, and a further £2,500 to be advanced in six weeks' time. Meanwhile, progress on the site was almost negligible and during February about half the men were discharged. In the middle of March notice was served upon the contractor to engage additional men within three days, but on the fourth Ritson was seeking to relinquish his contract. The Midland board conceded an honourable settlement in which it was arranged for the plant, equipment, and materials to be taken over at valuation. The work executed to date would be paid for according to the schedule of prices and the terms of the contract, and the contractor would receive £1,000 in addition to both the valuation and the balance due on the contract. The most unfortunate Ritson's downfall was thus brought about by his lack of adequate reserves of capital and the terrific upswing in costs and prices which accompanied the tremendous boom in railway construction in and around London during the early sixties.

For the South Construction Committee the position was a grave one, and the contract was shortly re-let to John Ashwell, who took possession of plant and materials on April 11, 1866. Work began the very same day and was kept going at a cracking pace. By June, Barlow was reporting considerable progress with the bridge under the North London Railway at sixty-nine chains, the Midland design for which had been approved by the North London's engineer at the start of the year. At seventy-nine chains the excavations for the St Paul's Road bridge were also under way and a heading for the covered way was then being driven under the Camden Road.

Barlow's September report shows conclusively that progress was now much more satisfactory. At Kentish Town the excavations for the engine sheds and workshops had been started, and beneath Camden Square the covered way was being tackled at two points. The masonry for the bridges beneath the North London line was about half built, and work for the northern end of the St Pancras Branch tunnel was also very well advanced. Taking the contract as a whole, work was in full-scale operation right round the clock with more than 1,100 men and eighty horses engaged; seventeen steam engines and four locomotives were also providing close support. In such greatly improved circumstances 1866 closed with Ashwell's section of the St Pancras Branch tunnel completed, with the work for the bridge beneath the North London line rapidly advancing, and the covered way beneath the Camden Road already about two-thirds finished.

The next year was an exceptionally anxious and difficult one for the Midland Railway Company in general, and the London Extension Committee in particular. However, the year opened with the excavations for the buildings of the Kentish Town engine sheds practically finished, and the foundations put in for half the outer walls. Ballasting and track laying also began that January, but perhaps an even better indication of the progress made was the completion of an engine road for the entire length of the No. 1 contract.

That March, John Ashwell offered to manufacture no less than 8,000,000 bricks that season—'well burned bricks at 30s per thousand delivered into the Midland Company's trucks at Kentish Town commencing about June 1st at the rate of 700,000 per month'. Nor was that the only offer of its kind made at that time. Competition was so keen that only two days later Joseph Firbank (by then in sole charge of Contracts 2, 3 and 4) also offered to produce 10,000,000 bricks at 35s per thousand delivered into Midland trucks at Boreham Wood, delivery commencing August 1867. Now, as the cost of transporting bricks was assessed at ½d per ton per mile, it will be readily understood why Ashwell's offer was accepted.

Since the banking failures of 1866 the economic situation had caused much anxiety, but during 1867 conditions deteriorated even more rapidly. Consequently, the London Extension Committee exerted every effort in attempting to get their new line to the St Pancras Goods Station opened on time, for in that way they would obtain the earliest possible return on the company's tremendous capital outlay. Even the Midland and South-Western Junction line between Brent and Acton for pouring Derbyshire coal on to the L.S.W.R. was temporarily shelved. In pursuing this emergency policy, arrangements were also rapidly made for installing just the first of the turntables needed at the Kentish Town engine sheds, the sheds themselves being three-quarters roofed and about one-quarter slated. The covered way beneath Camden Road and the St Paul's Road bridge were both receiving their last-minute finishing touches; and at Agar Town the northern wing of the completely re-orientated and re-modelled goods station was still unready. Consequently, when the line was brought into use on September 9th, the traffic was handled at only the southern end of the depot for the first month or so.

As let to Joseph Firbank in the sum of £238,741 18s 6d (actually the second lowest bid) in October 1864, the No. 2 Contract extended from the western end of Ritson's No. 1 at 1 mile 70 chains to the fourth milepost near West End Lane. No. 2 included four highly important engineering works, namely the bridge below the Hampstead Junction Railway at 2 miles; the very deep cutting between that point and the eastern end of Belsize Tunnel; the Belsize Tunnel proper (1,716 yards) below the southern flanks of Hampstead Hill; and lastly, the second interception of the Hampstead Junction line with an underbridge at 3 miles 62 chains, this having been made necessary by the easing of the gradient through the tunnel from 1 in 129 to 1 in 176.

As with Ritson's contract, the preliminary arrangements were completed by the close of the year, by which time temporary offices and stables had been set up at nearby Gospel Oak and also above the tunnel itself. Despite very stout opposition and delaying tactics by some of the local landowners, Firbank succeeded in obtaining possession of sufficient land for work to begin, and as Deputy Chairman of both the Midland board and the South Construction Committee, William Price laid the first brick for the No. 2 shaft of the tunnel on Friday, January 27, 1865. This was a severe winter, the ceremony being performed in a foot of snow, and to mark the occasion luncheon for the Midland party was specially provided on the site by the contractor. Work began immediately and within a month 3,500 cubic yards of the stiff London clay had been hacked out, mostly from the tunnel entrances. No. 1 shaft had been sunk to the level of the tunnel and a side length commenced; No. 2 shaft was within three feet of the top of the tunnel; shaft No. 5 had been sunk some twenty-six feet below the surface; and, although somewhat behind the others, No. 3 was completed in mid-April, by which time shaft lengths were being put in for shafts Nos. 1, 2 and 5, and also the side lengths for shaft No. 4. At this stage 612 men and sixty-one horses were at work on both the tunnel and the very deep cutting immediately to the east.

With the completion of the shafts, tunnelling operations commenced in April 1865; by June, seventy-two yards had been completed, and a further quarter's work raised that total to 328 yards. It was at this period that the Midland directors clashed with the ever-vigilant Board of Trade over the Derby application for official sanction to build their new line in a covered way immediately beyond the eastern end of the tunnel. Sanction was not readily forthcoming; in fact, work on the approaches to the tunnel and the tunnel proper was suspended as the result of an injunction. The working site was then inspected by Colonel Yolland, who reported to the Board of Trade in such terms that sanction was permanently withheld.

By this time the labour force on No. 2 contract had risen to 1,200 men and 175 horses, and with the resumption of work there was intense activity everywhere. But towards the end of the year tremendous pressure caused part of the tunnel invert to yield and this had to be corrected by the use of much heavier bricks. Despite this setback, work at all headings produced a grand total of 400 yards by the end of the year, a further 129 yards being added during the first quarter of 1866.

At this stage, Barlow was far from satisfied with the average of about forty-eight yards per month, and so a further shaft (the so-called No. 4a) was sunk to provide two extra working headings. Furthermore, shafts Nos. 3, 4 and 4a received improved gearing to ensure acceleration of the work. While these modifications were in progress there was some falling off in the general work, so that by the end of June 1866 the total length of tunnelling completed stood at 728 yards. Thereafter the figure improved by leaps and bounds, the figure for September being 986 yards, and for December 1,349 yards. Here the maximum monthly output of 134 yards executed in November compared most favourably with the seventy-seven yards recorded in November 1865. March 1867 found 1,636 yards finished, the remaining eighty yards being completed in only six more weeks. Thus, by mid-May the tunnel drains had been installed for about 600 yards, and ballasting and track laying were also well under way. Whereas four tracks were to be installed between Hendon

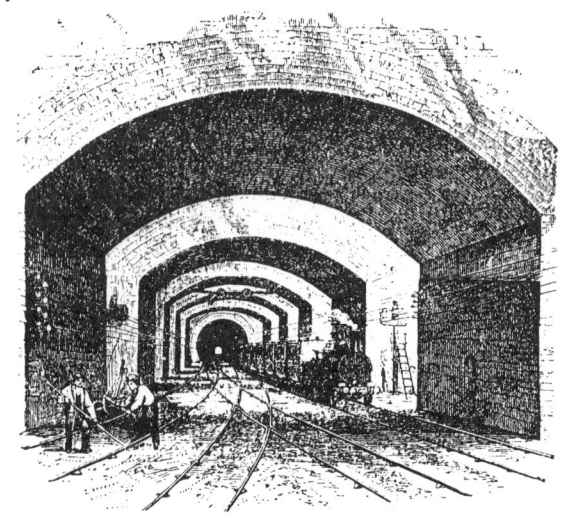

33. Up Midland train leaving Belsize tunnel, 1868

and St Pancras, the Belsize Tunnel constituted a bottleneck between Finchley Road and Haverstock Hill. Therefore, the two goods and the two passenger lines were 'gauntletted' between those two points in the manner so widely used during mid-Victorian times. Quite by chance, your author had the privilege of meeting some years ago a rather elderly gentleman who claimed that he clearly remembered helping to remove, at the turn of the present century, the last of the massive sleepers originally used for carrying the four lines through the Belsize No. 1 Tunnel. Obviously, then, the old sleepers lasted a good thirty years.

Even in the middle sixties, the old Belsize Tunnel undoubtedly constituted a major engineering feat. The five shafts for the tunnelling operations were reputedly sunk from the surface by miners from Co. Durham, who used the age-old colliery principle of commencing the brickwork at the surface and letting it down by gradual excavation, 10 in. × 6 in. bands of elm spaced at

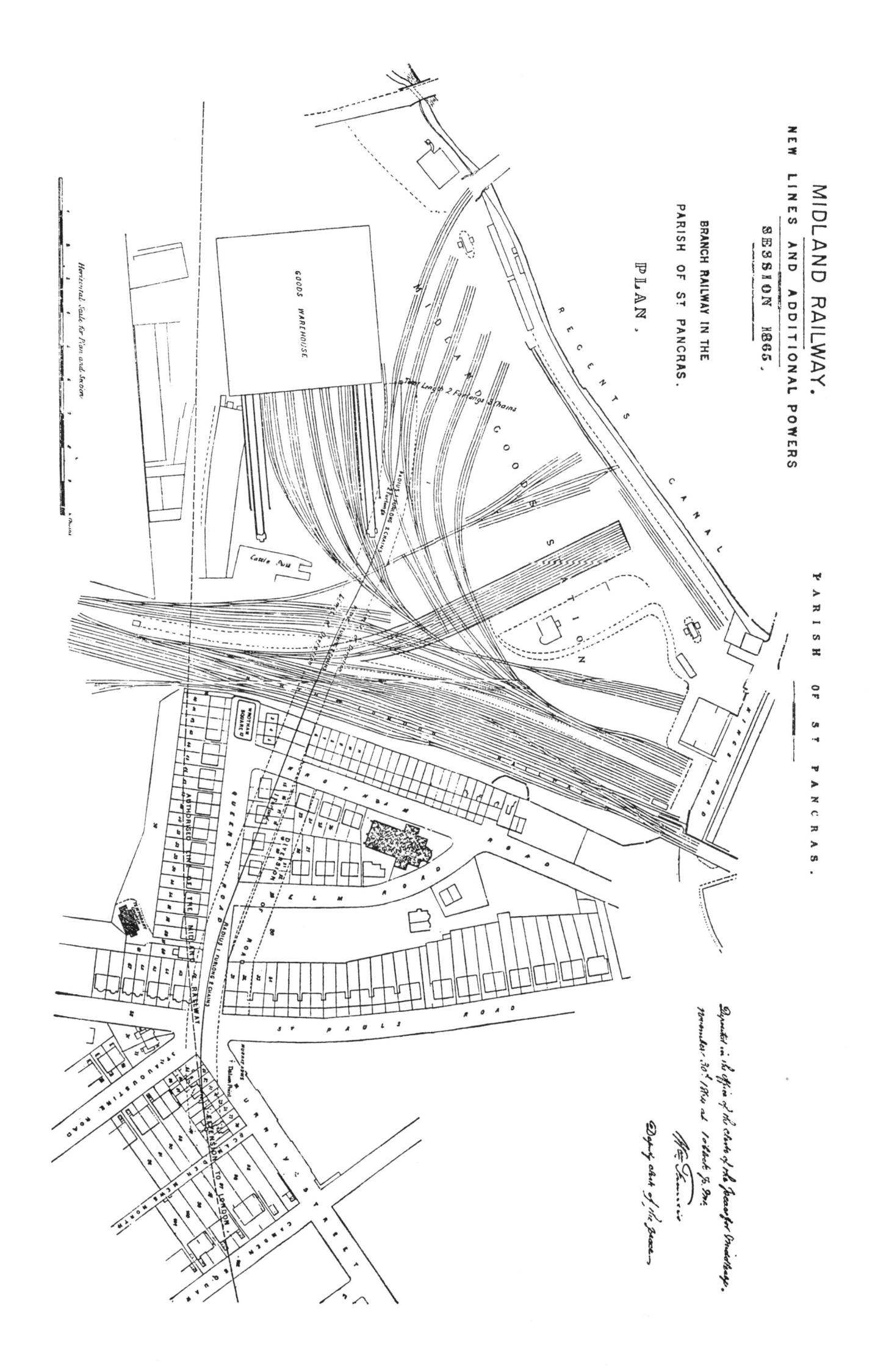

MIDLAND RAILWAY.
NEW LINES AND ADDITIONAL POWERS
SESSION 1865.

BRANCH RAILWAY IN THE
PARISH OF ST PANCRAS.

PLAN.

6-foot intervals being used to travel downwards. As two of the shafts (12 ft. and 15 ft. in diameter) were to be left as permanent ventilation shafts, both were lined with blue Staffordshire engineering brick, which is impervious to moisture. From these five shafts and the two tunnel mouths the mining was tackled from twelve headings, this number being raised to fourteen by the sinking of shaft No. 4a. Each heading was attacked by teams of twelve men, half of them wielding pickaxes and the remainder dumping the spoil in 1 ft. 7½ in. gauge trucks for removal. As the miners completed a 12 ft. length, the centres were set up and the bricklayers took over, the miners moving to the opposite heading. F. S. Williams, the Victorian railway historian, also observed that some of the navvies worked 'for two days and a night without cessation'. Quite clearly, then, Joseph Firbank employed some truly wonderful men, and their superb stamina may very well have been attributable to a diet of a nutritional value hardly known in this mid-twentieth-century era of mediocre and synthetic preserving techniques. When completed, the tunnel measured twenty-six feet from the crown of the arch to the invert by twenty-five feet across. The surrounding brickwork was, allegedly, 3 ft. 6 in. thick in cross section, with each lineal yard of tunnel containing thirty-three cubic yards of brickwork, and with every twelve-foot length accounting for 50,000 bricks. Therefore, something like 22,000,000 bricks, costing at least £35,000, must have been used in the execution of this work.

On New Year's Day 1867 an article in the provincial press announced that

'The extensive works at the Hampstead Tunnel, which have been carried on night and day for the last eighteen months, were so far advanced on Saturday (i.e. December 29, 1866) that communication was for the first time opened out from end to end. This communication is at present very imperfect and irregular, but it was sufficient to enable a small party of gentlemen . . . Entering it at the extremity (i.e. the Finchley Road end), the brickwork is entirely complete for many yards. Further on, however, the only communication is by narrow passages . . . shored up with very solid timber. The ordinary height of these passages is about six feet and the width about five. But in one case, the opening was not more than three feet by three feet for more than fifty yards . . . compelled to crawl by the dim light of candles, which the strong current of air threatened to extinguish. At another point where two sections of the works joined which were carried on at different levels, the only mode of proceeding from the lower to the upper was by climbing a timber support, technically called a 'raker', thirty-four feet in length, with thin strips of wood nailed upon it as steps and placed diagonally at a very abrupt inclination . . . It was found that solid brickwork three feet thick would not stand, and brickwork six feet thick has accordingly been substituted . . . It is expected that the whole of the works of the tunnel will be completed in about four months.'

This forecast proved surprisingly correct; however, the very last brick was specially laid by the chairman during a tour of the new London Extension by the directors on June 27th.

Of the two bridges permitting Midland trains to pass through the Hampstead Junction Railway embankments at 2 miles and 3 miles 62 chains, the plans for the first were sanctioned by the North London Company's engineer in July 1865, but permission for Joseph Firbank to proceed was withheld until March 1866, pending the settlement of a dispute between the two companies concerning the payment of a 'way leave' by the Midland in consideration of the mining operations. As to the bridge at 3 miles 62 chains, beyond the western end of the Belsize Tunnel, the plans were approved in May 1865 and work began that July. While these bridges were being built policemen were employed on the sites to ensure that North London drivers observed their company's instructions to cross the workings at a genuine walking pace. Wages for these policemen were paid in the first instance by the North London, which later recovered the cost from the Derby exchequer. In these much more amiable circumstances the bridges were completed by October 1866.

Contract No. 3 extended from 4 miles to 6 miles 20 chains at a point just south of the Brent Viaduct. Valued at £58,457, this contract was signed by Joseph Firbank in October 1865; work started the following month, being completed about a year

34. The bridge beneath the Hampstead Junction line

later. It was a comparatively straightforward job that does not warrant a very detailed description, except to mention that, as work on the Belsize Tunnel progressed, the men, horses and plant were steadily transferred from Contract No. 2 to No. 3, some 1,850 men, 150 horses, twenty steam engines and three locomotives being ultimately employed by the autumn of 1866.

By far the longest work in the whole of Barlow's district was Contract No. 4. Extending northward from near the River Brent at 6 miles 20 chains to milepost 14½, it was nearly half as long again as the other three together. From the Brent the line was to climb almost continuously to the local summit near the tenth milepost and then make a beeline for the lowest point in the Barnet Ridge at Elstree, which was to be pierced by a tunnel 1,058 yards long. In addition to the tunnel, the other engineering works would be quite heavy, with some very deep cuttings, several major embankments, and two brick-arch viaducts. In fact, the execution of all these works proved unexpectedly difficult and expensive, due largely to labour and financial difficulties. But from Barlow's viewpoint it was critically important that the work should be finished on time to enable the heavy freight trains to roll southward down into the metropolis, thereby providing the earliest possible return upon the Midland company's colossal capital outlay, pending the completion of the huge passenger terminus at St Pancras.

No. 4 Contract was staked out during the second half of April 1864, the next six months being spent in taking the longitudinal section, the preparation of land plans, and the serving of land notices upon local parties then in occupation. Finally, in the late autumn, the committee invited a number of firms to tender, and the contract was awarded to the second lowest bidder—Waring Brothers—in the sum of £222,721 on December 20, 1864. Early in the new year the committee's arrangements were badly upset by the contractor's acute difficulty in acquiring possession of the three-quarters of the land essential for beginning the works, due to the uncompromising attitude of numerous local landowners, and at Elstree only the tunnelling rights had been acquired as distinct from the outright purchase of the land. It was also impossible to begin the works on the embankments and cuttings, nor could a definite date be fixed for the completion of the contract; but sufficient land was obtained by July 1865, and a completion date was immediately fixed at July 26, 1867, with penalty clauses inserted for non-completion within the allotted time.

Waring Brothers made a very energetic start. Within a month the foundations had been laid for three of the piers for the nineteen-arched viaduct across the River Brent; by the end of September five piers had been fully concreted, and half a mile to the north work had also begun on the heavy cutting at Hendon. The first hint of trouble appeared in the autumn, when heavy and continuous rain brought work on the Brent Viaduct to a complete standstill. Further north, works on the cuttings at Hendon and Mill Hill and also the Stoneyfield Viaduct were similarly halted. Even the workings for the Elstree Tunnel which had begun in such a blaze of glory were brought to a complete standstill, though not before the first length of brickwork had been put in and the south face of the tunnel partly built. In many ways the halting of mining operations in the tunnel was the most serious matter of all, because it was through the completed tunnel that the materials taken from the pits near 'Radlets' would pass for ballasting the new line all the way into St Pancras.

There was a general resumption of work later that autumn and the Elstree Tunnel workings forged ahead until they were again slowed down, almost to a complete standstill, by a chronic shortage of bricks; still more delay occurred while a fresh supply was obtained. Thus, by the spring of 1866 the tunnel was roughly one-third completed with 326 yards built and 732 to go. With the resumption of work, Waring Brothers put on a tremendous spurt in a magnificent attempt to overtake the arrears, and by the following June the tunnel was approximately half built and a start already made upon the ornamental façade at the south portal. Viewed as a whole, however, the contract works were a long way behind schedule, and during the summer of 1866 Barlow was constantly urging the contractors to make ever-increasing efforts. Yet the acute shortage of bricks was so persistent that work on the bridges and culverts fell very far behind, with the most serious repercussions upon the earthworks. Both the Midland board and the London Construction Committee became so perturbed about the whole situation that the contractors were asked to attend the next Committee Meeting, which was held at Barlow's office in Westminster on September 19, 1866. There, in his report to the Extension Committee, Barlow explained that progress on the earthworks for No. 4 Contract was wholly unsatisfactory, by far the most important reason being the heavy loss of men who deserted the railway works for the harvest fields, as had occurred during the construction of the Leicester & Hitchin Extension ten years before.

Moreover, it was of vital importance that the large cutting at The Hale, Mill Hill, should be pressed forward with all possible speed. To date progress had been June, 15,700 cubic yards; July, 8,300 cubic yards; and August 6,700 cubic yards respectively. Eleven hundred and thirty-five men had been employed during July, but this number had fallen to 1,035 in August. Whereas in September the rate of excavation had improved, the bridgework and tunnelling had fallen off very sharply. The position now was that, although the date of completion had been fixed as July 26, 1867, the present rate of progress would result in the completion of the Elstree Tunnel in January 1867, the brickwork in January 1868, and the earthworks the following March. Financial cover might possibly last until October 1867.

Barely a couple of months after that meeting, Waring Brothers relinquished No. 4 Contract on Saturday, November 10th, the works being taken over as a temporary measure by Joseph Firbank the following Monday, November 12th. Thus, as with Ritson eight months earlier, Waring Brothers found themselves immersed in a tide of rapidly increasing costs and seasonal labour difficulties. Thereafter, the contract was shortly re-let in its entirety to Joseph Firbank, who thus assumed responsibility for the whole of Barlow's district west and north of 1 mile 70 chains. Firbank spared no effort to overtake the arrears. Work on the Elstree Tunnel and all the other major works was kept going night and day, especially during the closing weeks of 1866 and the early months of 1867. A further 500 men and thirty horses were put on to the works, these reinforcements being supplemented by the use of fifteen stationary and portable engines, and six locomotives. To ensure maximum progress, the Midland Locomotive Committee lent the contractor a couple of tank locomotives. Once again the official records do not disclose the numbers of these engines, but they may very well have been two of the four double-framed well-tank engines with 4 ft. 2 in. wheels and 16½ in. × 24 in. cylinders built at Derby for shunting purposes during 1857-58. They were built from scrap recovered from some old Kitson 0.6.0s which had originally been supplied in 1847 during Hudson's regime.

Barlow had obtained tenders for the supply of permanent-way materials for this section of the London Extension as far back as February 1866. He now took the most energetic steps to obtain tenders for the remainder of the materials needed, particularly for the points and crossings to be laid down for the stations at Elstree, Mill Hill and Hendon. These materials were to be delivered to the Great Northern station at Barnet, since that company's Edgware, Highgate and London Branch was still hardly ready for traffic.

On February 20, 1867, the engineer was able to inform the London Extension Committee that, apart from the wing walls at the northern entrance, the Elstree Tunnel had been completed and a single line laid right through from end to end. Elsewhere, the completion of the contract had become a race against time with work still proceeding night and day on the heavy cutting immediately north of the tunnel proper. At the Brent, nearly the whole of the preparatory brickwork for the nineteen-arch viaduct had been completed and the construction of the thirty-foot arches was already under way. By the end of March, four arches were completed. At The Hale, about three miles to the north, good progress had also been made with the large cutting where completion of the work on time was vitally important because material for the mile-long embankment immediately south of Mill Hill station would have to be brought from the cutting north of Elstree Tunnel—a run of more than three miles. Even though work was proceeding night and day, completion of the contract would take a minimum of three months more, and already at least ten days and nights had been lost through impossible weather conditions.

Firbank and his men kept the work going at a cracking pace, so that by the middle of May twelve of the nineteen arches for the Brent Viaduct had been completed. Within another month the remaining seven were completed and a double line of rails laid right across—the line being quadrupled during the next few weeks. But, as late as July, a gap of 134 yards in the broad embankment near Hendon still remained to be closed, and, with the work kept going night and day, this was completed in only a fortnight. In the meantime, work on the heavy cuttings at The Hale and north of the Elstree Tunnel was also proceeding night and day with the result that by September 1867, the whole of No. 4 contract was completed and the permanent way laid ready for traffic.

35. Brent Viaduct in 1867
(Second and third arches now occupied by the North Circular Road)

Following the recommendations set out in Liddell's section of the joint report presented to the South Extension Committee in September 1864, the heavy cuttings through the Chiltern Hills between St Albans and Luton, and again at Chalton and Ampthill, were 'gulleted' and the shafts for the Ampthill Tunnel completed by the end of February 1865. Even so, it was impossible to let the contracts immediately because of the obstinacy of many of the intermediate land occupiers, this being particularly the case in the immediate vicinity of St Albans, where very influential local interests fought tooth and nail to keep the railway at a respectable distance from the city centre. Eventually, the Midland people prevailed and by April it was found practicable to divide the whole of Liddell's length into three contracts (Nos. 5, 6 and 7) which were awarded to Brassey & Ballard, their value totalling £387,416. As mentioned previously, the separate contract for the Ampthill Tunnel went to John Knowles of Shefford, Bedfordshire. Sufficient land was eventually obtained to enable Ballard to make a start upon No. 7, and despite an apparent error in the wording of the contract, Ballard (although claiming full time for the work) promised to do everything possible to complete the work within two years from June 30, 1865. Meanwhile, steps had been taken in the spring by the Construction Committee to invite tenders for the supply of permanent way materials. In due course, the committee accepted the tender of the Park Gate Company for supplying the rails, and that of the Chilvers Coton Foundry in respect of the chairs, delivery being subsequently made to Bedford, Ampthill, Luton, New Mill End, Harpenden and St Albans.

With the site for the Bedford Junction, and the sites for the goods and passenger stations at Ampthill, Luton and St Albans settled that summer, Brassey and Ballard were enabled to make their final preparations, which included the use of four locomotives at various points along the contracts. Work on No. 7 began early in July 1865, but at first relatively little progress was made due to many labourers deserting the railway works for the harvest fields. But by September there came a great improvement; fencing and tunnelling proceeded at well above the average rate needed to ensure completion on time. Indeed, no less than 108 yards of the tunnel had been excavated, a really remarkable performance. During the next four months fencing and tunnelling had reached 74,633 yards and 346 yards respectively, that is double the average rate required, but bad weather had caused brickwork and masonry to fall to barely two-thirds of the requisite rate by March 1866. Despite this serious hindrance, there was still every prospect that the arrears could be overtaken by making a big effort in the spring. A very great effort was in fact made and by mid-July, 1866, Liddell was able to report very satisfactory progress. Of the eighty-six bridges and viaducts on his section, forty-six had been virtually completed, nineteen were in progress, and twenty-one about to be started. With work in operation at five faces, completion of Ampthill tunnel was expected by mid-October. However, bad weather that autumn caused serious dislocation, as the contractor was obliged to repair his access roads for coping with the approaching winter, which precautions proved only too well justified. Despite the fact that 1,500 cubic yards were being taken from the chalk cutting at Chalton daily and tipped at the end of a lead of four and a half miles, there was also a general tendency for the work to fall off, particularly with the onset of bad weather than December, with heavy rains continuing well into the new year (1867).

On No. 5 contract there was still more trouble, due to the inefficiency of a sub-contractor near St Albans. Despite repeated complaints from Liddell, the ganger there refused to increase the rate of output and progress was so poor that Brassey & Ballard were compelled to remove the work from the sub-contractor's hands. Yet, on Contracts 6 and 7 things were very much better, there being only two gaps in the embankments and two unfinished cuttings preventing the laying of a continuous line between Bedford and Luton. Indeed, ballasting and track-laying had already begun in earnest and five miles had been covered. By the middle of March 1867, Liddell was able to report a great improvement on Contract No. 5, and at Ampthill only a part of the south face of the tunnel remained to be completed. Elsewhere the brickwork was well under control, with plenty of bricks in hand.

That April numerous slips occurred in the vicinity of Flitwick which resulted in the base area of some of the embankments being increased by some 20,000 cubic yards. Despite this setback, progress on Contracts Nos. 6 and 7 still remained above average, and as men, wagons and materials became available they were transferred to No. 5, still somewhat in arrears. Late in June 1867, Liddell was able to announce that he considered Contracts 6 and 7 would be ready by August despite the effects of the embankment slips at Flitwick, which had lately proved very troublesome. However, Contract No. 5 was still a source of anxiety, there having been little improvement during May. Only one bank, at New Mill End, still remained to be closed, and that was expected to be completed in ten days, when the labour force would be turned over to ballasting. The remaining earthworks should take about ten weeks, and might even be ready by August. Twenty-two and a half miles of the permanent way had been ballasted and the track laid, and the buildings for the goods depots and stations had been commenced—although, here, progress had been slight due to the current shortage of bricks.

Liddell's July report shows that several more bad slips had occurred at Kempston and Flitwick, but that these had already been corrected and strengthened. Between those two points the down line had also been laid right through the newly-completed tunnel at Ampthill, and south of Luton only 400 yards of track remained to be laid between Chiltern Green and the Lea Viaduct.

Between Milepost 14½ and Bedford Junction the whole of the double-way was completed during the night of Saturday, August 24, 1867, that is about a fortnight before the new line came into operation. At first the London Extension carried only main line goods traffic running to and from St Pancras, since the construction of the intermediate stations and goods depots was still well behind schedule, as the South Construction Committee observed during their tour of inspection in June 1867.

At St Pancras, plans for building a goods and coal station on the waste ground behind the northern end of Agar Town had originally been hatched as far back as the spring of 1860, when Midland goods traffic was already overloading the facilities provided by the Great Northern Company at King's Cross. Then, in June 1862 the Midland people had found themselves 'evicted in the night' from the King's Cross sidings, and so the new Midland coal depot alongside the North London Railway embankment was brought into full-scale operation that August. Now, at that stage, the St Pancras goods station was only partly built. Construction work therefore continued throughout 1863 and 1864, being completed just as Ritson was preparing to begin work on the No. 1 Contract at Kentish Town about a mile away. The opening of the St Pancras goods station was reported by the *Illustrated London News* in a brief paragraph stating that 'the Midland Railway Company's extensive merchandise station in King's Road, St Pancras, and occupying a considerable proportion of Agar Town, was opened on Monday to the public for traffic (viz. January 2, 1865). The new station is furnished with twelve lines of rails for inward and outward traffic'.

With this new London goods station now safely operating, Derby proceeded to play yet another winning card. During the early eighteen-sixties the brewing industry in the Midlands underwent a tremendous expansion; but although Burton-upon-Trent lay astride the 'west branch' of their main line, the Midland company found it impossible to exploit the beer traffic to anything like its full extent, due to its acute lack of suitable storage facilities in the London area. Admittedly, Derby already leased a warehouse at Royal Mint Street, certainly a most useful asset, but even the capacity of those spacious premises represented but a fraction of the trade being filched from under the very nose of the Midland exchequer by the company's deadliest rivals, the London & North Western and the Great Northern. In fact, agreements previously signed with each of those concerns were now positively embarrassing the Midland cause.

While their new goods station was being built at Agar Town, the Extension Committee seized a golden opportunity to cater for the needs of Messrs Bass by erecting a huge ale warehouse upon a piece of ground sandwiched between the Regent's Canal and the King's Road. Thus, within about six weeks of the main goods station coming into operation, James Allport was writing to Bass and promising them occupation of the new warehouse by August 31st (1865), provided there were no delays through labour strikes. This date was most important because it would fit in so well with the beginning of the Burton brewing season. And even as Allport wrote his letter the new building was going up at a simply fantastic rate. On the second and third floors, well over 8,000 square yards of flooring were ready to receive the beer; on the fourth floor 2,000 square yards had already been laid, with ironwork for yet another 3,000 square yards being erected. Fifty carpenters were working at top speed, and about three acres of stowage were ready for use. Indeed, the storage of ale actually began on March 16, 1865, and six hoists were constantly kept busy transferring the barrels of beer from the warehouse into lighters lying in the Regent's Canal far below. In its subsequently completed form, the Bass warehouse was a hundred yards square, and the six acres of storage space enclosed within those walls were allegedly capable of accommodating no less than 100,000 thirty-six-gallon barrels of best Burton brew.

One very important problem remained to be tackled. As foreseen in 1864, the new all-Midland line would approach the St Pancras goods station from the north, whereas the existing outlet faced east, towards the Great Northern system. This new depôt already showed signs of becoming choked with traffic, and so, in the spring of 1866, the dual purpose plan was launched for both extending and completely re-orientating the layout of the depôt.

Work began with the demolition of the Agar Town slums, and by the end of June the east wall was up to rail level and a tremendous quantity of concrete laid at the south-east angle, close to what had so recently been the northern end of Salisbury Street. In another three months some 44,000 cubic yards (i.e. about two-thirds) had been excavated for the cellars, and some 500 girders were delivered ready for fixing. Thereafter the work proceeded at such a pace that by the close of the year tenders were obtained for the supply of hydraulic machinery.

The spring of 1867 found three of the five roof bays covered and partly slated and the connections between the old and the new sheds practically ready. Despite a temporary setback caused by a shortage of bricks, the eastern side of the enlarged goods station was roofed by June, by which time connections were also being laid in to link up with the main goods lines approaching from the virtually completed No. 1 Contract. As a temporary measure, the southern end of the remodelled St Pancras goods

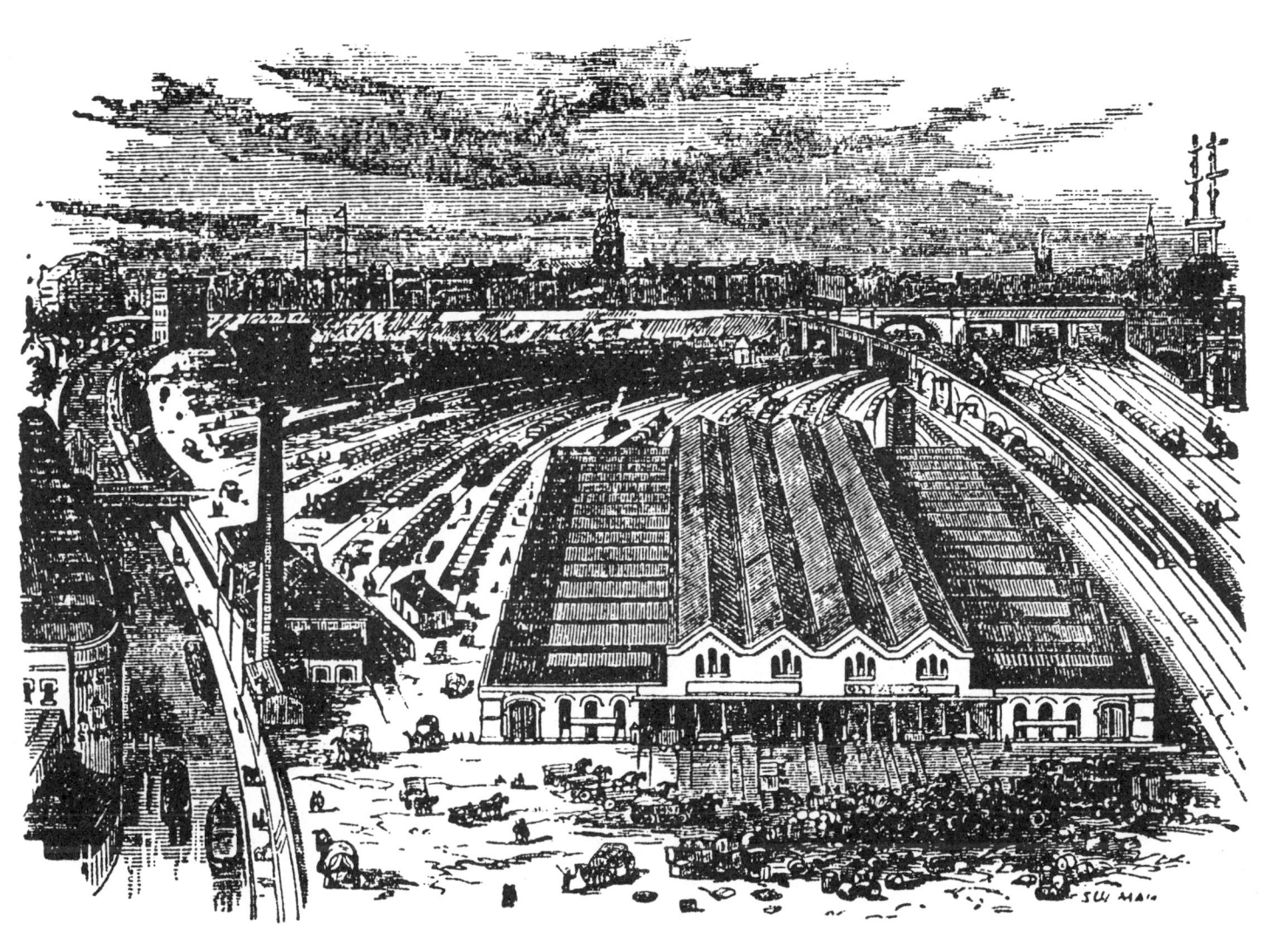

36. The new St. Pancras Goods Station in the early summer
of 1868
(Note the famous North London Incline giving access
to the N.L.R. in the background)

station was brought into use early that August pending the completion of the northern end. Of course, as the cuttings and embankments between Hendon and Elstree were still not quite ready to receive the permanent way, Midland goods trains still ran eastward from Agar Town to join the Great Northern Railway.

The London Extension was completed at the close of August 1867, and it was formerly opened on Saturday, September 7th, when at 10 a.m., a special train (double-headed) set out from Bedford on a trial trip. The party on board included Barlow and Liddell, F. Campion (resident engineer), Ashwell, Ballard and Firbank (contractors), Messrs Needham and Boylan (Traffic Manager and London District Goods Manager, respectively), and a number of guards and engine drivers. As the train drew into St Pancras Goods Station there came a resounding cheer from the workmen who had assembled there.

A somewhat similar run was made between London and Bedford on Sunday, September 8th. Leaving the goods station at noon, the train ran direct to Hendon. There, and at the intermediate points en route, the signals and equipment were carefully checked. Bedford was reached at 4.30 p.m., and shortly afterwards the train began the return trip and re-entered the London depot at about 7 p.m. The running throughout the trip has been described as 'remarkably smooth'.

Regular traffic began on the night of Monday, September 9th. This consisted of about a dozen main line trains running through the night, having been diverted at Bedford Junction away from the old route via Hitchin and the Great Northern Railway. Virtually no traffic used the new line by day because the finishing touches were still being applied to the works by the contractors. Because of this there was also virtually no intermediate traffic either until the local goods and coal stations could be brought into use. At Luton, for example, the freight facilities were apparently opened that December, and the price of coal promptly fell by 1s per ton. Further south, on Contract No. 4, the goods and coal stations at Elstree, Mill Hill and Hendon only came into operation in the spring of 1868, at which stage the famous North London Incline adjacent to the new St Pancras Goods Station was also brought into use. By means of the new incline, Midland freight traffic for the docks was diverted on to the North London Railway for almost two years, having previously reached that line via Rugby and the L.N.W.R. main line to Camden. A fresh route to the docks was secured with the opening of the Tottenham & Hampstead Branch in January 1870.

Having clearly achieved their primary objective with the opening of the London Extension as far as St Pancras Goods Station, the South Construction Committee now focused its undivided attention upon the completion of the 60-chain Pancras Extension and the huge passenger station fronting on to the Euston Road. To these tremendous tasks must be added the complications created by a rapidly deteriorating economic situation. The most critical testing time of all was at hand.

CHAPTER 11

THE PANCRAS EXTENSION AND THE ST PANCRAS BRANCH

The Pancras Extension, that is the 60-chain length between the goods yard and the Euston Road, proved to be a complicated, difficult, and particularly expensive undertaking. In preparing the parliamentary plans for this length at the close of 1862, Barlow found himself confronted by a continuous succession of major engineering problems. To reach the site chosen for the passenger station in the eastern part of Somers Town, the Midland main line would have to be extended southward from the goods station clean through the rubbish tips and the sordid slums of Agar Town, then obliquely bisected by the Regent's Canal. To the south of the canal lay the old St Pancras burial ground, beyond which the River Fleet, flowing more or less at surface level, was bounded to the west by the old St Pancras Road. The course of the canal was such that in order to preserve suitable gradients on the final approach to the passenger station, Barlow must choose between a high level or a low level terminus, the general elevation of which, in either case, must vary from that of the Euston Road by about twenty feet. Firstly, a low level station automatically implied very extensive and very expensive tunnelling operations beneath the canal, the burial ground, the Fleet, and the St Pancras Road. Secondly, the terminal facilities thus provided would impose completely impossible restrictions upon train movements as traffic later expanded. Such an arrangement would be both expensive and crippling in every way. Thirdly, a scheme providing for a high level terminus demanded that the approach lines should be carried upon an embankment. Fourthly, if that plan were adopted, the arrangements for the St Pancras Branch would require particularly careful consideration.

After much deliberation Barlow adopted the high level plan. To dispense with tunnelling beneath the canal and the burial ground, the St Pancras Branch was to leave the Pancras Extension where it crossed the old St Pancras Road to enter the terminus. Passing beneath the main line station on a steeply falling gradient, the branch would cross the Euston Road and fall very sharply to a proposed junction with the Metropolitan Railway immediately east of that company's King's Cross station. Due to their current operating difficulties on the Great Northern main line between Hitchin and King's Cross the Midland board was very seriously worried about the congestion which must surely arise on the one pair of Metropolitan tracks then about to open for public traffic. Moreover, the Metropolitan's engineer, John Fowler, attacked the Midland's proposal for establishing their junction at King's Cross (Met.), to the north-west of which station single line tunnels already linked the Metropolitan with the Great Northern main line. Consequently, when the Midland Railway (Extension to London) Bill came before Parliament in the spring of 1863, it was found that the clauses relating to the St Pancras Branch had been deleted, with plans in hand for a complete revision of the scheme and the presentation of a new Bill in 1864. By that time the point of junction between the branch and the Midland main line had been pushed north to St Paul's Road.

The discussions with the Vestry of St Pancras concerning the land needed by the Midland Railway Company were exceedingly difficult, and in November 1864 a bond of no less than £15,000 was paid to that body indemnifying the Midland Railway Company against the disturbance and damage which the railway works would certainly cause to the local sewers. The negotiations dragged on through 1865, a particularly difficult question being the terms upon which the Midland Company would be allowed to carry its main line across the canal and the burial ground, and also to build the mile-long St Pancras Branch Tunnel beneath those very same obstacles. Although the old burial ground had been closed and finally abandoned for some years, local public opinion still resisted the Midland scheme; but at length the Derby men prevailed and by the close of the year construction work became a distinctly practicable possibility.

The contract for the Pancras Extension was placed with Waring Brothers on February 12, 1866 (the contract price being a little over £319,000), for the construction of 'that part of the main line commencing at the Euston Road and ending at 60 chains, and the portion of the St Pancras Branch Railway commencing at the eastern boundary of the station and extending to a point nearly opposite to 60 chains in the main line'. Relevant to the crossing of the burial ground, the contract provided that no grave was 'to be disturbed without an order in writing from the engineer (Barlow), subject to agreement with the appropriate authorities'. A temporary timber staging was to be erected across the burial ground for the construction of the intended bridge at that place and for conveying materials across the burial ground. No staging support was to touch any grave, and the piers of the bridge across the burial ground were to be of cast iron cylinders and sunk into the ground. The cylinders were to be conveyed along the staging to their respective sites, all excavations and other work for sinking the cylinders were to be done from the inside, and the ground outside them must not on any account be interfered with or disturbed. The contract further specified that the cylinders for the bridge were to be 'perfectly upright and filled in with concrete and brickwork in cement, the brickwork to be capped with a block of Bramley stone not less than two feet thick and dressed to receive the underside of the girders. The cylinders at each corner were to be tested with a weight of 200 tons, applied before the cylinders were finished and before the girders were placed thereon. The two centre cylinders were to be similarly tested, but with 300 tons, all weights to be applied for a minimum of one week'. The company's rails could be used as weights, 'but on no account are they to be damaged'. Finally, the contract schedule was rounded off with the specification that no warm bricks were to be used, and that the brickwork was to be executed in English or Flemish bond throughout. The stonework was to be of Bramley Fall or Derbyshire gritstone, and granite from Aberdeen. Brickwork and masonry for the station were to be completed by June 1, 1867, and the remaining work by December 1, 1867.

Within days of the contract being let, John Crossley received orders from the Extension Committee to lay in several sidings for the benefit of the contractors, and thereafter Waring Brothers' demolition teams moved in against Agar Town. During March and April 1866 those hideous slums, sprawling between the new goods station and the St Pancras gasworks, were swept away for ever, and with them disappeared a menace to public health.

During May and June 1866 the equally sordid slums of Somers Town vanished in the same way; and with the whole length of the Pancras Extension then completely cleared, Waring Brothers made ready to tackle the general construction works. Already a temporary bridge was being thrown across the Regent's Canal, while Cambridge Street was about to be diverted and a bridge thrown across. With a temporary staging already built across the old burial ground, the piers had also been started for 16,000 square yards of brick arching immediately to the south for carrying the elevated line past the famous St Pancras gasworks. The north abutment was already being built for the permanent road bridges which would eventually carry the Midland tracks across the old St Pancras Road into the station proper. Thus, by the end of the year a contractor's line extended from one end of the contract to the other, St Pancras Road being temporarily spanned by a trestle bridge, over which quaint little locomotives hauled the construction wagons to and fro.

Work continued throughout the spring of 1867, and in June the South Construction Committee made their annual tour of inspection. Much to their satisfaction, they found the cylinders for the viaduct across the burial ground in their proper positions and fully tested, and even some of the girders fixed. Between the viaduct and the St Pancras Road the brick arches were three-quarters built. These two jobs were completed in October and November respectively; indeed, the arches had even been ballasted to receive the double-track permanent way. By the following month (December 1867), two of the four girder bridges across the St Pancras Road were finished, a third was nearly ready, and the fourth very well advanced.

The works for the St Pancras Branch Tunnel were co-extensive with those for the elevated main line extension from the enlarged Goods Station to the passenger terminus at the Euston Road, as well as those for the construction of the Metropolitan Widened Lines. With plans for the 'Second Line Tunnel' already taking shape, the idea of linking the Midland main line with the Metropolitan system by means of the St Pancras Branch was carefully reviewed by John Fowler in November 1863. A year before the old scheme proposed by the Midland board had been condemned by both Fowler and Colonel Yolland because of the dangerous gradients involved (1 in 40 and 1 in 30), so that when the Midland Railway (Extension to London) Bill came before Parliament in March 1863, the clauses relating to the St Pancras Branch were found to have been deleted. Following Fowler's latest consultations with Allport and Barlow, there now emerged completely new proposals wherein the gradients were vastly improved by establishing the point of junction with the Midland main line at St Paul's Road, seventy-nine chains north of the Euston Road. Secondly, to avoid fouling the Metropolitan old line, the Midland branch was to terminate in an end-on junction with a short spur from the new Widened Lines, a little to the west of the Metropolitan station at King's Cross.

The new proposals met with approval from all sides, and whilst the engineers of both companies were instantly instructed to make their surveys, a separate Bill was quickly drafted for presentation to Parliament in 1864. As before, the twin objects of the St Pancras Branch scheme were to enable Midland passenger trains to penetrate deep into the City via the Metropolitan tracks, which would also permit Midland coal trains to reach the L.C.&D. system via the newly promoted City Junction line. Here, the arrangements for the junction between the two systems were completely dictated by the Metropolitan Company's engineer, John Fowler, the Midland people having no say at all in the matter, as the following extracts from the Metropolitan Railway Commission Report, 1864, clearly show:

'Section 21. *Metropolitan Railway (Additional Powers).*

It is proposed to construct a Railway from King's Cross Station to join a Railway proposed to be constructed by the Midland Railway up to Skinner's Place, Euston Road, length 15·1 chains. The sharpest curve has a radius of 10 chains and the steepest gradient is 1 in 100. The line is shown as an open cutting.

It is also proposed to divert the existing lines connecting the Metropolitan Railway at King's Cross with the up and down lines to the Great Northern Railway. The lengths of these diversions are respectively 7 chains and 5 chains. Part of these diversions are on inclines of 1 in 50 and 1 in 46 and the curves are very sharp; viz. 6⅔ chains radius.

The proposed alterations are apparently brought forward to enable the Metropolitan Railway to have four lines of Railway at King's Cross and to place the junctions with the Midland Railway and the Great Northern Railway on the two new Northern lines of Railway.

Share capital of £450,000 to be raised, and £150,000 by loan.

N.B. Widening proposed by Metropolitan Railway: 1 line of 25 chains 50 links, and 3 lines of 27 chains 10 links.'

'Section 24. *Midland Railway (St Pancras Branch).*

This Railway 1 mile 0·83 chains in length commences at the authorized Midland Railway (Extension to London), at Camden Mews South, and proceeds in a southerly direction under the North London Railway and the Midland sidings adjacent to it, the Regent's Canal, Upper Cambridge Street, and ends near Skinner's Place, Euston Road, at a junction to be formed with a proposed Railway from the Metropolitan Railway at King's Cross. This Railway is in open cutting throughout, and for three-quarters of a mile is on a steep gradient of 1 in 60, falling towards the south; the sharpest curve has a radius of 10 chains.

It is proposed by this scheme and the Metropolitan Railway (Additional Powers) to connect the Midland Railway and the Metropolitan Railway at King's Cross. Such a junction should not, in my opinion, be sanctioned until there are four lines of Railway between King's Cross and Farringdon Street Station.

Capital of £150,000 to be raised by shares,
£50,000 to be raised by loan.'

The Bill for the St Pancras Branch was examined on April 21, 1864, by a Commons Select Committee functioning under the chairmanship of the Rt. Hon. Lord Stanley. Six petitions against the Bill had been presented on behalf of the Vestry of St Pancras, the Vicar and Churchwardens of St Pancras, the North London Railway, the Regent's Canal Company, the Metropolitan Road Commissioners, and the Metropolitan Railway, but in no instance did Counsel appear; only agents appeared in connection with the first four petitions; and, in the case of the last two, nobody appeared at all.

In presenting the case for the Midland Bill, counsel stated that at that time both the Great Northern and the London & North Western companies enjoyed tremendously powerful advantages over the Midland Railway inasmuch as they enjoyed access to all the shipping points on the River Thames, and by its existing branch to the Metropolitan Railway the Great Northern would secure entry to the heart of the City, the East End of London, and eventually to the London, Chatham & Dover system. Therefore, if the Midland company was to compete effectively against such opposition, it was essential that it too should have access to the Metropolitan Railway as now proposed.

In giving technical evidence on behalf of the Midland company on April 25th, William Barlow was questioned by Mr Vernon Harcourt, Q.C., and he explained how, in its original form, the St Pancras Branch had been abandoned as a direct result of the objections raised by the Metropolitan company's engineer. Then, the Midland plan had been for their branch to be connected with the Metropolitan line through a tunnel, and built on a curve of only eight chains radius, and falling to the junction on a gradient of 1 in 30. But this year the gradients on the new line consisted of a length of two chains at 1 in 300 and sixty chains at 1 in 60, the remainder being level—it was upon the last section that there occurred the sharpest curve of ten chains radius. Again, in deference to the objections raised in 1863 by Colonel Yolland, the St Pancras Branch in its latest form would effect a junction not with the original Metropolitan line but with that company's parallel or 'second line' at a point determined by Mr Fowler, the Midland company having no say in this matter. Whereas the cost of the 1863 proposals for the Midland branch had been estimated at £55,000, the scheme now proposed for 1864 should cost £150,000, due to the more elaborate arrangements made. Replying to further questions, Barlow informed the committee that generally speaking the branch as now proposed would be twenty-six to twenty-eight feet below street level, and the crown of the arch would be six feet below the surface, although that could be taken down to twelve feet if required, thereby providing sufficient depth for the support of ordinary buildings. Barlow was also questioned very extensively about Midland plans for burrowing beneath the old St Pancras burial ground, which had been rendered necessary by the greatly increased length of the St Pancras Branch, that aspect of the work having lately caused a public outcry. In view of that outburst, the Select Committee's decision was temporarily deferred, but the Bill was subsequently sent on to the Lords where the Midland case was found proven and the measure sanctioned that July (27 & 28 Vic. cap cxxxi, July 25, 1864).

For thousands upon thousands of ordinary working-class people in the parish of St Pancras, 1866 was a particularly loathsome and disastrous year. With the destruction of Agar Town virtually completed by the end of that April, the demolition teams moved on to the eastern part of Somers Town. During the spring and summer the desperate wretches displaced by those operations simply herded into the nearby districts, where overcrowding had already reached simply alarming proportions. Pauperism was increasing apace, and during the twelve months ending July 1866 the number of people throughout London in receipt of relief rose from 90,000 to 103,000. Due to such conditions both the immediate and long-term effects of the huge Overend & Gurney banking failure meant precious little to the population of St Pancras, where the depressing scene was transcended by the arrival of the latest spectre—cholera. Small wonder, for a major cause of the trouble was undoubtedly to be found in the revolting condition of the River Fleet, which between Camden Town and St Pancras was virtually an open sewer. The outbreak assumed such menacing proportions that on July 21, 1866, an Order in Council called for the appointment of a special medical committee comprising six medical officers and seven medical assistants supervised by the Medical Officer of Health. This team visited 7,000 separate families in the parish and quickly found that 'the sanitary arrangements were most defective'. Whereas the brunt of the outbreak was borne by Somers Town, throughout the parish more than 5,000 cases of simple diarrhoea and eighty-six cases of cholera were treated, of which 122 cases were removed to hospital ('an arrangement for that purpose having been entered into by the committee with the hospital authorities. A cab suitably fitted up at a cost of £14 was purchased for the conveyance of patients to the hospitals'.), whilst more than 16,000 persons 'suffering from diarrhoea sought and obtained gratuitous relief; 232 streets and places were supplied gratuitously by the water companies with an extra supply of water, and the sewers were continuously cleansed with disinfectants'. The cost of all these corrective measures totalled £1,582 16s ½d, a very substantial sum a century ago; even so, more than 300 deaths occurred throughout the parish, including, most tragically, that of the M.O.H. himself.

Amid all this activity work for the St Pancras Branch Tunnel began at three separate points in May. With the arrangements already well in hand for the diversion of Cambridge Street, a month found the brickwork for the tunnel being built very close by between 34½ and 37½ chains. By July, 100 yards of the side walls and arching had been completed. Below the northern end of the future passenger terminus the side walls for the tunnel were completed at 13 and 17 chains, and a start also made at 21 and 25 chains near the site already earmarked for the bridge across the Pancras Road and the River Fleet. Beyond the Regent's Canal and close to the southern end of the new goods station at 54½ chains work on the tunnel was also very well in hand; in fact, regardless of the cholera epidemic, Waring's 'brickies' were working like beavers throughout the length of the contract. With the outbreak at last subsiding, October found the tunnel excavated for 40 chains (i.e. about half its length), and the arch turned for 5 chains (110 yards).

At least one good result emerged from those recurrent outbreaks in the big official drive made by the new Metropolitan Board of Works to enclose London sewers, and with the construction of the Pancras Extension the new Board seized this golden opportunity to insist that where the Midland extension crossed the Pancras Road the Fleet Sewer should be diverted into huge iron pipes specially designed to carry the stream across the St Pancras Branch tunnel. This project proved particularly difficult and hazardous, but to the very great credit of all concerned the

37. Enclosing the Fleet Sewer at St. Pancras, December 1866

work was most successfully executed during November and December without a really serious accident.

November 1866 produced a further outburst of public opinion. In 1864, at the parliamentary stage, the intention had been to dig a 145-yard length of the St Pancras Branch tunnel beneath the burial ground. It had then been estimated that by building the crown of the arch at a depth of twelve feet below the surface there should be little need to disturb the graves, but it was now found that the graves lay much deeper than had been realized. This was due probably to the burial ground having been built up layer by layer with the passing of the centuries. There was now no alternative to opening the burial ground and completing the construction of the tunnel by the cut-and-cover method. It became necessary to remove a great number of coffins for re-interment either behind the old St Pancras workhouse or in other cemeteries at Kensal Green and Highgate. This task began in November 1866 and continued for the next three months, the graves mostly affected being those of political refugees of French, Hungarian, Italian and Polish origin, who had died in London during the first half of the nineteenth century.

38. Railway works in old St. Pancras churchyard
(*Illustrated London News*, August 11, 1866)

Incidentally, a story persisted for some years concerning a French emigré bishop who was buried there and how his family took the opportunity of having his remains returned to France. Upon opening the grave, Waring's labourers were confronted by three sets of bones, which caused quite a headache until one of the men hit upon the idea that since they had to locate the remains of a foreign gentleman, the darkest set of bones must surely be the ones required. The French reaction to this procedure does not appear to have been recorded.

The sinking of the six cast-iron cylinders (for carrying the girders of the main line bridge across the burial ground) had involved the removal of 300 bodies, and the disturbance caused by the tunnel workings (estimated by the Incumbent of old St Pancras at 10,000 graves) brought a fresh roar of protest from the public. But the work continued unabated, and the completion of the arching took a further three months. By the autumn of 1867 Barlow was able to inform the South Construction Committee that the tunnel for the St Pancras Branch was approaching completion with ballast and the permanent way laid in between 10 and 60 chains.

Completion had originally been scheduled for January 1868, but due to the onset of the slump that autumn (1867), the severe winter, the difficulty in acquiring possession of a short length known as West's land, and the big effort made to complete the 170-yard tunnel beneath the front of St Pancras station for carrying the Metropolitan 'second line', the end-on junction with the Metropolitan Railway was not ready before February 1868. Close by, at King's Cross, the Metropolitan Railway was also striving to complete the remodelling of the two underground junctions with the up and down spurs connecting with the Great Northern main line, for which purpose Great Northern services had been suspended since July 1867. Upon completion, Great Northern goods trains ran on to the new Metropolitan 'second line' from February 17th, followed by passenger services to Farringdon Street on March 1st. All this, of course, delayed the completion of the short length of tunnel linking the St Pancras Branch with the 'second line'. Derby therefore began a flood of correspondence in which the Metropolitan board was bluntly informed of the loss in time and money they were causing the Midland exchequer. Again, whereas 'Metropolitan Junction' was ready by February 1868, the special terminal facilities at Moorgate Street were still not ready, and Midland trains from the St Pancras Branch were delayed until the following July.

Before leaving the subject of the extensive tunnelling operations at King's Cross and St Pancras, it should be stated that the 'second line tunnel' extending westwards beneath the steps of the Midland terminus formed part of the Metropolitan plan to quadruple their line between Moorgate Street and Praed Street Junction. Whereas in 1865 the Metropolitan had sought powers to build their own tunnel, their proposals were most successfully opposed by the Midland company which, under the provisions of the Metropolitan Railway (Additional Powers) Act of 1866, actually undertook the work on behalf of the Metropolitan company. This contract (valued at about £23,500) was also placed with Waring Brothers on November 30, 1866. In this instance, work was due to start within fourteen days, and to be completed by September 1, 1867. It actually began in February 1867, and was finished in January 1868, that is about five weeks before the completion of the end-on connection with the neighbouring St Pancras Branch tunnel the following month.

Particularly interesting light is thrown upon the mid-Victorian wage structure by the contents of the contract schedule:

Navigators or Labourers	4s. 6d. per day
Bricklayers, Masons, Carpenters, and Smiths	7s. 6d. per day
Strikers	4s. 0d. per day
Fitters	10s. 0d. per day
Miners	8s. 0d. per day
Platelayers	6s. 0d. per day
Boys	3s. 6d. per day
One horse, cart, and driver	12s. 0d. per day
Two horses, cart, and driver	21s. 0d. per day

The contractors were to find and provide at their own expense as many policemen on the site of the tunnel and the works as the Midland company or magistrates might think necessary for the preservation of the peace, the sum of £100 being payable to the Midland company for each breach. The contractor's employees were to be paid at least at fortnightly intervals, and the contractors were to erect near the site any temporary cottages needed for accommodating the men. No workman engaged upon this contract was to be allowed to work on Sundays other than where required in connection with absolutely essential works covered by an engineer's certificate. Nor were the contractors allowed to retail any article of consumption to the workmen—the sum of £100 to be paid to the Midland Railway Company in respect of every breach. It was also stipulated that the contractors were not allowed to create spoil dumps whether of a temporary or permanent nature. Consequently, the spoil from these new workings was dumped in the Great Northern single line tunnel swinging westward from Maiden Lane, which was at this period abandoned. Today, the 'second line' tunnel is utilized by the eastbound 'Circle' line at King's Cross (L.T.B.) Station opened in 1941. The original Metropolitan station there was almost entirely destroyed in the blitz.

When work had begun upon the Pancras Extension in March 1866, the Midland board had resolved that it would be most desirable for their local trains to secure direct access to the heart of the City by running into the Metropolitan terminus at Finsbury Circus, subject to the arrangement of suitable terms, of course. James Allport was given the task of conducting the negotiations which continued throughout the year. The seeds of a firm agreement appeared in the spring of 1867, when Allport was able to inform his directors of the proposed agreement for Midland trains to use Metropolitan stations between King's Cross and Moorgate Street, where separate terminal facilities were to be provided. The Midland would also obtain access over the Metropolitan Widened Lines to the London, Chatham & Dover system. These negotiations continued well into the summer, the chief obstacle to a definite conclusion being the settlement of the proportion of expenses to be borne by each of the parties; but early in August 1867 Allport announced that agreement had been reached on the following points:

1. Midland trains were to use the Metropolitan company's widened lines from the junction near King's Cross to Moorgate Street, the Midland Railway fixing the number and the times of the trains it would operate.

2. The Midland was to pay the Metropolitan company a mileage proportion of the receipts derived from the traffic. A minimum of £4,000 would be paid for the first year, £5,000 for the second, £6,000 for the third, and £7,000 for the fourth and successive years.

3. For the use of the intermediate Metropolitan stations at King's Cross, Farringdon Street and Aldersgate Street the Midland company would pay £5,000 for the first three years, and £4,000, £5,000 and £6,000 respectively at Moorgate Street.

4. For goods traffic the Midland undertook to pay 6d per ton; 4d per ton for coals up to 50,000 tons, and 3d per ton for quantities in excess of 50,000 tons. In short, the Midland would pay the Metropolitan company at least £14,000 per annum.

Very shortly afterwards, in December 1867, the Metropolitan reached a somewhat similar agreement with the Great Northern, which was also anxious to secure terminal facilities at Moorgate Street. There were also three-way negotiations between the Metropolitan, the City of London Corporation and the L.C.D.R. regarding the latter company's plans to build the Smithfield spur. One of the major outcomes of all these multi-lateral discussions was that in November 1867, John Fowler had produced his design for the new station at Moorgate Street which was to be built for the accommodation of the Metropolitan company and its three 'tenants'.

By this time the St Pancras Branch tunnel was nearing completion. However, due to the difficulty experienced in acquiring West's land for the final five-yard length of tunnel works, the connecting tunnels just west of King's Cross were not ready before the middle of February 1868, when the second notice was given to the Board of Trade. Immediately east of the Midland junction with the Metropolitan line, the reconstructed junctions with the Great Northern were already completed and having been suspended since the previous July, Great Northern local trains began running over the widened lines to and from Farringdon Street as from March 1, 1868. Subsequently, on June 29th, the new Midland junction near King's Cross was inspected on behalf of the Board of Trade by Colonel Yolland, but due to the tendency for the smoke to hang in the tunnels he was quite critical of the general arrangements. Despite these criticisms, which in later years proved very well founded, the new facilities were sanctioned by the Board of Trade.

E. M. Needham, the Midland Superintendent, was now anxious for the company's local trains to come into service on July 6th, but following a discussion between John Fowler and Matthew Kirtley on the subject of the locomotive power to be used by the Midland, this move was deferred until the following week, July 13th. This subject had originally been dealt with by the Midland board in January 1867 and, following the preparation of a report by Matthew Kirtley, six 2.4.0 side-tank engines had been ordered in July from Beyer Peacock of Manchester at a cost of £2,600 each, the number being increased to ten on August 20th. In general dimensions these engines were very similar to the 2.4.0. tender engines of the 170 class, delivered by the same firm in connection with the opening of the New Mills extension that spring. Both series had 6 ft. 2½ in. driving wheels, 16½ in. × 22 in. cylinders, and the 140 lb. boiler pressure standard at Derby at that time, but for working through the Metropolitan tunnels the new tank engines were specially fitted with condensing apparatus. Delivered in the late spring of 1868, the ten newcomers were absorbed into the Midland stock as Nos. 230-239, inclusive. Thirty carriages for working 'the short Metropolitan trains' had also been ordered at Derby in April 1867, that number being doubled the following August. Comprising all three classes, these carriages were originally fitted with oil lamps, but in June 1868, barely a month before they went into service, they were modified for gas lighting at a cost of £25 per vehicle employing three lamps apiece, a further £2 being charged for each additional set of lamps supplied in excess of three. For charging these carriages with gas, a steam boiler was specially installed at St Pancras at a cost of £300.

Following Colonel Yolland's inspection of the underground junctions at King's Cross on June 29, 1868, the 230 class tank engines and the carriages provided for the Midland services were promptly inspected by the Metropolitan engineer, John Fowler, who stated quite adamantly that the 16½-foot rigid wheelbase of the 230 class machines was far too long for negotiating the sharp curves on the new Metropolitan lines. Indeed, Kirtley admitted that the 230 class had not been specifically designed for working the widened lines, but had been adapted at rather short notice and that specially designed engines would be obtained as soon as possible. Fowler refused to certify the Midland engines as being fit for service on his company's lines, and on the following day Kirtley reported to the Midland Locomotive Committee that the Metropolitan company was now demanding the use of a four-wheel bogie instead of the rigid leading wheels. Yet, to meet immediate Midland needs, Fowler had consented that the 230 class tanks should be permitted to work over the new widened lines for a limited period only, provided that side-play was given to the leading and trailing axles. For regular service, though, he insisted that the Midland should obtain tank engines of the type about to be delivered to the Metropolitan by Beyer Peacock. Derby immediately placed an order with that firm for six similar machines, which would be adequate for initial traffic requirements. As for the ten engines of the 230 class, these would have to be withdrawn and altered in due course and provided with new tenders for working main line trains between St Pancras and Bedford, the estimated cost being £300 per machine. The 230 class engines were gradually converted during 1869, but whereas the earlier 170 class had been equipped with Beyer, Peacock 1,600-gallon tenders, the converted 230 class were paired off with 2,000-gallon tenders of the new Derby standard pattern.

Amid all this hectic activity, Midland local services began on Monday, July 13, 1868. On the 14th the Midland Locomotive Committee accepted Beyer, Peacock's tender to supply 'six Locomotive Condensing Tank Engines for £2,600 each, made exactly to the same plans and specifications as the engines now being built for the Metropolitan Railway Company'. The first of these engines was to be delivered by December 1, 1868, and thereafter at the rate of one a week, so that delivery would be completed by the first week of the New Year. However, as Beyer, Peacock were already building some tank engines of precisely the same type for the Metropolitan company, the Midland board offered the firm that August an extra £75 in consideration of each of the first six of these machines which it might be found possible to divert to Derby. At first Beyer, Peacock found it impossible to accede to that request. However, by the end of August three-way negotiations resulted in the Metropolitan allowing Beyer, Peacock to divert four of their new engines to the Midland, who would reciprocate when their own engines were ready for delivery. Thus, by mid-September we find the first four machines ready for delivery to Derby at the original price of £2,600 apiece. Of course, they had already been allocated Metropolitan names, but these were hastily deferred and superceded by Midland numbers. Thus, the debut of the new 204 class bogie tanks virtually coincided with the opening of the main line station at St Pancras on October 1, 1868, upon which date the whole of the local services were completely recast and retimed. Thereafter, the stopping services from Bedford, Luton and St Albans were diverted to St Pancras, and the 'London District' services from Moorgate Street terminated at Finchley Road and Hendon. Whereas the Moorgate Street services were hauled by the 204 class, the 230 class took charge of the stopping trains to Bedford. Generally speaking, the two classes were kept well segregated, and, as previously mentioned, the 230 class were soon progressively withdrawn to Derby works and converted to tender engines, after which they returned mostly to the Kentish Town shed.

The Midland company's local passenger services to and from the City came into operation in the most unpretentious manner during the summer of 1868. With only a fortnight's advance publicity the service was opened on Monday, July 13th, by the 6.20 a.m. from Kentish Town to Moorgate Street. Having briefly halted at Camden Town (6.23), this inaugural train was turned off the main line at Paul's Road Junction whence it ran down the St Pancras Branch tunnel beneath the still far-from-ready main line terminus to pass on to the Metropolitan widened lines at Metropolitan Junction. Following stops at King's Cross (Met.), Farringdon Street and Aldersgate Street, this Midland train steamed without fuss or bother into the company's new City terminus at 6.35 a.m., to the intense interest of the early morning commuters. This train left Moorgate Street at 6.48 a.m., called at all stations to Kentish Town, ran non-stop to Mill Hill, thence all stations to Luton, where it arrived at 8.10 a.m. The 6.48 was followed by the 7.50 and 8.25 a.m. 'government trains', calling at all stations to Finchley Road and Hendon respectively, this pair being followed by the 9.10 a.m. 'government train' to Bedford. The 51¾-mile journey took 2 hours 20 minutes, an average of 22·2 m.p.h. inclusive of stops, a performance which compared most favourably with the 30 minutes allowed for the run from the City to Hendon, barely 18 m.p.h. All told, there were twenty-three Midland departures from Moorgate Street that day, comprising one train to Kentish Town, seven to Finchley Road, eight to Hendon, three to Luton and four to Bedford. Sunday services consisted of ten 'government trains', eight to Hendon and two to Bedford.

The 6.20 a.m. from Kentish Town was followed into the City by the 7 and 7.38 a.m. from Hendon, the 7.22 a.m. from Luton, the 8.51 from Finchley Road and the 9.2 from Hendon, and the 8.29 ex Luton which omitted the Chiltern Green, Hendon and Finchley Road stops, the latter points being respectively accommodated by the 9.53 a.m. and 10.15 a.m. trains to the City. From Bedford the first train to Moorgate Street was the 8.38 a.m., which took 2 hours 12 minutes In all, there were twenty-four up weekday services with five from Bedford, two from Luton, nine from Hendon, six from Finchley Road and two from Kentish Town. In September the addition of two more trains from Hendon raised the total to twenty-six. Up Sunday services during July, August and September of 1868 consisted of ten 'government' trains, two from Bedford, seven from Hendon and one from Kentish Town, and, with only a few relatively minor exceptions, these local services remained in force for about eleven and a half weeks until the main line station at St Pancras could be brought into use. Even so, they were already clearly organized into two well-defined groups, i.e. the inner or 'London District' services between Moorgate Street and Hendon, and the 'outer services' terminating at Luton and Bedford. As from October 1st, the opening of St Pancras station resulted in the distinction being even more clearly marked than before.

The inauguration of the Midland suburban services was not without incident. Exactly three weeks after the City services began, the 10.48 a.m. Moorgate Street-Hendon train was partly derailed at 11.15 a.m. on Monday, August 3rd, when running at about 40 m.p.h. down the 1 in 200 bank immediately south of the Brent Viaduct. The train consisted of a tank engine running chimney first and hauling ten vehicles comprising a brake-third, a third-class coach, a second-class, two firsts, another second, one first, two seconds, and a brake-third carrying the head guard. Near the bottom of the incline the engine began lurching violently, throwing the crew from one side of the footplate to the other. The driver managed to shut off steam, and the engine became steadier, but half way across the viaduct his attention was drawn by the Brent Junction signalman pointing vigorously to the rear; looking back he saw that some of the carriages were derailed. Immediately he reversed and whistled for brakes, the fireman applying the engine handbrake simultaneously. Thus, the train was halted on the rising bank of 1 in 396 about 280 yards south of Hendon station. Only then was it found that the rear guard's van had been derailed and the head guard thrown headfirst from his van and fatally injured. No passengers were hurt.

At the subsequent inquiry, Lt.-Col. F. H. Rich, R.E., concluded that a subsidence had occurred in the clay bank extending some distance south of the Brent Viaduct, this bank having occasionally given previous trouble through sinking and slipping. At the time of the accident the permanent way was still in the hands of the contractor and not in good order. Rich therefore recommended that lower speeds should be employed until a reasonable quantity of good gravel ballast could be added to the burnt clay. He also criticized the arrangement of leaving the maintenance of new railway lines to the contractors, as well as the fact that neither of the two guards nor the signalmen operating the new line had been provided with timepieces as had been promised by the Midland company's officers when the line was officially inspected immediately prior to opening. Therefore, he recommended that a timepiece should be installed at the Brent Junction signal box without further delay.

Yet another teething trouble arose in connection with the new London Extension when the manager of the Metropolitan Railway wrote to Derby complaining about the impurity of the coke used by Midland engines working over the City Widened Lines. So, while the Locomotive Committee was busy enquiring into the grade of coke used by the Great Northern and Great Western engines which also worked over the Metropolitan lines, the Midland's contractor was asked to quote in respect of 'hand picked coke identical in all respects to that supplied to the Metropolitan company'. At the beginning of September, Kirtley informed his Committee that he had received an offer of 20s 9d per ton delivered at Normanton; but this price was considered excessive, and the Locomotive Committee directed that their new tank engines should continue to burn the original grade of fuel. What the Metropolitan people had to say about that decision does not appear to have been recorded for the benefit of a generation accustomed to the designation of smokeless zones.

CHAPTER 12

ST. PANCRAS STATION UNDER CONSTRUCTION 1866-1873

Since 1868 the majestically proportioned roof of St Pancras station has proudly dominated the local skyline, thereby dwarfing into comparative insignificance its traditional rival King's Cross. Almost a century later the old Midland terminus still stands as a magnificent memorial to the professional capabilities of both William Henry Barlow and George Gilbert Scott who were respectively responsible for designing and erecting the station roof and the hotel buildings. But in the summer of 1863, when Parliament sanctioned the London Extension scheme, Somers Town was nothing but a warren of slums and hovels surrounding a brewery, and following the acquisition of the Somers Town site for erecting the passenger station the brewery was served during October 1864 with notice to quit.

Relevant to the planning of the huge station, 1864 was a year of decisive importance, for at this stage the L.N.W.R. was most actively campaigning for the construction of four lines of railway connecting Euston with the South Eastern company's terminus at Charing Cross, thereby providing a direct north-south link for the benefit of through passengers. The Great Northern company was also seriously interested in the possibility of pushing a spur from their King's Cross terminus to connect with the proposed line, and at Derby the prospect of Midland participation in the scheme by means of a connecting line leaving the Pancras Extension at Somers Town was being most carefully considered. At length, Derby declined to participate, and the whole scheme subsequently foundered because of the highly prohibitive costs of acquiring the necessary land.

Following the rejection of those joint proposals, Samuel Beale's Extension Committee reverted to their original scheme for a completely independent Midland terminus at Somers Town, and Barlow promptly resumed his surveys for the construction of a station fronting upon the New Road. At the outset, he conceived the idea of a passenger station covering a site of two acres, and roof spans 120 feet across would rise to about ninety feet above the level of the rails. But this arrangement suffered from a number of inherent drawbacks of a technical nature. Firstly, the girders and brickwork for a twin span roof would certainly extend far below the surface of the huge embankment upon which the elevated platforms were to be built, right down to ground level at least. Consequently, some of the station roof supports must obviously rest upon the crown of the newly sanctioned St Pancras Branch Tunnel which was to curve beneath the main line station on its final approach to the end-on junction with the Metropolitan Widened Lines. But, as James Allport observed to the Midland board, numerous spans supported by internal columns and intermediate brick walls would most certainly prove completely inflexible items when the time came for a major reorganization and remodelling of the station as the traffic expanded. Accordingly, Barlow again revised his plans and early in 1865 there emerged a still more ambitious scheme for a terminus beneath one huge unsupported span. Yet another revolutionary idea adopted at this stage was directly related to the company's drive for securing a far greater share of the Burton beer traffic. Barlow's earlier scheme had envisaged using the spoil taken from the St Pancras Branch Tunnel for providing a solid foundation for the station platforms, as well as meeting Parliament's requirements prohibiting the creation of spoil dumps in the immediate locality. Barlow and Allport now hit upon the idea of utilizing the space beneath the platforms as a gigantic beer store. This scheme was threefold in its conception, for not only were these ground level premises ideally located for their task, they were eminently suited to maintaining a constant temperature, and would be vast enough to provide storage facilities upon a scale likely to prove attractive to the rapidly expanding brewing industry and its distributing trade. Equally important was the very substantial income which the Derby exchequer would receive from the cellerage charges. These new suggestions were received most enthusiastically by the Midland board, and so it was certainly no accident that the principal girders for supporting the famous gothic arch roof were

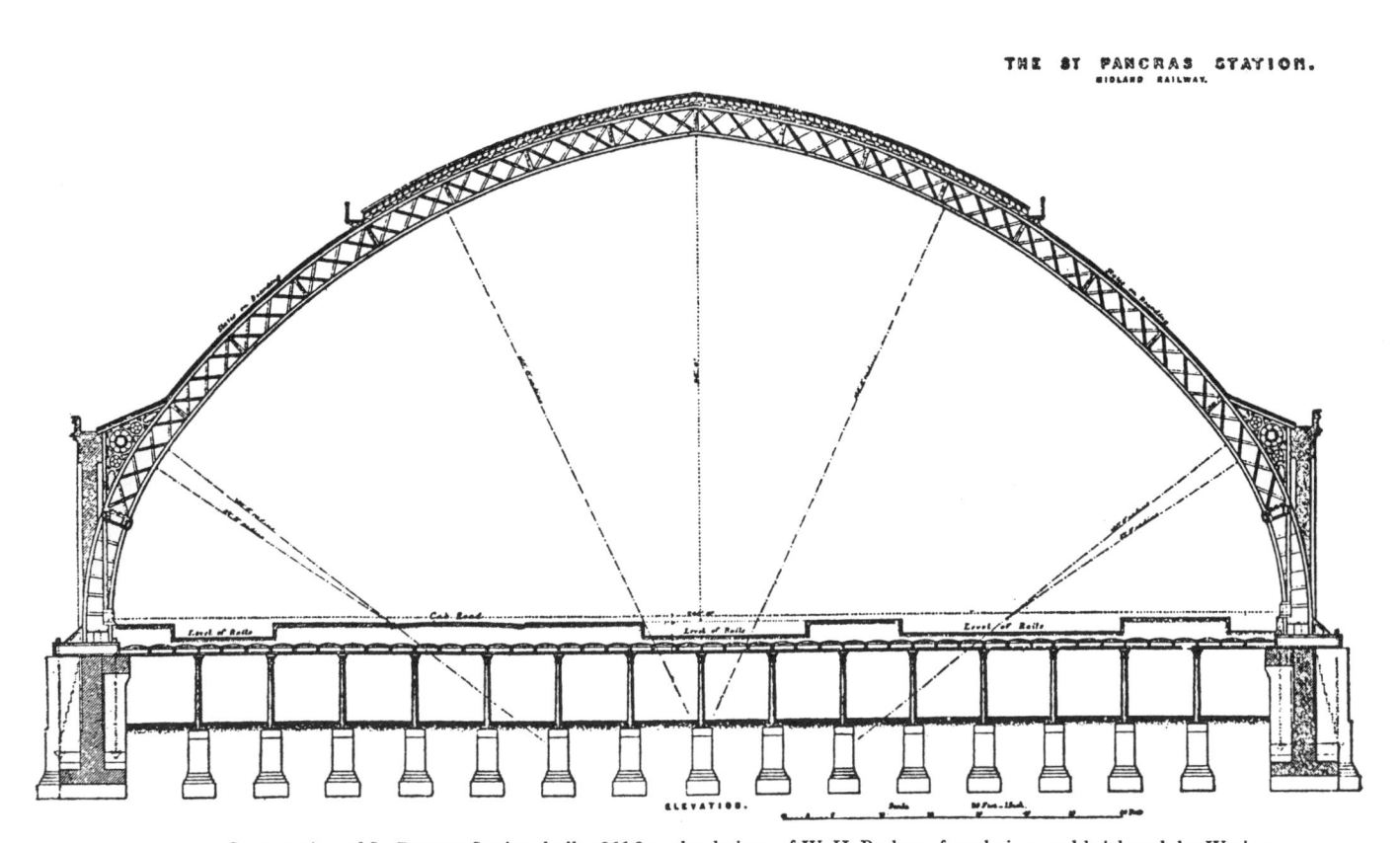

39. Cross section of St. Pancras Station, built 1866-8 to the designs of W. H. Barlow—foundations and brickwork by Waring Brothers—ironwork manufactured and erected by the Butterley Company

eventually erected at 29 ft. 4 in. centres, a dimension most carefully adopted since it was a multiple of the girth of the old-fashioned English beer barrel. Based upon such profoundly important considerations as these, there now emerged Barlow's final design providing for one huge roof span of simply fantastic proportions, 689 feet long, 245 feet wide, and rearing more than 100 feet above rail level.

To carry such a gigantic structure the foundations had to be adequate both in area and in depth, nor must they foul the roof of the St Pancras Branch tunnel. Upon such a massive base would rise the brick piers for supporting nearly 700 columns on which would rest a meshwork of 2,000 girders carrying the elevated tracks and platforms more than twenty feet above the general street level. Obviously, the massive roof girders must be capable of retaining their correct shape under all conditions of stress produced by their own weight, not forgetting the effects of wind, rain, frost, snow and ice. Therefore, the sectional area of each girder must be completely adequate yet not excessive; and, equally important, all arch sections must be correctly jointed and riveted to provide continuity of form.

The general architectural style to be adopted for the hotel buildings was derived by placing the whole scheme on a fully competitive basis to a number of carefully selected architects during the spring of 1865. The prize-winning design was submitted by George Gilbert Scott, and after sanctioning Barlow's revised plans for the station shed in the spring of 1866, the Midland board asked Scott to submit more detailed plans and a more definite estimate of the cost of the hotel and station buildings. Scott's proposals were very elaborate, even lavish, but in view of the rather uncertain economic outlook the board very wisely decided only a fortnight later to secure an estimate for the erection of the hotel, but with Scott's original plan reduced by one floor. Consequently, the broader plan for eventually transferring the company's headquarter offices from Derby to the London terminus was shortly abandoned in the disastrous slump of 1867.

The huge station was subsequently built in four main sections:
1. Foundations and lower station walls (Waring Brothers).
2. Upper walls for the station shed (Waring Brothers).
3. Ironwork for station cellars, floor and roof (The Butterley Co.).
4. Station buildings, hotel and clocktower (built in instalments between 1868 and 1873 by Jackson & Shaw).

The construction of St Pancras station was a mammoth scheme, the first step being the clearance of the four and a half acre slum site at Somers Town. Having completed the demolition of Agar Town by April 1866, Waring Brothers' demolition teams moved southward across the Pancras Road and within two months the eastern half of Somers Town met precisely the same fate. So the end of June found the whole of the Pancras Extension between the goods station and the New Road razed to the ground and cleared. Next, the demolition workers were succeeded by Warings' excavation gangs and bricklaying teams, so that by July more than a thousand men were already hard at work, whilst fifty horses and eighteen stationary steam engines were providing close support. Warings' 'brickies' were particularly active, and by the autumn the massive north wall for the new station was already partly built. South of the wall, on the station site proper, the excavation for the station foundations suffered a sharp setback while temporary tramroads were laid in for expediting the removal of the spoil, and although a locomotive was then put to work further serious delays were caused by intermittent shortages of bricks and a spell of extremely bad weather during October and November. Consequently, the close of the year found brick piers built for carrying only 150 of the 688 cast iron columns needed for carrying the ironwork forming the station floor. Immediately north of the station, a temporary bridge had been thrown across the Pancras Road thereby completing the contractors' temporary line between the goods station and the New Road, and a second locomotive put to work. Summing up, the progress of the works during the second half of 1866 was rather spasmodic and somewhat disappointing.

In June 1866 the Butterley Company had won the huge contract for the supply and erection of the ironwork for the station with their offer of approximately £117,000. Several of the clauses embodied in the schedule to the contract placed with the firm that July cast fascinating light upon the original intentions of the South Construction Committee concerning the construction of St Pancras station, and also the wage structure then in force:

'Clause 61. The delivery and erection of the columns and girders is to commence on 1st September next and to continue at the rate of 30 columns with their cross girders and plates per week. The work is to commence at the south end of the station and to proceed evenly towards the northern extremity.
62. The first principal of the roof is to be delivered and erected by 1st November, 1866, and the work is to continue at the rate of one principal with all other work necessary to complete one bay per week until the whole work is completed.
63. The whole work is to be delivered up complete including the gables by 1st August, 1867.
64. The southernmost principal is to be erected first and the work is to proceed regularly towards the northern end.
65. The timber framing employed in erecting the roof of this Station shall be such as to permit trains of Passenger Carriages to pass under it, so that the southern extremity of the Station may be used for traffic as soon as one half is completed.'
Regarding wage rates, men engaged on day work were to be paid as follows: Labourers, per day of ten hours, 5s 2½d; Plumbers 8s 4d; Slaters 7s 11d.

In actual practice things proved very different. The Overend and Gurney banking failure of May 1866 produced a nationwide reaction, and at Liverpool, Derby and Nottingham there were particularly bad crashes. Thus, by the autumn prompt delivery of the ironwork proved impossible. In fact, these materials only began arriving on the station site in January 1867, by which time a full meeting of the Midland board (held under the chairmanship of W. E. Hutchinson on December 5, 1866) had already launched a full-scale economy drive. In view of the situation, Scott was now formally requested to keep expenditure to bare minimum wherever possible, in response to which directive he immediately produced plans for saving £20,000. A meeting of the Extension Committee held in London on December 19th was equally purposeful, and on that occasion Scott was asked to ascertain the terms upon which 'Mr Gripper of Nottingham will undertake to supply faced and ordinary bricks into wagons at Nottingham for the construction of the St Pancras Station buildings, the Midland Railway to find the necessary trucks to carry the bricks at ½d per ton per mile to the Midland Goods Yard at St Pancras'. Scott rose to the occasion in a magnificent manner, his success being due in no small measure to the loyal support of his nominee, John Saville, the newly-appointed clerk of works.

The year 1867 was a desperately anxious one for the Midland board. Quite apart from the cost of the London Extension, the company was also heavily committed in respect of its extension to New Mills and Manchester, and it was only after overcoming many technical setbacks that the new line was opened for traffic. In the spring a through main line passenger service was opened between Manchester (London Road), Derby, Leicester and King's Cross. At this stage, of course, construction work for the London Extension was very well advanced, with the one major exception of the Pancras Extension and the passenger station proper. A tremendous effort was now launched, resulting in the laying that January of the foundations for the massive towers at the northern end of the station. February produced a further intensification of the economy drive and, following the outcome of Scott's enquiries, the committee ordered the station buildings and the front of the hotel to be faced with Gripper's top-grade bricks, whereas cheaper bricks were to be obtained elsewhere for the side and interior walls. By the spring the station foundations were advancing rather faster than hitherto, and very close behind about one-third of the brick piers had been built. Consequently, it now became possible for the Butterley Company to begin the erection of the cast iron columns for supporting the floor girders. Thus, May found the lower section of the massive side walls about half built, whilst anchor plates and springers for six of the main roof ribs had been installed at the northern end. Obviously, the contract schedule had been reorganized to meet the difficulties of the situation in general, and of the contractors in particular. Again, the western walls for the lower part of the station were advancing faster than those on the east, with nine anchor plates installed on the west against two on the east.

At this juncture the worsening slump was dominating the economic scene, and at the urgent request of the Construction

Committee, Scott produced detailed plans for the front elevation of the station buildings with provision for the work to be limited to the great archway, together with the basement, the ground, and the first floors east of that point. Nothing whatever was to be built to the west of the main gateway, and here the moral is obvious. Delighted with these proposals, the Midland board took immediate steps to obtain tenders covering two possible courses of action, namely:

1. Construction of the station buildings to this emergency plan, or
2. Construction of all the buildings, whether or not this be executed by means of one continuous building operation.

With the appearance of Scott's crash programme, Waring Brothers pushed on harder than ever with the foundations, and these were closely followed up by the brick piers. Although the lower station side walls were advancing so slowly, the ironwork was even further behind schedule, as the South Construction Committee observed when they toured the works in the whole of Barlow's district on June 20th. Even in July the engineer was far from satisfied with the progress of the ironwork to date, and as late as October 1867 only one-third of the station columns had been erected, whilst the springers and anchor plates for the main ribs were still only creeping forward. Therefore, at Derby on October 15th, Barlow placed before the Midland board his own three-point crash programme which received immediate sanction:

'1. The price to be paid for the gables according to the working drawings shall be £25 per ton.
2. To expedite the work, the Butterley Company shall forthwith build a second staging to a design approved by the engineer (i.e. Barlow himself) and to supplement the staging at present in progress.
3. Time of Completion—The roof to be erected, slated, glazed and completed for a length of 450 feet from the Northern end and including the Northern gable on or before May 1, 1868, and the remainder including the Southern gable to be completed on or before October 1, 1868.'

Thus, the policy originally set out in clause 61 of the contract schedule was completely reversed, for it will be recalled that the erection of the main ribs was to commence at the southern end of the station and then proceed northward.

Far more cheerful was the Butterley Company's statement in November that their first timber staging was now ready for service. Built in three independent sections, the staging was a massive affair 240 feet in breadth, 100 feet high, and 90 feet deep, and weighing about 1,300 tons in full working order. The colossal structure even ran upon specially laid rails eventually extending the whole length of the station site, and whenever necessary each of the three sections was literally manhandled along the rails by whole teams of navvies who inserted 'spraggs between the spokes of the wheels and heaved in unison to the booming note produced by the ganger striking an iron plate 'gong'. In this most laborious fashion the staging was moved about 1½ in. per stroke, that is about 3 in. each minute, and since the huge ribs were erected at 29 ft. 4 in. centres, moving the staging from one position to the next must have kept those magnificent navvies heaving for two hours at a stretch. With the completion of the first Butterley staging, the first rib (No. 3, measured from the northern end) was erected in November 1867, but nothing further was done, due to the intercession of the slump and exceptionally severe frosty weather which brought operations to a halt, by which time the foundations for the station shed were nearly completed, whilst those for the station offices were well advanced and those for the station hotel only just begun.

By now, the economic situation was becoming desperate, so that the Midland board stepped in and arranged that the construction of the hotel and even the station buildings should be postponed for at least a year. Tenders for this work already received from several firms were left unopened in Gilbert Scott's office, and upon receipt of Waring Brothers' tender for £64,844 for the erection of the upper walls of the station shed and the adjoining offices, Scott was asked to prepare a fresh schedule of prices. The position was so bad that the architect was then paid five per cent on the outlay on the work done to date and in respect of his working drawings and professional services.

The close of 1867 produced the most serious challenge to Midland finances since the collapse of the 'Railway Mania' twenty years before, and from the latest peak of £7 7s 6d in 1864 the company's dividend slumped to £5 10s. With their huge commitments in respect of their extensions towards Manchester and London, the Midland board faced a major crisis, and it was essential that a further £5,000,000 should be raised, of which sum no less than £2,150,000 was to be earmarked for the London Extension.

Exactly a week before Christmas 1867, the shareholders received a circular letter outlining the position and calling a special general meeting early in the new year in order to consider the propriety of making an appeal to Parliament during the approaching session.

At that meeting, held at Derby on January 15, 1868, the chairman, W. E. Hutchinson, explained that relevant to the London Extension, much of the money was accounted for by the steep rise in property values after 1862, which had also affected the rates of compensation paid for land taken for the company's purposes. Close to London the rise had been very rapid indeed; and to keep the cost of land purchase to a minimum sufficient ground had been bought and overbridges built for four lines throughout. At the moment, only two lines had been built between Hendon and Bedford, but these would be quadrupled as soon as the traffic justified such a step. Then, on the four-track section between St Pancras and Hendon steel rails had been laid instead of iron following the conclusion of trials made by the London & North Western company which had revealed that the working life of steel rails was ten times that of iron. In past years adverse gradients had caused the Midland company much delay and expense, and so on the new London line the gradients had been generally improved from 1 in 176 to 1 in 200, and in the tunnel from 1 in 129 to 1 in 176. Yet another important and expensive item had been the provision of increased capacity. For example, St Pancras station, originally designed to cover about two acres, had been increased to more than four. Iron columns had been used for supporting the roof of the beer store instead of the earth filling originally envisaged, and on the final approach to the terminus three and a quarter acres of arching had been adapted to provide coal drops capable of handling 250,000 tons a year, and the cellars beneath would also yield an income for the storage of coal.

The company had also been caused very much inconvenience and expense by the special works stipulated in the Parliamentary Act for the benefit of very influential bodies. The covered way through Camden Square, and the passage of the surface and the underground lines through the St Pancras burial ground had all proved difficult and expensive. Similarly, extensive drainage schemes insisted upon by the Metropolitan Board of Works, and the nineteen-arch viaduct across the Brent demanded by the Grand Junction Canal Company had proved very costly, as also had the provision of two extra lines for all railways crossed on the approach to the Metropolis.

Separate from these items, expenditure had exceeded the original estimates by £200,000, this being largely attributable to increased labour costs which had risen sharply since 1863. This was particularly true of the Belsize Tunnel which had to be strengthened and lined. An increase in prices had caused three contractors to abandon their works, and there had been further losses transferring the plant and equipment to new people.

Referring to the cost of St Pancras station, Mr Hutchinson said that the magnificent single-span roof had cost £4 per square yard as compared with the £5 per square yard provided in the Parliamentary estimate for the double span. The steel rails, he said, would cost £13 per ton, compared with £6 per ton for iron, and there were hundreds of tons used in every mile of track formation. Lastly, to forestall rising land costs, 407 acres instead of 209 had been bought near London, and 710 instead of 368 for the remainder of the route to Bedford.

Hutchinson was very loudly applauded at the conclusion of his speech, and then a committee of consultation, with Edward Baines, M.P., at its head, was set up to consider to what extent the company's new works could be postponed or even relinquished. After conferring with the directors, the committee's report was presented to the shareholders at the half-yearly meeting held at Derby on February 19, 1868, in which the committee expressed its whole-hearted support for the policy recently pursued by the company's directors, and that the proposed Money Bill for

£5,000,000 should be approved in its entirety by the shareholders in readiness for its presentation to Parliament that spring.

With the arrival of the new year (1868), work on St Pancras station shed was still a very long way behind schedule. Only about one-third of the ironwork for the station floor had been fixed, and only No. 3 principal fixed. The effects of the slump were further protracted by the arrival of extremely frosty weather, and in calling upon the Butterley Company to build a second staging, Barlow now demanded the working of both day and night shifts. Thus, with the arrival of better weather a most heroic effort was made by all concerned, and in the single month of February more than 180 columns were installed, whilst main ribs 4, 5 and 6 were fully completed, and a start also made on Nos. 7 and 8. These were finished in March, by which time the four girder-bridges across the St Pancras Road at the north end of the station were also completed and handed over to the painters. Throughout the spring of 1868 day and night shifts kept the construction work going all round the clock, and progress on the Butterley contract can most easily be summarized as follows:

Balance of the ironwork still to be tackled

	April	1868 May	June
Main Floor Girders (in feet)	1,686	596	Nil
Intermediate Floor Girders	1,283	433	Nil
Cross Girders	819	500	265
Columns	105	11	Nil

Of about 9,000 buckle plates which were ultimately used in the formation of the station floor, nearly 1,150 still remained to be fitted at the end of June.

Terrific efforts were also made by Waring Brothers' bricklayers as they raced along, keeping pace with the Butterley ironworkers. The whole scene was one of frenzied yet systematic activity. The brick piers for the cast iron columns were completed in April, and the columns in May. Three more principals (Nos. 1, 2 and 9) were also erected that April, this figure being increased to thirteen the following month. Woodwork for the roof was already being delivered to the site, and work had even commenced upon enclosing the roof, with five bays ready for slating. Indeed, slating was already under way. But now came a serious setback, this being occasioned by the non-delivery of materials, so that by mid-June only two more ribs were erected, there now being only a little more than three months left in which to get the station ready for traffic. Delays in the delivery of bricks from Nottingham also had a serious effect upon the progress of the brickwork during June and July, and so every effort was made to obtain alternative supplies from Leicester. In mid-September—that is barely three weeks before the station was opened for traffic—the last of the main ribs was erected and glazing was also 'in very active progress'. The highly competitive spirit between the glazing teams is illustrated by the fact that by mid-September sixteen bays had been fully glazed on the eastern side of the roof, seventeen on the western side. Far below the glaziers, the 'brickies' were every bit as busy, and with the station platforms built for a distance of about 400 feet, Barlow and Kirtley were conferring upon the installation of the terminal buffer stops. Close at hand, James Allport was busy negotiating with 'Mr Walker of London' for the provision of a suitable station clock. Even when St Pancras was opened for traffic on October 1st, the station was still far from finished, although such a feat would have been quite impossible without the use of the second timber staging. Passengers used a temporary booking office, and at the northern end of the station Barlow's magnificent gable still awaited glazing. Meanwhile, one of the Butterley stages had been dismantled and cut up, the timber thus recovered being used for surfacing platforms 5 and 6, as we know them today. At the other end of the station, the second Butterley staging was being modified in readiness for the erection of Scott's gable, and, by way of contributing to the general air of completion, the last of the roof glazing was being executed. However, the acute shortage of bricks was proving a constant embarrassment to the harassed clerk of works, John Saville, and those supplies which were available were allocated on a priority basis to Waring Brothers. The middle of December found poor Saville still struggling to close the great southern screen in his attempts to protect the otherwise exposed station interior, and with the floor concreted and the window tracery installed, he was still optimistic about having the main booking office ready

40. The Midland Grand Hotel, St. Pancras, as it appeared in 1873

by Christmas. This, then, was how the new station appeared at the close of 1868 some three months after it had been opened for traffic.

It will be recalled that work on the hotel at the southern end of the station had been suspended at the end of 1867. With the all-round economic improvement arrangements were soon put in hand for the resumption of construction work, although the completion of the hotel and the general tidying up and consolidation at St Pancras took at least four more years. At the very outset Simms and Barre had temporarily provided two types of station lamp for trial purposes, and in January 1869 James Allport was authorized by the Extension Committee to negotiate with that firm for the supply of the permanent lamps (in those gloriously ornate copper frames) at a cost of £11 10s. apiece. Arrangements were also sanctioned for the construction of the famous clock tower, George Scott being further asked by the Midland board to prepare drawings for the clock room; but, in June, Scott's amended designs for the ornamental dial were rejected on the grounds of the cost involved. Meanwhile, Barlow had been instructed to obtain tenders for the erection of the clock house, ladder and dial framing. Although the construction of the clock tower was soon under way, the question of the clock itself hung fire for more than two years until, in December 1871, 'Mr John Walker's estimate of £355 for the four dial frames glazed with white glass, gilt band centre work, and hour and minute hands painted blue' met with the approval of the Midland board.

Following up the recommendations made by Scott on June 15, 1869, the completion of the hotel and station buildings at an estimated cost of rather more than £59,000 was fully endorsed by the General Meeting of Midland shareholders held at Derby on August 31st and, after further discussion, Scott's suggestion that these buildings should henceforth be completed by Jackson & Shaw to the scale of prices furnished in their original tender was also adopted. Work began almost at once, but the project was so vast that even two years later, in September 1871, the western part of the hotel had still not been started. In fact, work on the huge square tower had only just begun, and so the construction of the western section took almost two more years, the magnificently furnished hotel being ultimately brought into use on May 5, 1873.

Like so many huge undertakings of the day, St Pancras station experienced some minor upsets and teething troubles, a typical case occurring when, on March 1, 1870, the South Construction Committee referred a complaint concerning smoking waiting-room chimneys to John Saville for immediate attention. As Saville subsequently explained, the fault was caused by a fierce down draught caused by the contours of the huge arched roof; remedial measures had been taken. Other finishing touches made to this wonderful terminus during 1870 sprang from the approval bestowed by the committee upon Scott's amended design for the front station gates, and the installation of the gas mains the following December for lighting Scott's magnificent chandeliers. The flight of steps leading down from the eastern end of the elevated station forecourt to the corner of Pancras Road dates from 1872.

The construction of St Pancras station and the approaches thereto reputedly consumed 60,000,000 bricks, 80,000 cubic feet of dressed stone of more than a dozen types, and 9,000 tons of ironwork. The main ribs of that famous roof, together with their ornamental spandrils, even cost more than £1,100 apiece. Whereas Barlow was closely associated in later years with the construction of the Second Tay Bridge, the completion of his truly wonderful station at St Pancras undoubtedly placed the seal of success upon his whole career, whilst the prize-winning design for the St Pancras Hotel subsequently earned a knighthood for George Gilbert Scott.

CHAPTER 13

EARLY DAYS ON THE LONDON EXTENSION

St Pancras passenger station was brought into use early in the morning of Thursday, October 1, 1868. The night had been damp and cold, and a few hours later, in the first pale streaks of that chilly autumn dawn, the new Midland terminus presented a very incomplete appearance far different from the highly sophisticated group of buildings so familiar to subsequent generations of travellers. In 1868 the new station comprised merely the elevated platforms sheltered from the full force of the elements by Barlow's wonderful single-span roof, the lower sections of this gigantic structure being completely screened by Waring Brothers' massive side walls. Since the summer, teams of glaziers and slaters had been racing the clock night and day— and racing each other—in their heroic attempts to complete the fabric of the four-acre roof in time for the opening. A press report of the day reveals that 'half way up the roof has been slated, but the crown is all glass and iron. More than two and a half acres of glass have been used'. At the northern end of the station 'the upper opening of the great arch is half covered in by a wrought iron screen weighing 200 tons which is to be partly glazed to break the force of the wind'.

By this time the first Butterley timber staging built in the autumn of 1867 for erecting the roof girders was being dismantled. Of the 6,000 men and 1,000 horses formerly employed on the station works, few traces now remained. The last of the labourers and riveting teams were beginning to disperse, and everywhere the finishing touches were being added with teams of painters most industriously engaged among the gothic arched ribs, the girders and the ancillary ironwork. Throughout, the colour then employed was brown, but as this gave the station interior such a dark and heavy appearance, further discussions between Allport, Barlow and Scott culminated in the under surface being later repainted light blue.

Far below the gigantic roof canopy the station layout consisted of 'a single line for local traffic, then a platform (today

41. St. Pancras Station shortly after opening for traffic

Nos 1 and 2), next eight lines of rails, with room for another two, the space at present being used as a cart road, next a double platform (No. 5), then a carriage road, a platform (No. 6), then two lines, and lastly a platform next the wall (No. 7)'. Incidentally, the eight lines of rails between the major platform faces were partly used for the accommodation of empty coaching stock, and several trains of empty carriages had already arrived upon the scene.

Pending the construction of Scott's beautifully elaborate screen, the second Butterley timber staging was still in use, otherwise, the southern end of the gothic arch roof was completely exposed to the Euston Road, access to which at ground level was dependent upon specially constructed exit ways. In front of the station shed, only the foundations had been prepared for the now world-famous clock tower and the adjoining hotel buildings, all other building work for these projects having been completely suspended in 1867 until the arrival of better times. Even the station booking hall and the associated offices were only just beginning to go up, and in October 1868, Jackson & Shaw's men were still working night and day in a superbly successful attempt to have those facilities ready in time for Christmas. Until these were completed, though, passengers used a temporary booking office.

So, in this far from finished state, the new Midland terminus was brought into operation without any formal ceremony whatever to mark the occasion; indeed, shortly after midnight on Wednesday, September 30th, the company's London booking staff were simply transferred, together with their equipment, from the Great Northern terminus at King's Cross to their new temporary quarters across the Pancras Road. This move was executed with typical Derby despatch, and early that dark autumn morning St Pancras was ready for business.

According to Stretton, the first main line train to reach St Pancras was the 10.5 p.m. overnight mail train from Leeds which at 3.10 a.m. was turned on to the London Extension at Bedford Junction, whence it ran non-stop to the new London terminus. Hitherto, this train had run non-stop from Bedford, reaching King's Cross at 4.15 a.m., but in view of the slightly increased mileage now occasioned by the new extension, five minutes were added to the running schedule. Consequently, the revised time of arrival at St Pancras now became 4.20 a.m. and so, compared with the old 40 m.p.h. run between Bedford and King's Cross, the average speed over the new route rose to 42·6 m.p.h.

Despite the complete absence of official celebrations, though, the driver apparently upheld the honour of the Midland company with a private celebration of his own, and having made the run from Bedford at 45·8 m.p.h. he pulled into St Pancras at 4.15, the old time of arrival at King's Cross. Such a gesture was clearly aimed at the Great Northern and the North Western people studying the situation with the keenest interest from either flank. However, at this stage Derby was maintaining a very discreet silence.

The first train to leave the new Midland terminus that morning was the Leeds newspaper express. Until the previous day, September 30th, this train had left King's Cross at 6.25 a.m., but as from October 1st it was retimed to leave St Pancras at 6.15, to halt briefly at Luton (6.59), and, having made a four minutes' stop, to leave Bedford at 7.30—that is one minute earlier than hitherto. The 6.25 was followed by the former 7.20 a.m. 'government' and the 9.10 a.m. 'morning' Midland trains from King's Cross to Leeds now retimed to leave St Pancras at 7.45 and 9 a.m. respectively, and a completely new stopping train for St Albans was also brought into service at 8.20.

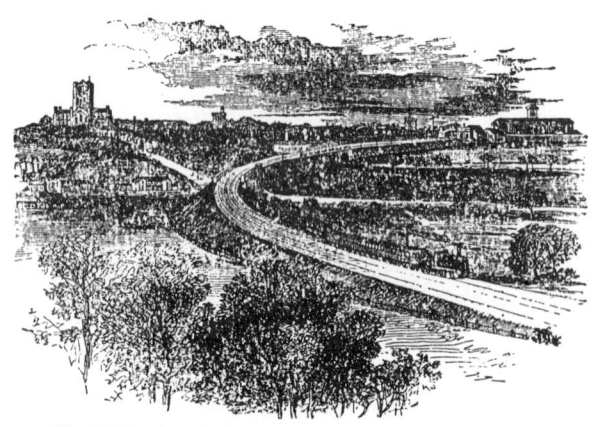

42. Up Midland train leaving St. Albans for St. Pancras, 1869
(Note Great Northern Railway Station immediately left of Midland Railway Bridge across the London Road)

Less than a couple of hours later, Derby tossed a bombshell into the London railway political arena. For the past eighteen months a service of Midland trains had operated between King's Cross and Manchester (London Road). These trains had not been very fast, but at 10 a.m. that Thursday morning a completely new express taking only five hours for the journey left St Pancras for Manchester. Leaving Kentish Town at 10.6, this newcomer covered the next ninety-seven and a half miles to Leicester (Campbell Street) in 2 hours 14 minutes non-stop, arriving there at 12.20 p.m.—a sustained average of 43·6 m.p.h. between Kentish Town and Leicester, or 42·5 m.p.h. throughout. Now, in view of the tiny locomotives then in service, this run was a truly wonderful performance; indeed, such a feat then constituted a world record non-stop run. There was also a complementary afternoon service leaving St Pancras at 4.40 p.m., Kentish Town at 4.46, and maintaining a precisely similar cracking pace to Leicester compared with that set up by the morning train. Naturally enough, the King's Cross and Euston hierarchies were in a state of uproar, but there was still more to come. Determined to show their opponents that this was no mere flash in the pan, the Midland board had directed that there would also be two new 'up' services taking exactly five hours between London Road and St Pancras, the departure times from Manchester being fixed at 9.45 a.m. and 3.30 p.m. Having called for ten minutes at Derby (at 11.20 a.m. and 5 p.m.), and for five minutes at Leicester (12.20 and 6.5 p.m.), both trains were booked to run non-stop to Kentish Town (2.40 and 8.25 p.m.), finally reaching St Pancras at 2.45 and 8.30 p.m. respectively. Incidentally, an extra minute was allowed (on paper, at any rate) for the up runs from Leicester to Kentish Town, but in actual practice this time was most likely spent in discharging passengers and luggage at Kentish Town where the now completely reorganized local services provided really tip-top connections for the City. Similarly, the ten-minute stop at Derby also facilitated excellent connections for Leeds, Sheffield, Nottingham, Lincoln, Birmingham, Gloucester and Bristol.

The up and down morning trains passed each other at Leicester, and there the sight of such a lively performance was certainly a source of pride and inspiration to all ranks of the Midland staff during those exhilarating times. In 1868, engines were changed at Derby, and between Manchester and Derby the locomotives used were the 6 ft. 2½ in. 2.4.0s of the '170 class' delivered by Beyer Peacock about eighteen months previously in the spring of 1867. South-east of Derby, however, the new trains were hauled by the 6 ft. 8 in. Derby-built 2.2.2s of the '25 class' built specially for the London traffic between 1863-1866 and, therefore, still quite new machines. But from the summer of 1870, Leicester was found more convenient as the changing point.

Bradshaw's timetable for October 1868 indicates sixteen main line departures from St Pancras. Of these, ten stopped at Bedford on their way north, whereas the Manchester expresses did not. The remaining four services provided for two stopping trains terminating at Bedford, and two at St Albans. Up weekday services into St Pancras consisted of a single stopping train from Luton and two from Bedford, nine long-distance trains from the north which stopped at Bedford, and the two up Manchester expresses which ran straight through—fourteen arrivals in all.

Sunday services were comparatively sparse and comprised only four trains each way. In the up direction there were the 3.0 a.m. and the 2.40 p.m. 'government trains', together with the 10.5 p.m. night mail train from Leeds, supplemented by the 5.30 p.m. 'government train' from Derby. At St Pancras the respective arrival times were 12.35 p.m., 10 p.m. and 4.15 a.m. for the Leeds trains, and 9.40 p.m. for the Derby train. In the circumstances, 4 hours 10 minutes for the run between Derby and London was not such bad going since it represented an average of about 30 m.p.h., inclusive of stops. The four down services were the 6.30 a.m. 'government train' from St Pancras to Leeds which took 12 hours 35 minutes in the process, the 2.50 p.m. to Leeds (7 hours 10 minutes), the 5.15 p.m. 'government train' to Leicester, and the 8.35 p.m. mail train to Leeds (6 hours 25 minutes). At Derby the 6.30 a.m. and the 2.50 p.m. gave off connections for Manchester, reaching London Road at 5.45 and 8 p.m., and there were also several up trains from Manchester which connected at Derby with the 2.40 and 10.5 p.m. trains from Leeds. At Derby really excellent connections were also established with the cross-country main line services to and from Birmingham and the West of England.

With the opening of St Pancras passenger station in the autumn of 1868 the weight of Midland trains operating between London and Derby had risen very rapidly indeed, and during the first few months of the new year increased to such an extent that by the early summer of 1869 the gallant little 2.2.2s of the '25 class' were having difficulty in maintaining their former speeds across the Desborough and Sharnbrook banks. Double-heading had also been commonplace for some time, and the story goes that the main line drivers sent a deputation to Derby pressing for the provision of much more powerful machines. The party was received personally by the company's locomotive superintendent, Matthew Kirtley, and the company records clearly justify the popular legend of the wonderful *esprit de corps* so carefully built up and maintained throughout all ranks within the Midland Locomotive Department following Kirtley's appointment in 1844. Here, Kirtley kept faith with his men by starting work at once upon a new type of express engine completely revolutionary by former Midland standards. Out on the road, the new design achieved instant popularity with the crews and later it came to be regarded in many quarters as Kirtley's *chef d'oeuvre*.

The new design was centred round the 2.4.0 wheel arrangement, which had been so successfully employed for the company's heavy excursion and local stopping trains for the past ten years, but at Derby the use of coupled wheels for express engines was a revolutionary innovation. These were 6 ft. 8 in. in diameter (c.f. the 6 ft. 8 in. driving wheels employed on the 25 class 'singles') with outside cranks and bearings, the running plate to be suitably curved to clear the throw of the cranks; and whereas the driving wheels were to be encased by ornamentally slotted, semi-circular splashers, the trailing pair of wheels were to be enclosed by rather austere rectangular splashers adjoining the footplate. The 16½ in. × 22 in. cylinders used on the 25 class were to be henceforth abandoned in favour of 17 in. diameter cylinders having a stroke of 24 in., these being mounted at 2 ft. 6 in. centres between newly-designed frames of colossal strength. Boiler tubes and firebox would provide a total heating surface of 1,088 sq. ft., whilst the working pressure of 140 lb. p.s.i. formerly used for the 'singles' was to be retained for the new type. The distinctive boiler mountings typified Kirtley's practice of the day. His tall, slim chimney, cast in three sections, was provided with a conspicuously flared top. The round-topped dome was also tall, generously proportioned, and provided with an externally loaded safely valve—the whole sturdy assembly being mounted on the centre ring. Each locomotive was to be provided with a 2,000 gallon tender, the new standard recently adopted at Derby.

Acting upon the recommendations of the Locomotive Committee, the full board of directors resolved that forty-eight of these new machines would be needed for their forthcoming traffic requirements, and since the company's works could turn out but a dozen during 1870 and six more the following year, the remaining thirty would have to be obtained from outside contractors. Consequently, following the scrutiny of competitive tenders, the Midland board resolved on September 14, 1869, that the thirty machines would be ordered from Neilson's of Glasgow at a cost of £2,275 apiece. So, this one order alone was worth nearly £70,000 to the firm.

Resplendent in their mid-Victorian livery—bluish green boilers picked out by very thin white and black lines with neat brass numerals mounted immediately beneath the dome, the whole assembly carried on dark red frames—the first six of these new Neilson machines were delivered to Derby and then placed on the road during June 1870 as Midland Nos. 800-805 inclusive, the remaining twenty-four engines (Nos. 806-829) being delivered in batches of six per month until delivery was completed by the following October. Now, although all thirty thus received the consecutive numbers 800-829, they were far from identical in layout for whereas the first ten (800-809) had vertical screw wheel reversing gear (a feature which involved No. 809 in a fatal accident late in 1880), the remaining twenty (Nos. 810-829) were equipped with the more usual horizontal reversing wheel. But in very sharp contrast to these arrangements, all eighteen of the Derby-built machines received lever and quadrant gear.

Prior to 1870 the West Riding expresses had been hauled between Derby and Leeds by the old No. 1 class 'singles' built at Derby works between 1859 and 1861; and for just that very purpose Nos. 1-10 had been stationed for the past decade at Derby, whilst Nos. 11-20 were housed at Leeds. However, all this was changed in 1870 by two very important developments. Firstly, the arrival of the new, powerful 2.4.0s of the 800 class ensured that henceforth Leicester could be much more conveniently utilized as the true half-way house between London and Leeds for engine changing purposes. Secondly, the opening for traffic in February 1870 of the new direct line between Chesterfield and Sheffield had placed the latter centre in main line communication with both Derby and Leeds. Now, a moment's reflection will recall that during the Parliamentary hearing of the North Midland Bill in 1836 a direct line had been suggested by Charles Vignoles of the Midland Counties party, but Parliament had come down in favour of George Stephenson's line through the chain of river valleys. Naturally, Vignole's line would have been very costly to build, and it is hardly surprising that the new Midland line opened in 1870, with its heavy engineering works and its long, steep descent through Heeley into Sheffield, also proved very difficult and extremely expensive to construct.

Of the thirty engines of the '800 class' delivered by Neilson's, Nos. 800-811 were given steaming trials at Derby and then were sent straight up to the London District shed at Kentish Town during June and July 1870. In August, Nos. 812-819 were allocated to Leeds, with Nos. 820-829 being put to work on the West of England main line during September and October. Contemporary with these developments another twelve machines (Nos. 165-169 and 60-66) were also emerging from Derby works and taking up their duties at Leicester, where they henceforth provided the intermediate engine link between St Pancras and Leeds. The last six of the whole class (Nos. 3, 22, 23, 93, 138 and 139) were built at Derby in the following year (1871), and they were mostly stationed at either Skipton or Carnforth for handling the company's Scottish traffic. Thus, the close of 1870 found Midland locomotive power between London and Leeds modernized and reorganized for strengthening the West Riding expresses against the steadily mounting competition from the Great Northern Railway for the business between London, Sheffield, Leeds and Bradford; and thanks to Kirtley's efforts Derby was able to secure her fair share of the business. Before the year was out every member of the '800 class' was steaming into battle with superb gusto matched only by the invincible skill and the completely indomitable spirit of the Midland crews.

The effect upon Midland suburban services produced by the opening of St Pancras main line station has already been briefly mentioned. As from October 1, 1868, the whole of the local services on the London Extension were completely recast to create two clearly defined spheres of operation, namely the London District proper and the outer suburban area. Henceforth, the London District trains were restricted to the nine-mile run between Moorgate Street, Kentish Town and Hendon, whereas stations between Hendon and Bedford were to be served by main line stopping trains running to and from St Pancras. This complete reorganization of the suburban services also enabled excellent connections to be established at Kentish Town with the main line trains to and from the North. Such facilities were vitally important to the Derby board because the Midland Railway's arch enemy, the Great Northern, had secured access to the Metropolitan station at Farringdon Street as long ago as 1863; even so, the Midland had still managed to steam into Moorgate Street the better part of a year ahead of her rival. But there again, the 'North Western company's terminus at Euston Square was also situated within comparatively easy reach of the Metropolitan station at Gower Street (now the Circle Line station at Euston Square), so that as early as January 1863 the north country traveller had enjoyed a comparatively direct method of reaching the City by rail. So, if Derby was to secure anything like its fair share of the through City traffic, really first-class connections at Kentish Town were absolutely essential.

Until September 30, 1868, Midland local trains on the London Extension had run to and from Moorgate Street. Now, with effect from Thursday, October 1st, the reorganization provided thirteen trains from Moorgate Street to Kentish Town, four to Finchley Road and nine to Hendon. On October 4th the new Sunday service of ten 'government trains' was brought into operation between Moorgate Street and Hendon. On the main line the weekday services were augmented by two completely new stopping trains which left St Pancras for St Albans at 8.20 a.m. and 6.35 p.m., and two others for Bedford at 1.45 and 4.45 p.m. respectively. So, with the opening of the London Extension for main line traffic, the train services between London and Bedford were both trebled and accelerated, Hendon became the outer suburban terminus, and Kentish Town assumed a greatly enhanced importance. Even so, some further adjustments were made during the last quarter of 1868 when the 8.20 a.m. was retimed as the 9.10 a.m. semi-fast to Luton, and the 6.35 p.m. was extended to Luton. Further south, the thirteen weekday services between Moorgate Street and Kentish Town were reduced that November to six; whilst three new trains were put on between the City and Haverstock Hill, the four trains to Finchley Road were stepped up to six, and the nine to Hendon increased to seventeen. Finally, at 6.20 p.m., a completely new business train left Moorgate Street for Hendon, St Albans and Harpenden; but this train was probably something of an experiment for by the end of 1870 it had been withdrawn. Still, it does demonstrate the awareness of the Midland board of the need to explore the traffic potential which might very well arise from the outer residential districts. Summing up, at the close of 1868 there were thirty-three down weekday services from Moorgate Street, and on Sundays ten 'government trains' to Hendon. In the up direction there were nineteen weekday trains from Hendon to the City, five from Finchley Road, two from Haverstock Hill, and six from Kentish Town. At the last-mentioned point three other trains (one from Bedford and two from Luton) were divided into portions for both St Pancras and Moorgate Street, thereby providing a total of thirty-five Midland services into Moorgate Street every weekday. Sunday services consisted of nine trains from Hendon, one from Kentish Town.

Stretton has recorded for posterity that in the summer of 1868 Midland local services to and from the City were hauled by the ten 2.4.0 tank engines of the '230 class' between Moorgate Street and Kentish Town where they were detached and replaced by main line machines. Against this, though, scrutiny of Bradshaw's timetables for August 1868 suggests that these tank engines most probably took their trains right through to Hendon. Now, almost coincident with the complete reorganization of the local services on October 1st, Beyer Peacock were preparing to deliver the first of the six 4.4.0 Metropolitan type tanks of the 204-209 series. So, with delivery completed by the close of the year, Midland surburban services were soon rescued from their teething troubles and so quickly settled down into their normal working rhythm; but even with this safely accomplished the Derby board simply could not afford to rest upon its laurels, and with the arrival of the new year (1869) numerous schemes aiming at the expansion of the London District traffic were launched without further delay.

Since the early eighteen-sixties it had become abundantly clear that Midland ambitions knew no bounds, and long before the completion of the St Pancras Branch Tunnel leading to the Metropolitan Widened Lines, the Midland board were hard at work investigating ways and means of sending their coal trains rolling across the Thames towards the highly lucrative markets just ripe for exploitation in the south-eastern counties beyond. Naturally, such a bold scheme was completely dependent upon the ability of the distinctly impecunious London, Chatham & Dover company to complete the City Junction line leaving the Chatham & Dover Metropolitan Extension near Ludgate Hill and falling steeply to an end-on junction with the Metropolitan Widened Lines at Snow Hill. Even in face of appalling financial difficulties, the prospect of the tolls which would most certainly be derived from the Midland coal traffic was an extremely attractive one that encouraged the Chatham & Dover board to persevere with such a critically important project. After a stupendous struggle, the City Junction line was opened for traffic on January 1, 1866, and toward the end of that year an invitation was issued for one Midland director to sit on the L.C.D.R. board. Needless to say, Derby accepted this invitation with alacrity and then followed up the advantage by concluding with the Metropolitan company (in August 1867) the traffic agreement whereby Midland goods and mineral trains secured access to the end-on junction at Snow Hill, as well as entry to Moorgate Street for Midland passenger trains, of course. Whereas the company's passenger trains began running into their new City terminus on July 13, 1868, the very next day found Derby actively seeking running powers to Herne Hill and Stewart's Lane on the L.C.D. system. Then, in the spring of 1869 came the suggestion that Chatham & Dover suburban trains should also work through to Kentish Town via the Metropolitan Widened Lines and the St Pancras Branch, and that in the opposite direction Midland local passenger trains should run through to Herne Hill. Indeed, these arrangements came into operation on June 1st, and at the end of eighteen months the northbound services from the L.C.D.R. consisted of four trains to Kentish Town, one to Crouch Hill (on the recently opened Tottenham & Hampstead Branch), and eight to Finchley Road—thirteen trains in all. In the southbound direction there were ten services, eight from Finchley Road and two from Crouch Hill. On Sundays there were no trains in either direction. Later, in the summer of 1875, Midland passenger trains were extended to the Chatham & Dover station at Victoria, there being three from Hendon, three from Finchley Road, five from Kentish Town, and one from South Tottenham. In the opposite direction, five services terminated at Kentish Town, two at Finchley Road, two at Child's Hill, and three at Hendon. These cross-London services operating to and from Herne Hill were an instant success and boosted still further the importance of Kentish Town as an interchange point for Midland passengers. Soon, so many people were travelling to and from South London stations that by October 1869 it became necessary to instal special re-booking facilities upon the up platform at Kenish Town. Nearby, a new siding was laid down the following month 'for holding the short Metropolitan trains'.

Back in the early autumn of 1868 the negotiations then in progress between the Midland and the Chatham & Dover boards were obviously proceeding so favourably that Midland goods and mineral trains would soon be rumbling southward across the Thames at Blackfriars. Now this cheerful prospect raised fresh problems for Derby concerning the locomotive power to be employed; with John Fowler's protests against the long rigid wheelbase of the 230 class 2-4-0 tanks still fresh in their minds, the Midland Locomotive Committee clearly foresaw that use of their 360 class tender 0-6-0s over the Metropolitan Widened Lines between Midland Junction and West Street Junction (near Snow Hill) was absolutely out of the question. Consequently, Matthew Kirtley was instructed at quite short notice to solve the problem by designing a powerful mixed traffic bogie-tank locomotive capable of hauling the company's trains up the 1 in 40 incline leading to the Widened Lines side of Farringdon Street station, and the even steeper bank beyond Snow Hill, as well as meeting every stipulation made by the Metropolitan company's engineer, John Fowler. Kirtley's new design proved to incorporate a number of revolutionary features, and in sharp contrast to the 4-4-0 wheel arrangement formerly employed for the 204 class machines, he now adopted the reciprocal plan whereby 5 ft. 2½ in. coupled wheels having outside cranks preceded the trailing four-wheel bogie truck mounted beneath the footplate. Between the double frames, 17 in. × 24 in. cylinders were employed in conjunction with a boiler producing a working pressure of 140 lb. p.s.i. As pioneered by the 204 class among Midland engines, special condensing gear was also provided for working through the St Pancras Branch and the Metropolitan tunnels.

Having received Kirtley's new design with the utmost enthusiasm, the Midland Locomotive Committee promptly recommended to the full board (in November 1868) that six of the new bogie tank engines should be ordered from Beyer Peacock at a cost of £2,500 each. This was in fact done, and following delivery in the spring of 1869 the whole batch was allocated Midland numbers 690-695 and sent straight up to Kentish Town shed. There they promptly settled down to a long and honourable career, mostly spent in hauling Midland freight trains between Kentish Town and L.C.D. depots in South London. For many years one of this class was constantly stationed outside Farringdon Street station for banking Midland trains up to Ludgate Hill, and from time to time they also assisted with the passenger trains to Herne Hill, and, after 1875, to Victoria (L.C.D.R.). These 690 class tanks proved particularly sturdy machines and lasted about sixty years, thereby outlasting their contemporaries of the 204 class by a good quarter of a century.

The agreement reached between the Midland and the L.C.D. boards in the spring of 1869, whereby the latter company's passenger trains began rumbling northward to Kentish Town and Finchley Road that June, whilst their Midland counterparts ran to Herne Hill, was not without purpose. For some years now Derby had been intent upon establishing a chain of Midland coal depots on the Chatham & Dover system, and in pursuance of this policy James Allport was instructed in December 1869 to open separate negotiations for the acquisition of a piece of land adjacent to the Walworth Road just south of the Elephant & Castle. Allport was so successful that in August 1870 an additional fourteen acres were also purchased from the L.C.D.R. Taken together, these two acquisitions cost the Midland exchequer about £6,500, and by 1871 Derby was able to open a depot with a capacity of 100 wagons. The results were so highly successful that within only two years the new Midland coal station at Walworth Road was handling six trains daily from Kentish Town, yet another task heaped upon the 690 class tanks. With so much extra traffic running to and from the Kentish Town yard the cattle pens there were more systematically enclosed in November 1869 to prevent animals destined for the Caledonian Market from straying across the running lines. Then, in February 1870, the sidings themselves were completely reorganized, a further reorganization being effected only a year after that. Modifications at West End Lane also made it possible to eliminate thirty-four trains formerly passing through the Belsize Tunnel daily, thereby leading to a further saving of three locomotives.

At St Pancras the London goods station had been completed by the close of 1867, and south of the parent goods station the construction work for the Pancras Extension was very well advanced. When finally completed, the elevated tracks for this sixty-chain length would span the Regent's Canal, the old burial ground, no less than 16,000 square yards of brick arching, and lastly the Pancras Road before entering the huge passenger station. As early as December 1866, Allport and Barlow had earmarked the brick arching flanking the Pancras Road as eminently suitable for the site of their new London coal station; and with those arches virtually completed, Allport was using a scale model, in October 1867, in demonstrating to the South Construction Committee a vastly improved type of tipping apparatus lately invented by Samuel Plimsoll (of mercantile marine fame). Although very favourably impressed, the committee's reaction was tempered by the rapidly increasing severity of the trade slump; therefore, Allport was instructed to have just one tipper installed upon a purely trial basis. However, this proved so successful that a further sixteen were sanctioned in February 1868, of which eight were brought into use on May 18th, the remainder following just a few weeks later.

Yet another important development in the latter part of 1867 was the acquisition of a site immediately north of the Cambridge Street diversion for constructing the St Pancras Basin, whereby coal could be speedily transferred from the railway wagons into lighters for shipment along the Regent's Canal to London's dockland and the East End. This contract also went to Waring Brothers, then most busily engaged upon the general works for the Pancras Extension, the construction of the St Pancras Branch Tunnel, and, above that, the foundations, brick piers and the side walls for the St Pancras station shed. At the very outset, arrangements were made for the 'stuff' excavated from the St Pancras Basin site to be removed in the Midland company's wagons and dumped at the Brent, for which service the contractors were charged freight rates appropriate to a normal business transaction. Once under way, work on the St Pancras Basin continued throughout the whole of 1868; but the effects of the worsening slump and the all-out effort to erect Barlow's gigantic roof for the station shed caused the task to fall well behind schedule. Once the station had been opened for traffic, however, Barlow began pressing Waring Brothers to complete the basin with all speed possible, so that the excavations were finished by January 1869, after which the finished basin was filled with water from the Regent's Canal the following spring. It was only then that water was detected percolating through the brickwork of the nearby St Pancras Branch Tunnel, this defect being promptly remedied by providing a lining of blue engineering brick. By the summer of 1869 the dock was in full-scale operation and a hive of furious activity.

No opportunity of expanding their coal traffic was ever missed by the Midland board. In the autumn of 1868 accommodation for 200 more wagons had been provided immediately north of St Pancras station, and only six weeks after that the ground between Cambridge Street and the old burial ground was selected for erecting still more coal drops. After that, every nook and cranny south of the Regent's Canal became a target for the committee's expansionist activities. With the opening of the North London Incline that spring, Midland freight traffic was transferred to the North London Railway for redistribution to the northern and eastern districts of London, and the Thames-side depots at Poplar, Blackwall and Royal Mint Street. At that time the northern suburbs were expanding very rapidly; not only was there a highly lucrative market for Derbyshire and Nottinghamshire coals, but also for bricks and Leicestershire granite. Only a little further afield, the east end also formed a very important market, and in the docks the displacement of the old sailing ship by the coal burning vessel had already created another booming market which the Midland board was determined to exploit to the full, and which would soon become an extremely important source of revenue to the Derby exchequer. Some idea of the extent of this colossal traffic can be gleaned from the fact that during 1869 Derby paid the very substantial sum of £9,500 in tolls to the North London company.

The Midland Railway had first secured a footing in dockland as far back as 1860 when agreement had been reached with the London & Blackwall Railway for the provision of Midland depots at Royal Mint Street and Blackwall. Five more years had seen the acquisition of land at Victoria Docks, and now, in May 1869, plans were being hatched for yet another Midland coal station near Blackwall at an estimated cost exceeding £7,000. So extensive was the Midland freight traffic in the docks that in May 1870 it was resolved to build an engine shed to be known as London Docks; but with nearly £10,000 being paid yearly to the North London company, the Midland board was already casting round for a fresh route to the docks that would prove cheaper. Therein lay the intense Midland interest in the affairs of the Tottenham & Hampstead Junction Railway.

The little Tottenham & Hampstead Junction was something of a white elephant on the London railway scene of the eighteen-sixties. It had been promoted with the express intention of inducing the North Western company's dock traffic to leave the parent system at Willesden, then to proceed over the newly-completed Hampstead & City Junction line to Gospel Oak, and there turned on to the little Tottenham & Hampstead Junction. Beyond Tottenham the through traffic was to pass on to the Great Eastern main line and so roll southward through Stratford to the Docks. Such was the theory behind the scheme, but in practice the L.N.W.R. had for years sent its traffic, and that of the Midland, along the East & West India Docks and Birmingham Junction line to Poplar. Under the more compact title of North London Railway, many of that company's shares had been acquired by the North Western when seeking an easier and cheaper means of reaching the docks. Having amalgamated to that extent, neither of the two partners was at all anxious to divert such a lucrative freight traffic from the fully integrated North London route, and so the Tottenham & Hampstead Junction promptly lost much of its *raison d'être*.

In spite of these difficulties, the T.&H.J. party decided to press on; upon the receipt of a Great Eastern offer made in June 1862 to work their line from the opening, they went forward to obtain their Act exactly four weeks after the Midland coal traffic was 'evicted' from the Great Northern sidings at King's Cross. The new Act did not escape the attention of the Derby board, and when their London Extension was being planned in readiness for the Parliamentary session of 1863 the potential value of the Tottenham line to the Midland cause was instantly appreciated. Very astutely, Derby also realized that the housing estates already creeping out from North London would certainly swallow up the open country along the Tottenham & Hampstead route, and there lay the foundation of a heavy suburban traffic in the years to come. Of course, the Tottenham & Hampstead concern could never survive without the effective support of large and powerful neighbours, and in May 1864 an agreement was reached whereby the Midland and the Great Eastern companies undertook to lease this unfortunate undertaking. This development was quickly followed up when the Midland obtained an Act (on July 25th) sanctioning the construction of a branch linking the Tottenham line with their main line in the vicinity of Kentish Town. In this move the Midland was also supported by the Great Eastern which had its sights trained upon securing access to a 'West End terminus', for which purpose St Pancras would prove most admirable.

Construction of the Tottenham & Hampstead line duly got under way, and this provided the Midland, as joint lessee, to appoint William Price as a co-director of the struggling organization. As predicted, the little company's finances proved most precarious, and by March 1866 (when Agar Town was being cleared) the Great Eastern and the Midland companies agreed to purchase the Tottenham & Hampstead shares in equal proportions. The financial climate was such that in June the Gloucestershire Banking Company appears to have done a 'Disraeli' by purchasing and holding for the Midland Railway £30,000 worth of Tottenham & Hampstead Junction shares at fifty per cent discount! Nevertheless, the little concern battled on with the intention of opening its line for traffic in the autumn of 1867, but the works were all but extinguished by the slump which came perilously close to causing even the mighty Midland to abandon work on their majestic hotel at St Pancras for a year or two. So the little line really did remarkably well in opening for passenger traffic on July 21, 1868, by which time Midland local trains had been running to and from Moorgate Street for just over a week. As no connection had yet been put in between the Midland and the Tottenham & Hampstead systems, locomotives and rolling stock for the new line were provided by the Great Eastern which also put in the Tottenham South Curve to facilitate the through running of their passenger trains between Fenchurch Street and Crouch Hill. But with only one train in each direction daily, it is small wonder that receipts failed to cover working expenses, and thus even this sparse service was withdrawn on January 30, 1870.

Still, that was not the last to be heard of the little concern for while the line was still under construction a meeting was held at Leicester in August 1867 between the Tottenham company's chairman, Captain Arrow, and his Midland counterpart, W. E. Hutchinson, where it was agreed that:

'1. The Tottenham & Hampstead Junction Railway Company would grant the Midland Railway Company the right to build and operate either a permanent or temporary junction between the two systems at Kentish Town.
2. The amount to be paid by the Midland company for the use of the Tottenham & Hampstead Junction land at Kentish Town to be settled by arbitration.
3. This arrangement was to be considered as provisional and temporary only and would in no way prejudice the claims of the Midland company to require the construction of the two junctions in the vicinity of Kentish Town as previously sanctioned by Parliament.'

The tentative nature of this agreement is reflected in the onset of the economic depression, and already the Midland exchequer found itself paying off a creditor threatening to seize a piece of land right in the middle of what was to become the T.&H.J. six-foot way. By the autumn of 1867 the slump was depressing railway property everywhere, and even the Midland was fighting tooth and nail in an all-out effort to complete the Pancras Extension. Consequently, Derby's plans for developing the Tottenham line hung fire for at least a year, and from the spring of 1868 Midland traffic for the docks was routed via the North London Incline and the North London Railway, as previously mentioned.

With the arrival of better times in 1868, Midland interest in the Tottenham & Hampstead was rekindled, and Barlow was instructed that November to make all the necessary arrangements for the construction of the connecting line. This was to leave the Midland main line immediately beyond the Kentish Town Road, climb at 1 in 48 and then swing across the main line to join the Tottenham & Hampstead Junction line near the Highgate Road. The contract for the ironwork needed for the bridge across the Midland main line went to the Park Gate Iron Company; and that for the earthworks was awarded to John Ashwell who had so successfully taken over the No. 1 contract in the spring of 1866, and then gone on to build the Kentish Town engine sheds.

Construction work for the new branch began in January 1869, and by the time the L.C.D.R. trains began running through to Kentish Town and Finchley Road the following June, the bridge for the fly-over across the main line was already half built. By the autumn both the earthworks and the bridge had been completed and the permanent way was being laid in. In November 1869 a further meeting between the representatives of both the Midland and the Great Eastern boards was held under the provisions of the 1864 Act. This proved to be a very amicable affair which resulted in the formulation of an agreement whereby Great Eastern passenger trains would use the Midland terminus at St Pancras and the approach thereto from Kentish Town, of course. In exchange for these facilities the Midland would be allowed to send its freight trains over the Great Eastern line between Tottenham, Stratford and the docks for practically next to nothing.

No time was lost in putting this agreement into effect, and on

43. The London Extension, 1871

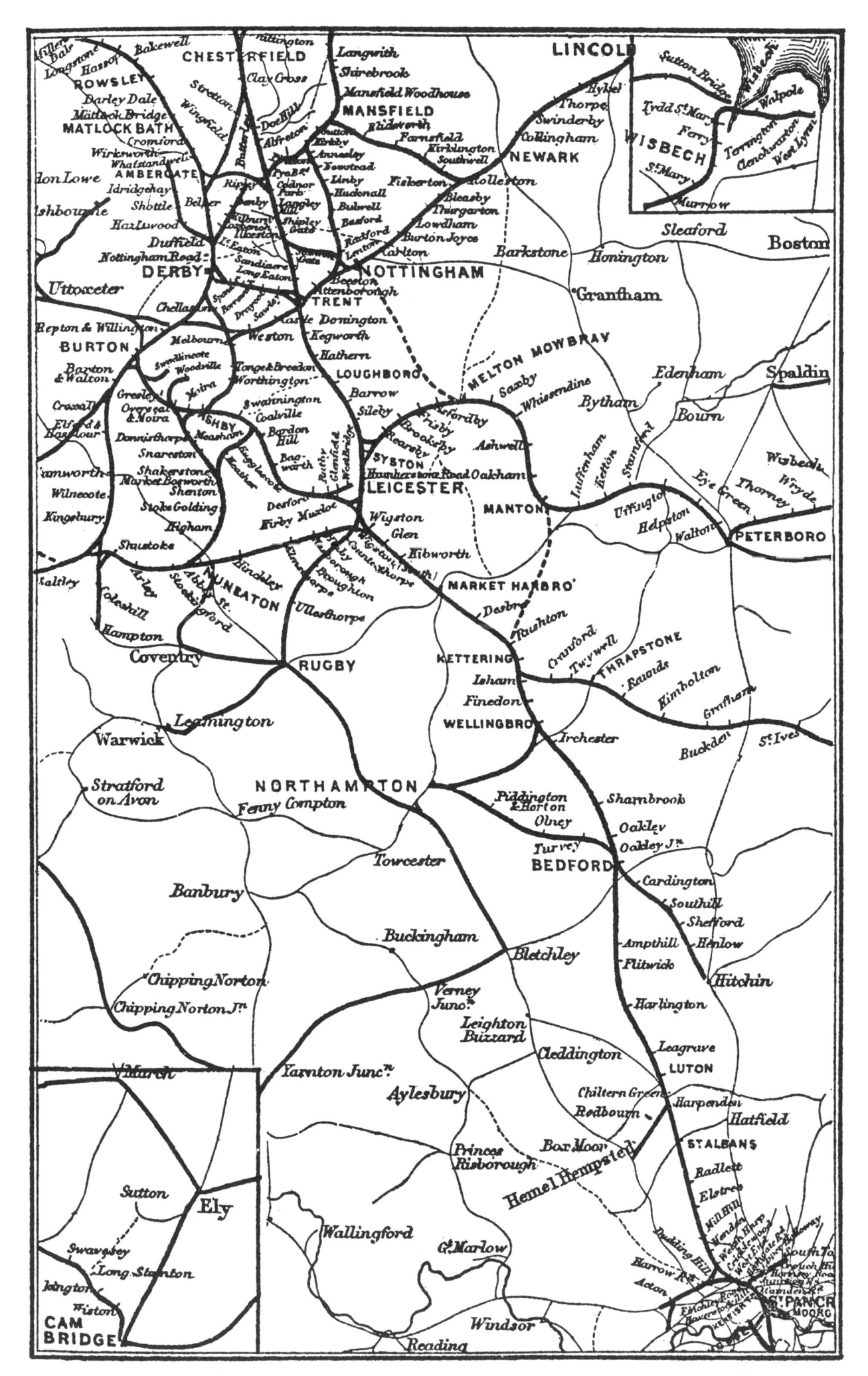

January 3, 1870, Midland trains for the docks were diverted to the Tottenham & Hampstead line. Thereafter, the previous North London route was virtually abandoned after an effective working life of barely two years. The engines used on the new route were the 'old faithfuls' of the 360 class, now about fifteen years old and working harder than ever before. As the Board of Trade had not yet sanctioned the carriage of passengers on the new branch, Great Eastern trains did not reach St Pancras before July 1st when a service of six up and five down trains was inaugurated, with connections made at Tottenham with that company's main line trains to and from Shoreditch.

In any event, the Midland people were caused no direct hindrance by Board of Trade delay in sanctioning the operation of passenger trains along the new branch as Derby was then still engaged in a prolonged tussle with the Metropolitan company which was refusing to allow the Midland working expenses in respect of the trains then being planned to run between Crouch Hill (on the T.&H.J. line) and Moorgate Street. Agreement was eventually reached, however, and from October 1, 1870, Midland suburban trains began running between Crouch Hill, Kentish Town and Moorgate Street, there being five up trains and nine down. Besides these, there were three trains each way between St Pancras and Crouch Hill, two through trains from the L.C.D.R. to Crouch Hill, but only one in the opposite direction. Sunday services apparently consisted of four down trains starting at Kentish Town and six up trains terminating at Kentish Town, and thus underlined the essentially weekday character of those early Midland through commuter services. Within only seven months, on May 1, 1871, the Midland trains were extended to South Tottenham.

The intensification of, firstly, the London District services between Hendon and the City, and then the extensions to the L.C.D.R., to Crouch Hill and to South Tottenham, caused Derby to order from Dubs in September 1869 twenty 0.4.4 tank engines having leading dimensions quite similar to those of the '690 class'. Costing £2,086 each, four were delivered in January 1870, and the others followed at the rate of six a month until delivery was completed. The newcomers were numbered 780-789, and they were immediately allocated to the Kentish Town shed as the prelude to a very long working career which extended well into the nineteen-thirties.

As previously mentioned, the Midland freight trains between St Pancras Goods Station and the docks were hauled along the Tottenham & Hampstead Junction line by the 360 class 0.6.0s, and these machines performed a very efficient job. All went well for about two months until March 1870 when Mr Davies, the Great Eastern company's engineer, decided to erect a fairly low footbridge in the vicinity of Stepney station, and which would be fouled by the chimneys of the Midland engines. Consequently, some members of the 360 class had their boiler mountings cut down, but Matthew Kirtley seems to have taken the hint because, when Beyer Peacock built ten freight tanks with 4 ft. 2 in. wheels for Kirtley in 1871, they were fitted with very short chimneys. Furthermore, the safety valve levers were specially mounted on very short columns set at an obtuse angle well forward of the dome centre line, thus producing a most unusual effect. All ten were numbered 880-889.

In the seventies the pace of London life began to quicken. It may have been more leisurely for the more prosperous members of society living in the remoter rural areas, but examination of the records shows that commuters had already appeared on the London scene rushing hither and thither between the advancing suburbs and their places of employment, just as they do to this very day, and quite a few seem to have come to grief. Closely adjacent to the suburbs now sprawling at the foot of Hampstead Heath, the Midland station at Haverstock Hill seems to have been a favourite place for passengers to alight from trains still on the move. On July 16, 1872, for instance, a male passenger injured his leg in this way. Six weeks later, on August 25th, another injured his hand and knee; on December 7th somebody else was luckier in escaping with only a heavy shaking; still, barely three weeks after that, on December 27th, a fourth man was slightly injured in precisely the same way.

So much, then, for the miscalculations of passengers. Even train crews began to participate. On the afternoon of September 1, 1871, the 3.32 p.m. Great Northern train from Moorgate Street to King's Cross was approaching Farringdon Street station at 8 m.p.h. when the driver caught sight of the 3.5 p.m. Midland train from Herne Hill to Kentish Town converging from the Ludgate Hill line. With very great presence of mind, the Great Northern driver remembered that his leading coach was fitted with gas lighting, and threw on steam. Thus, it was his second (oil lit) vehicle which was struck at about 2 m.p.h. by the Midland tank engine which had skidded down the 1 in 37 bank from Snow Hill. Now, although the Midland driver was subsequently accorded the blame, the Inspecting Officer, Lt. Col. Hutchinson, R.E., took the opportunity of criticizing the local signalling arrangements.

September 1871 was a particularly bad month for Midland trains in the London District. On the morning of Monday, September 11th, the 9.27 a.m. South Tottenham to Moorgate Street was running six minutes late as she approached Kentish Town. At the foot of the 1 in 48 incline giving access to the main line from the new Tottenham & Hampstead Branch, the fourth coach was derailed as it negotiated the crossing outside Kentish Town station, being followed by the eighth, ninth and tenth coaches. Later, it was found that a cast iron chair supporting a wing rail had been fractured during the passage of an earlier train, and the wing rail distorted.

The year 1872 proved even worse than 1871. On Tuesday, March 5th, an over-zealous Midland driver misjudged the speed of his train upon entering the terminus at Moorgate Street, and the engine struck the buffers—six passengers being injured. Five months later, on August 4th, a train of empty carriages setting back into a siding at Kentish Town was struck by a train from Hendon, approaching at about 10 m.p.h. One passenger was shaken by the force of the collision. Described as 'an eight-wheel tank engine with trailing bogie running tank first', the engine of the Hendon train appears to have been one of the 0.4.4T of the new 780 class. Only three days after that, a train from Luton was in collision with a light engine just outside St Pancras. No one was hurt. Just as though this chain of mishaps was of little consequence, there was a triple smash near Snow Hill Junction caused when a Great Northern train was struck by a Chatham & Dover train that had over-run the junction signals. Both engines were damaged, six Great Northern coaches were derailed, the latter being struck by a Midland train of empty wagons.

Last in this tale of woe from the early seventies is the accident which occurred at Elstree on Wednesday, July 22, 1874. Elstree station then consisted of two through platforms, of which the rear of the southern end of the up main platform formed a bay. At 9.15 that evening an excursion train left the bay platform carry a party of schoolchildren back to Haverstock Hill, and, due to the negligence of a twenty-one-year-old porter who omitted to operate a set of safety points, the train ran along the siding instead of turning out on to the main line, and thus struck the earth-filled buffers. 'Sixteen children and four adults complained of injury.'

All these accidents underline the tremendous expansion which was then taking place everywhere along the whole length of the London Extension; and under the ever-watchful eye of the Midland board at Derby all sorts of schemes for increasing the company's business were constantly receiving the most careful consideration. At Mill Hill, for example, the provision of a house for the stationmaster, ordered in March 1869, was followed in January 1871 by the erection of a small waiting room on the 'up' platform; and three miles further north, at Elstree, steps were taken in August 1869 to complete the station approach. Much further out, at Flitwick, a new passenger station was opened in May 1870, a development which was followed that autumn by a scheme for the provision of a refreshment room at Bedford. Incidentally, this most interesting structure still survives at the time of writing and provides a clear idea of the very similar buffet which originally stood at the head of No. 1 platform at St Pancras.

Within the London District proper, that is between Hendon and the City, the suburban services also came in for a tremendous amount of detailed attention. Quite apart from the twenty new break vans and the twenty 'third-class composite breaks' ordered in the autumn of 1868, further sidings for holding the 'short Metropolitan trains' were laid in at both Finchley Road and Hendon (August 1868), and at Kentish Town (November 1869). To facilitate safer working, the sidings at Kentish Town underwent a major reorganization during November 1873, there being a similar reorganization at Hendon in October 1874.

Nor did the newly-opened stations escape review. In March 1870 additional office accommodation was provided for the stationmaster at Hendon, where the footbridge and steps were also enclosed. Then, in the following November, the platforms at Finchley Road were ordered to be roofed over in order to compete with the facilities already provided by the St John's Wood Railway at their Swiss Cottage station situated but a few minutes' walking time further down the Finchley Road. In tapping the then rapidly developing suburbs at South Hampstead, this Metropolitan offshoot had commenced work three months ahead of the Midland Railway, and there were through trains between Swiss Cottage and Moorgate Street until March 1869, at which stage these were cut back to Baker Street. The Midland people also had to contend with the ban placed upon their 230 class tank engines by John Fowler, the Metropolitan engineer, not forgetting the problems raised by the opening of their main line extension to St Pancras. Here, the whole situation was eased by the arrival of the Beyer Peacock 4.4.0 tanks of the 204 series, a development which is reflected in the following summary of the Midland services between Finchley Road and Moorgate Street during the second half of 1868:

	July & August	September	1868 October	November & December
'UP' SERVICES Finchley Road to Moorgate Street				
Weekdays	22	23	18	27
Sundays	9	9	9	9
'DOWN' SERVICES Moorgate Street to Finchley Road				
Weekdays	22	23	13	24
Sundays	10	10	10	10

Yet a further indication of the tremendous expansion within the London District was the appearance of L.C.D. trains on the Midland suburban system in the summer of 1869. At first, the newcomers terminated at Kentish Town, but they were quickly extended to Haverstock Hill and Finchley Road; by 1870 there were eight weekday services each way between Finchley Road and the Chatham & Dover system, but on Sundays there were none. This development alone shows to some extent the way in which Londoners were abandoning the old idea of 'living in' at their places of employment and moving out toward the new suburbs. Furthermore, the appearance of public holidays was already making it possible for thousands of Londoners to flock out to the entertainment centres then beginning to spring up around the metropolis; and in order to tap their fair share of this new type of traffic the Midland board opened two new stations at Child's Hill (5¼ miles) and Welsh Harp (6¾ miles). These came into operation on May 2, 1870, and quickly created a tremendous amount of work for the new 0.4.4T engines of the 780-799 series, the first six of which arrived at Kentish Town sheds that year to reinforce the earlier 4.4.0T Nos. 204-209.

CHAPTER 14

TOWARDS A GOLDEN FUTURE

With the appearance of the revolutionary '800 class' 2.4.0s in the summer of 1870, the Midland Railway rapidly consolidated its grip upon the West Riding traffic, and thereafter began moving forward towards a period of completely unprecedented expansion and prosperity. Almost overnight the opening of St Pancras station had transformed the status of the company from that of a London line to that of a railway of national importance. And, yet, the Midland Railway could scarcely be described as a national trunk line, especially as the company's Scottish traffic was such a skimpy affair and largely obtained second-hand through the condescending graces of the 'North Western and North Eastern companies. Because of this most of the traffic petered out in the midland counties, whereas the cream of the Scottish traffic to and from London was handled at either Euston or King's Cross. At Derby this situation was completely unacceptable, and to remedy the position the Midland board had already launched, in 1869, an audacious plan for building their own fully independent line from Settle to Carlisle. Under the direction of a young Tasmanian engineer named Sharland, construction work was already under way, and within only six more years Midland expresses would be thrusting northward high across the Westmorland Hills to the bleak, desolate wastes of Ais Ghyll, then go hurtling down the Eden Valley to rendezvous with their Scottish partners, the Glasgow & South Western and the North British, at the border city.

To expand still further Derby's share of the English passenger traffic a revolutionary scheme was already very well in hand, and very soon now third-class passengers would be carried by *all* Midland trains instead of the traditional and desperately slow 'government trains' of the last quarter of a century. Indeed, when this latest stroke was delivered in the spring of 1872 there was a tremendous uproar in railway circles, and the prophets of doom were unanimous in condemning Midland tactics; but the greatly increased length of Midland trains and the simply fantastic increase in passenger receipts left the critics completely confounded, while at Euston and King's Cross the rival empires found it absolutely impossible to restore the old *status quo*. Much of the credit for taking such an enlightened step undoubtedly belonged to the company's general manager, James Allport.

Since the opening of their London Extension, the Midland board had gained a tremendous amount of ground, and now Midland competition was so fiercely effective that even the Great Northern company was obliged to admit third-class passengers to many of their more important expresses. By 1872, third-class passengers could travel by most Great Northern long-distance trains; but, of course, there simply had to be one diehard exception on the Great Northern, the crack 10 a.m. Scottish express, the 'Flying Scotsman'. But to clearly emphasize the new democratic policy an almost identical train catering for all three classes was also instituted. This left King's Cross at 10.10 a.m. and ran at precisely the same speeds as the 'Flying Scotsman', but as a compensatory bonus to first and second-class passengers, the latter was accelerated by a full hour between London and York, this journey being covered at an average of 44 m.p.h. throughout.

Shrewd and far-seeing, the Midland board proved uncannily correct all along the line, and with the appearance of a long succession of distinctly lean years after 1872, the tremendous expansion in the company's receipts from third-class passenger traffic told its own story. To cope with such a colossal growth, no less than sixty-two 2.4.0s of a new class, even sturdier and more powerful than the '800 series' of 1870-71, were placed on the road between 1871 and 1875. Although based upon generally similar leading dimensions, i.e. 6 ft. 8½ in. coupled wheels and 17 in. × 24 in. cylinders, there were many important design and structural differences, particularly in connection with the frames. As originally laid out, the 1½ in. tubes and the 92 sq. ft. firebox of the new class gave a total heating surface of 1,112 sq. ft, compared with the total of 1,088 sq. ft. of the '800 series' in their original form.

With the completion of the 800-829 batch in 1870, Neilson's turned out the first twenty of the new class (Nos. 890-909) in the following year. Six more emerged from Derby works in 1872, the remaining thirty-six following up between 1873 and 1875. At first glance the forty-two Derby-built machines appeared to have been numbered on a simply chaotic basis, but in actual fact they 'inherited' their numbers from a previous generation of engines (largely old 'singles') only recently sent to the scrap heap. From about 1875 onward even the '890 class' was rebuilt and enlarged.

As Kirtley died on May 24, 1873, at the relatively early age of sixty, the '890 class' proved to be the last main line passenger engines built during his lifetime, his '1070 class' 2.4.0s being delivered in 1874. Kirtley's death also severed another link with the early pioneering days during which the development of the British railway system had been so effectively moulded by the giants—by the Stephensons, father and son; and by the greatest railway administrator of the age, George Hudson—all of whom had directly influenced his career at its critically important stage.

In making his preliminary survey of the locomotives of all shapes and sizes 'inherited' from the amalgamation of 1844, Kirtley had instantly perceived the marked superiority of the Stephenson six-wheeled heavy freight engines built for the North Midland over the diminutive Bury type four-wheelers supplied to the Midland Counties, and promptly adopted the 0.6.0 as his own standard wheel arrangement. For some years yet the 2.2.2 reigned supreme on the lighter semi-fast trains and expresses, but by the early fifties local passenger trains were beginning to be hauled by 2.4.0s. At first, new machines and rebuilds were obtained from carefully selected contractors, but with the recovery from the Hudson débâcle, Kirtley convinced the Midland board of the wisdom of setting up their own works at Derby. The first engine to emerge from the new works, in 1851, was probably a 2.4.0 with 5 ft. 8 in. coupled wheels, No. 158, built to replace an obsolete machine acquired during Hudson's regime. During the course of the fifties the fleet of 0.6.0s expanded steadily, and from 1852 the main line 2.2.2s were progressively replaced by bigger engines. Of these, many still came from contractors due to the strictly limited capacity of the new Derby works. However, during the sixties, Kirtley was occasionally criticized, particularly by those contemptuous of his apparent lack of technical education in the theoretical field, but he was in fact a thoroughly capable engineer who knew precisely what he was doing, from the hard school of practical experience. With the weight of main line trains rapidly increasing throughout the sixties, he abandoned the 2.2.2 at the end of 1866 in favour of the 2.4.0. From 1866 onward, Derby built 2.4.0s of the 6 ft. 2½ in. 156 class, and these were quickly followed by those of the 170 class specially built by Beyer Peacock in readiness for the opening of the New Mills Extension in the spring of 1867.

The death of Matthew Kirtley in 1873 marked the end of an era both in Midland locomotive history and administrative policy, for as Locomotive Superintendent he had also been responsible for the design, construction and maintenance of the company's rolling stock. With their tremendous expansion programme now so close at hand, the Midland board resolved that Kirtley should be followed by two superintendents—one for the Locomotive Department and the other to assume control of the newly-created Carriage and Wagon Department. Before considering the appointment of his successors, though, it should be remembered that Kirtley's latest and most valuable addition to the Midland locomotive stock occurred only a few months before his death. Taken together, the 800 and the 890 class 2.4.0s then provided rather more than eighty modern, powerful, and altogether highly successful engines, and within the next couple of years that figure would be increased to 110. Both classes were very well capable of handling the most important trains on the Midland system, and although they solved that problem, they created another—the need for greatly improved brakes. Even by the standards of the seventies, braking technique was still extremely primitive and completely inadequate. In fact, the eighteen-sixties were littered by serious accidents, the grim effects of which were directly attributable to the question of brakes. As late as 1872 a typical case occurred near Dronfield when an engine travelling at speed burst a tyre. In reporting upon this accident, Captain Tyler recommended the use of continuous brakes, and the Midland board responded by making prompt arrangements for prolonged trials to be made with the

Westinghouse Air Brake. For this purpose, several Midland trains were specially fitted up for working down the St Pancras Branch, and this began a series of experiments which continued for the better part of ten years. Very soon, the Westinghouse Brake was also being tried out on the main line engines, particularly extensive trials being made with engines operating on the London Extension. One such engine was No. 809, one of the twelve Neilson engines allocated to the Kentish Town shed in 1870. About two years after these trials began, No. 809 was involved in a serious smash at Elstree on November 7, 1874. She was then hauling the 1 p.m. Manchester to London express (seven vehicles) which, by normal standards, should have arrived at Leicester at 4.3 p.m. for combination with the 12.50 p.m. from Leeds and the 3.15 p.m. ex-Nottingham, ready to leave Leicester at 4.9 p.m. On that day an earthslip at Marple Tunnel delayed the departure from Manchester by sixteen minutes. Thus, when the train reached Leicester the other two portions (due at St Pancras at 6.40 p.m.) had already been sent on. At about 6.42 p.m. the belated portion from Manchester dashed through Elstree station at about 45 m.p.h. Barely a minute later the engine and tender began violently shaking and bucking. Shutting off steam, the driver was fortunate enough to bring the train to a halt inside the Elstree Tunnel about 1,000 yards south of the station. Climbing down from the footplate, he was astounded to discover that only the leading guard's van and the first of the three composites were still attached to the tender, the six-wheeled composite having lost one pair of wheels. From the underside of the locomotive footplate, an iron cylinder of circular section (measuring 2 ft. 5½ in. in diameter and 2 ft. 8¾ in. long, and used for storing compressed air for the Westinghouse braking system), having fouled an unknown object lying between the rails, had been ripped right away. Walking back along the track towards the station, the astonished driver now found in the darkness the third vehicle lying smashed across the line, the fourth on top of the third, and the front end of the fifth stove in. By something resembling a miracle, only one passenger had been killed and eight others injured. Two hours elapsed before lifting gear could be brought from Kentish Town and the unfortunate man's body recovered. At the subsequent enquiry, the ever-vigilant Colonel Yolland drew the newly-appointed S. W. Johnson's attention to a flaw in the iron bracket used for securing the cylinder to the underside of the footplate. This was the first really serious main line accident on the London Extension. Unfortunately, it wasn't the last.

No. 809 must have been an 'unlucky engine', for in 1880 she was involved in the Kibworth accident when hauling the 9.15 p.m. night Scotch Express between St Pancras and Leicester. Having halted in a very dark cutting for temporary repairs, the driver accidentally restarted the engine in reverse gear, and at 4 m.p.h. the express backed into the engine of a stationary mineral train. The last two coaches were badly damaged, and five passengers hurt.

For some considerable time the Midland board had been contemplating the creation of a separate Carriage and Wagon Department. During the sixties the company's rolling stock lagged far behind that of its principal competitors, both in design and amenities, and this situation was clearly emphasized with the arrival of the new 2.4.0s of the 800 and 890 series from 1870 onward. Of course, the Great Northern and the London & North Western companies were exerting themselves to the utmost to snatch the business at competing points such as Bradford, Leeds, Manchester, Sheffield and Nottingham, and in the matter of design their carriages were years ahead of current Midland practice. But with the opening of their main line extensions to New Mills and London the Midland board began to take active steps to remedy that situation.

Whereas twenty brake vans and twenty third-class brakes were ordered in September 1868 for use on the London Extension, a further sixty brake vans were ordered in August 1870. Only a month later it was resolved that the standard of amenities in the company's second-class carriages should be improved to match those of its rivals, and in November 1870 no less than 1,000 footwarmers were ordered to be fitted in second-class compartments. Then, James Allport drew the attention of the board to the fact that the North Western already had a highly successful saloon carriage; therefore, the Midland should have one, too. But that was not all. In 1871 a first-class composite carriage was ordered from Klett of Nuremberg, but due to the intervention of the Franco-Prussian War, delivery was delayed until the middle of 1872.

The question of modernizing and improving the company's rolling stock was of such critical importance that, in 1872, James Allport was sent to the United States where he made a 6,000-mile fact-finding tour of the American railroad system. In North America the devastation caused by the Civil War had produced a post-war boom in long-distance railway transportation, and this was accompanied by a nationwide demand for greatly improved standards of comfort, a trend which a gentleman named George Mortimer Pullman was quick to exploit. During his tour, Allport was immediately impressed by the luxurious amenities afforded by the vehicles of the Pullman Palace Car Company, already an integral part of the American scene, and, upon returning to Derby, Allport introduced Pullman to the Midland board. Using a magnificent scale model, the American businessman demonstrated his proposals for introducing his palatial standards of comfort into Britain, and this was a most important proposal in view of the forthcoming intensification of the Midland campaign against the Euston and King's Cross empires. At Derby, reaction to George Pullman's proposals was typically Victorian. Sustained discussion was rounded off with the traditional British solution of compromise. Acting upon Allport's instigation, the Midland board (in November 1872) expressed its willingness 'to run Mr Pullman's cars upon the Midland line by way of experiment finding the Engine Power, but on the understanding that the Company is not bound to buy, rent, or repair any of the stock'. With this major obstacle safely negotiated, Pullman returned to demonstrate his plans to the shareholders at the Half-Yearly Meeting held at Derby on February 8, 1873. Things began to move much faster and within a further month the Midland Carriage and Wagon Committee had settled the arrangements for the provision at Derby of the sheds needed for the re-assembly of the new Pullman cars due to be delivered from June onward.

In Detroit, USA, the manufacture of the cars was being subjected to the traditional North American hustle. After being made they were shipped in parts across the North Atlantic, imported into the United Kingdom through Liverpool, and then moved inland for re-assembly at Derby. There, the work was in charge of a certain Mr Longstreet, reputedly a relative of the American general, and during the next few years no less than thirty-six parlor and sleeping cars were re-assembled for service on the Midland Railway. In the later stages of the programme a number of closely similar cars were also turned out for use on other lines, perhaps the most well known being the Dining Car 'Prince of Wales' which appeared on the Great Northern Railway in 1879. Thirty-two other carriages generally similar in appearance to the original Pullmans were also built, but these were the property of the Midland Railway and provided accommodation for passengers of all three classes—the third-class vehicles also incorporated baggage compartments.

Much has already been written elsewhere about the original Pullmans, but mention should be made here that these wonderful carriages were magnificently proportioned and stately in appearance. For their day they were extremely heavy (about twenty-two tons apiece) and they were slung not on their native American style, six-wheel bogies but upon British bogies having four 3 ft. 6 in. wheels of the famous Mansell pattern. At that time, there was widespread criticism in British technical circles concerning the alleged rough running of those long, heavy vehicles, and the bogie centres were apparently adjusted at this stage from 41 ft. to 39 ft. The first two Pullmans to be re-assembled at Derby were probably the sleeping car 'Midland' and the parlor car 'Victoria'. Both were fitted with the recently introduced Westinghouse air brake which acted upon cast-iron brake-blocks applied to all wheels. These arrangements proved very smooth in action, there being a complete absence of vibration during application, a point which must have made them very popular with passengers using the sleeping cars.

Progress was such that by January 1874 James Allport was able to report that trials with the new Pullman Cars had been held on every section of the line with the one important exception of the old North Midland line between Ambergate and Leeds. Generally speaking, these tests had proved highly successful, but the Marple Tunnel proved to be a solitary exception, and so it was proposed to modify the tunnel in conjunction with the M.S.&L.R., of course, at an estimated cost of £23,000.

On Saturday, February 21st, a special train marshalled from four of the new cars made an exhibition run from St Pancras to Bedford and back for the benefit of the press. One report claims that about eighty guests were carried on this trip, and that the keenest interest was shown in the saloon carriages which could be adapted within but a few minutes to provide sleeping accommodation for sixteen people. Upon the conclusion of that demonstration, the cars were restored to their original appearance. Then, the exhibition car was rapidly converted into an 'hotel car', small tables being fitted up and covered with snow-white table cloths in readiness for the serving of a first-class lunch. This included the serving of wines and spirits which, allegedly, remained steady in their glasses even when the train was running at 50 m.p.h. Judging by all accounts of this event, everything seems to have been highly successful. The gentlemen of the press had a right royal time, Spiers and Pond provided their catering services, and, having footed the bill, particularly for the wines, George Pullman received the benefit of glowing publicity.

According to the Victorian author, C. E. Stretton, a further trial run was made on St Patrick's Day, 1874, when engine 906 (a 2.4.0 of the 890 class) hauled two of the new Pullman Cars (with a party of Midland directors on board) at very high speed between Derby and St Pancras, parts of the trip being run off at 75 m.p.h. The trip included two stops of three minutes each (presumably at Leicester and Bedford) and the whole journey was completed in two and a half hours, being apparently made to review the proposed timetable arrangements under practical conditions. The sights afforded by this brand new, gleaming and luxurious train hurtling down the Sharnbrook Bank for mile after mile and, finally, gliding gracefully to a halt at St Pancras, must have produced reactions little short of sensational.

On the Midland Railway the Pullman Car service came into regular operation on Monday, June 1, 1874. A so-called Pullman train marshalled from two full-scale Pullmans and three of the Midland-owned American type cars built for passengers of all three classes, left Bradford (Market Street) at 8.20 a.m. After numerous stops en route, the train reached Bedford at 1.12 p.m., ran non-stop to Kentish Town (2 p.m.), and reached St Pancras five minutes later. The down train left St Pancras at midnight and, maintaining corresponding speeds, reached Bradford at 5.45 a.m. Incidentally, sleeping-car passengers were allowed to board the empty train at St Pancras from 10 p.m. onward, and upon arrival at Bradford the cars had to be vacated by 8 a.m. Whereas in June 1874 the train ran via Derby, from July 1st it was diverted down the Erewash Valley line, thereby running direct from Chesterfield to Trent. Furthermore, the departure time at Bradford was changed to 9.20 a.m., and at St Pancras the time of arrival became 2.35 p.m., i.e. a net saving of thirty minutes during the whole journey. A further saving of twenty minutes was effected that August by the cancellation of the Chesterfield and Trent stops which enabled the train to be kept running at continuously high speeds, and for the arrival time at London to be reduced to 2.15 p.m.

On June 1, 1874, there were six full-scale Pullman Cars at work on the Midland system. These six comprised the sleeping cars *Midland*, *Enterprise*, *Excelsior*, and the parlor cars *Victoria*, *Britannia* and *Leo*. Very shortly after this, another two sleeping cars, *St George* and *Princess*, were placed upon the road on June 28th and July 17th respectively, by which time the pioneer sleeping car *Midland* had been shipped across to the Continent where she spent the next three years acting, presumably, as a mobile shop window for George Pullman's wares. Eventually, however, she reappeared on the Midland Railway in June 1877.

At the very outset, in 1874, the earliest of the Pullman Cars were fitted with American pattern Miller automatic couplings. Accordingly, the tenders of some of the 890 class 2.4.0s were specially fitted up to haul these vehicles. Again, the cars possessed no buffers in the ordinary British sense of the term, and such shortcomings quickly earned the displeasure of the Midland people, so that by the end of June 1874, T. G. Clayton, the newly-appointed Carriage and Wagon Superintendent at Derby, drew his committee's attention to the desirability of replacing the Miller couplings with normal draw gear and buffing gear. The cars also suffered from prolonged lubrication troubles, and at the outset Midland fitters and greasers rode with the cars and lubricated any hot axleboxes that developed en route. The trouble was persistent and has been attributed to the excessive length and weight of the cars. Be that as it may, one unfortunate Midland greaser lost his life that June when his head came into violent contact with an iron pillar as one of the cars entered Market Street station at Bradford.

Some idea of the public response to the introduction of these Pullman Cars may be gauged from the fact that by September no less than 198 passengers were being carried in the up direction daily, and 38 by the midnight down sleeping car service. A little later that autumn, on October 17th, yet another sleeping car, *Transit*, was added to the existing fleet. So, ignoring *Midland* which was away on her continental tour, there were then eight Pullman-owned vehicles at work on the Midland system—five convertible sleeping cars and three parlor cars. By the close of the year a booking office for the exclusive use of Pullman passengers appeared at St Pancras, and in the following spring the pioneer Pullman services underwent a pronounced expansion.

After Kirtley's death in May 1873, T. G. Clayton (formerly second in command at Swindon) was appointed the first independent Carriage and Wagon Superintendent at Derby. A prompt review of the existing coaching stock quickly convinced him that even the main line vehicles were positively archaeic in design, and luggage racks were still being fitted to the roofs of brand new carriages, even though such practices had long been abandoned by rival concerns. Clayton opened his campaign with a drive directed at the main line stock, and in February 1874, as the massive American Pullmans began to appear at Derby, thirty composites with luggage compartments and one hundred third-class coaches were ordered from outside firms in preparation for the summer traffic. A further one hundred third-class vehicles were also ordered that June, by which time the luxurious Pullmans sponsored by James Allport had just made their debut. By the end of the year the new Superintendent was showing the Carriage and Wagon Committee plans for sixty-foot carriages mounted on six-wheel bogies. Clayton did his work supremely well and thus laid a magnificent foundation upon which the Midland Railway subsequently established its world-wide reputation for elegance and comfort. No less significant was the appointment of S. W. Johnson as Kirtley's successor as Locomotive Superintendent at Derby. Upon taking up his new post he displayed equal promptitude in preparing an extensive programme of rebuilding and replacement spread over many years.

The close of 1874 thus found Derby straining every nerve and ready to unleash the revolutionary campaigns of 1875 and 1876 that were to expand the company's business by completely unprecedented leaps and bounds. There again, the Settle & Carlisle line had been under construction since 1869, and soon, in the early summer of 1876, the company's trains would secure direct access to the border city and their rendezvous with their new-found Scottish allies of the Glasgow and South-Western and the North British lines. This link-up at Carlisle would instantly transform the Midland Railway into a national trunk line fully capable of competing there on equal terms with the L.N.W.R. for a very substantial share of the Anglo-Scottish traffic. At the London end of the system, the Midland board had already most successfully drawn abreast of the company's traditional rivals at Euston and King's Cross.

Viewed as a whole, the past thirty years had been a period of heroic struggles, setbacks and resounding triumphs that had lately culminated in the completion of the London Extension. Nor had all this been achieved without a colossal expenditure on the part of the Derby exchequer, particularly during the past decade. Whereas the Leicester & Hitchin Extension had cost £1,750,000 to build and equip, the London Extension had cost no less than £9,000,000. Even the empty shell of the company's London showpiece, the St Pancras Grand Hotel for accommodating 600 guests, had accounted for £350,000, a further £15,000 being added to the bill by the furniture and decorations. No effort had been spared anywhere, and with so many of the company's major objectives previously attained in such a masterly fashion, the whole system was now poised ready for Midland trains to steam at full speed into the golden future of the late Victorian era.

BIBLIOGRAPHY

B.T.C. Historical Records.*
House of Lords Record Office (minutes of evidence).
Bradshaw: 1857, 1858, 1867, 1868, 1870.
British Museum Newspaper Library, London, N.W.9:
The Times, 1836-75.
Railway Times, 1845/46/47.
Bedford Mercury, 1854/55/56/57.
Bedford Times, 1854/55/56/57.
Berrow's Worcester Journal, 1839/40.
Bedfordshire Independent, 1854/55/56/57.
Birmingham Herald, 1838.
Derbyshire Chronicle, 1837-40.
Derbyshire Courier, 1837-40.
Derby Mercury, 1837-40.
Derby & Chesterfield Reporter, 1837-40.
Gloucestershire Chronicle, 1840.
Leeds Intelligence, 1837-40.
Leeds Mercury, 1837-40.
Leicester Chronicle, 1839-40.
Leicester Journal, 1839-40.
Midland Counties Herald, 1834-44.
Northampton Mercury, 1854/55/56/57.
Nottingham Mercury, 1844.
Nottingham Review, 1839-40.
Sheffield Iris, 1837-40.
Warwick & Warwickshire Advertiser, 1839-40.
Worcestershire Chronicle, 1838-44.
Miscellaneous sources:
Early British Railways (Lewin).
The Railway Mania and Its Aftermath (Lewin).
The Midland Railway, etc. (F. S. Williams).
History of the Midland Railway (C. E. Stretton).
History of the Great Northern Railway (Grinling).
The Story of Agar Town (Rev. Conyers Morrell, M.A.).
A Geographical Study of a London Borough—St. Pancras (Cooke).
St. Pancras (Miller).
St. Pancras Through the Ages (Denver).
Illustrated London News, 1865/66/67.
The Railway Fly Sheet, June 1874.

Official Minute Books of the undermentioned Midland Railway Committees:
Board of Directors, Committee of Management, Locomotive Committee, Carriage & Wagon Committee, Ways & Works Committee, Leicester & Hitchin Committee, South Construction Committee (embracing London Extension Committee), Traffic Committee.

Extracts from Birmingham & Gloucester Railway Company official records:
Board of Directors' minutes, Birmingham Committee, minutes of meetings.

APPENDIX

	Engineer(s)	Act	Line opened
Birmingham & Derby Junction Railway	G. Stephenson	May 19, 1836	August 5, 1839
Leicester & Bedford Railway, 1847	R. Stephenson	July 9, 1847	—
Leicester & Hitchin Railway	C. Liddell	Aug. 4, 1853	April 15, 1857(M) May 8, 1857(P)
Leicester & Swannington Railway	R. Stephenson	May 29, 1830	July 17, 1832
Liverpool & Manchester Railway	G. Stephenson	1826	Sept. 15, 1830
London & Birmingham Railway	R. Stephenson	May 6, 1833	Various dates July 20, 1837 to Sept. 19, 1838
Midland Counties Railway	C. Vignoles	June 21, 1836	May 30, 1839 May 4, 1840 June 30, 1840
Midland Railway	—	May 10, 1844	
North Midland Railway	G. Stephenson	July 4, 1836	May 11, 1840 July 1, 1840
Nottingham, Newark & Lincoln Railway	R. Stephenson	June 30, 1845	August 3, 1846
Sheffield & Rotherham Railway	G. Stephenson	July 4, 1836	October 31, 1838 1839
York & North Midland Railway	G. Stephenson	1836	May 11, 1840 July 1, 1840
Syston & Peterborough Railway	R. Stephenson, C. Liddell	June 30, 1845	Sept. 1, 1846 to May 1, 1848
London Extension St. Pancras Station to M.P. 14½ M.P. 14½ to Bedford Junction	W. H. Barlow C. Liddell	June 22, 1863	Sept. 9, 1867(G) July 13, 1868(P) Oct. 1, 1868(P)
St. Pancras Branch	W. H. Barlow	July 25, 1864	July 13, 1868

INDEX

ACCIDENTS involving
1 CONSTRUCTION WORKERS, 149
2 JUVENILES, 150
3 EARLY LONDON COMMUTERS, 292
4 TRAINS:
  Ashchurch (1845), 121
  Camp Hill (1845), 122
  Colney Hatch (1865), 176
  Elstree (July, 1874), 294
  Elstree (November, 1874), 301
  Farringdon Street (1871), 292
  Gloucester (1844), 119
  Hendon (1868), 250
  Hitchin Junction (1859), 165
  Hitchin Junction (1862), 174
  Kentish Town (1871), 293
  Kentish Town (1872), 293
  Lickey Bank explosions, 112, 115
  Market Harborough (1862), 174
  Moorgate Street (1872), 293
  New Barnet (1862), 175
  Snow Hill (1872), 293
  St. Pancras (1872), 293
  Welwyn (1864), 176
  Welwyn Junction (1867), 178
  Welwyn Tunnel (1866), 177
AGAR, WILLIAM, 191
AGAR TOWN
  Origins of, 191
  Epidemics in, 192
  Preliminary purchase by M.R., 167
  Demolition of (1866), 235
ALLPORT, JAMES
  General Manager, B.andD.J.R., 60
  General Manager of M.R.
    gives parliamentary evidence (1860), 168
    negotiations with G.N.R., 171
    gives evidence before Commons Select Committee (1863), 197
    gives evidence before House of Lords (1863), 202
    tours American railroads (1872), 303
    reports trials with Pullman cars (1874), 304
AMPTHILL TUNNEL, 225

AVON AND GLOUCESTERSHIRE TRAMWAY, 97

BARLOW, WILLIAM HENRY, Engineer
  Reports to Committee of Investigation (1849), 131
  Surveys and plans for London extension (1863), 203
  Plans for St. Pancras branch (1864), 238
  Plans for St. Pancras station (1864/65), 253
  Emergency plan for St. Pancras station (1867), 259
BEALE, SAMUEL, M.P.
  Chairman Agar Town Committee (1859/60), 166
  Chairman Midland Railway, 167
  Gives evidence before Parliament (1860), 168
  Chairman South Construction Committee, 205
BEDFORD
  Bridge across R. Ouse (1856), 153
  Joint station proposed (1856), 153
  Railway level crossing, 148
  Leicester and Hitchin Line opened (1857), 158
  Bedford Junction, Site for, chosen (1865), 225
BELSIZE TUNNEL
  Under construction (1865/67), 214
  Works and labour force, 214
  Excavation techniques, 218
  Gauntletted tracks, 215
BIRMINGHAM AND BRISTOL LINE
  Through railway scheme proposed (1824), 97
  Through line finally consolidated by M.R. (1854), 126
BIRMINGHAM AND DERBY JUNCTION RAILWAY
  Official opening (1839), 42
  Rolling stock for, 43
BIRMINGHAM AND GLOUCESTER RAILWAY
  Proposed (1832), 99
  Openings (1840), 112

BRAKES, CONTINUOUS
  Trials with Westinghouse air brake, 301
BRASSEY, THOMAS
  Contractor for Leicester and Hitchin Extension (1854), 145
BRENT VIADUCT
  Construction begun (1865), 221
  Construction completed (1867), 224
BRUNEL, I. K., Engineer, 99
BUTTERLEY COMPANY, THE
  Ironwork for Trent bridge, 31
  Contract for St. Pancras station (1866), 256
  First timber staging (1867), 257
  Second timber staging (1868), 259

CANALS
  Early in Midland counties, 14
CHELTENHAM AND GLOUCESTER TRAMWAY, 100
CHURCH, DR. WILLIAM, 114
CLARKE, SEYMOUR
  General Manager of G.N.R., 171
CLAY CROSS TUNNEL
  Construction of, 47
  Opened for traffic (1840), 52
CLAYTON, THOMAS G.
  Appointed M.R. C.andW. Supt., 307
CONTRACTORS FOR LONDON EXTENSION
  No. 1 Ritson (1864), 209
        Ashwell (1866), 211
  No. 2 Firbank (1864), 213
  No. 3 Firbank (1865), 219
  No. 4 Waring Bros. (1864), 221
        Firbank (1866), 223
  Nos. 5, 6, 7 Brassey & Ballard (1865), 225
CRIMEAN WAR
  Effects of, 147
CROMFORD CANAL, 47
CUBITT, WILLIAM, Engineer, 80

DEE'S ROYAL HOTEL, Birmingham, 101
DELAYS TO M.R. TRAINS
  South of Hitchin (1861/62), 200
DENISON, EDMUND, 58
DEODAND, 115

DERBY
  Works for N.M.R. begin, 47
  Temporary station opened (1839), 30
  N.M.R. station opened (1840), 53
  Loco. shed, N.M.R., 51
  Headquarters of M.R. (1844), 65
  Loco. policy (1844/49), 90
  Economy drive (1849), 135
DICEY, T. E.
  Chairman M.C.R., 27
DICKENS, CHARLES
  Protests against speed of M.R. trains, 180
ELLIS, JOHN
  Promotes L.andS.R. (1829), 18
  Deputy Chairman of M.R. (1844), 66
  Chairman of M.R. (1849), 132
  Chairman of Leicester and Hitchin Extension Committee, 142
  Negotiates with G.N.R. party (1857), 162
  Death of (1862), 186
EREWASH CANAL, 13
EREWASH VALLEY RAILWAY SCHEME (1832), 21
EREWASH VALLEY
  M.C.R. Extension, 41
ELSTREE TUNNEL
  Tunnelling rights for, 221
  Work begins (1865), 221
  Work completed (1867), 223

FLEET RIVER
  Enclosed at Kentish Town (1865), 210
  Enclosed at St. Pancras (1866), 240
FITZWILLIAM, EARL (1838), 49

GLOUCESTER
  Bell Hotel (1838), 100
  Break of gauge (1844), 120
GLYN, GEORGE CARR
  Financier; Chairman of London and Birmingham Railway, 39
GRAND JUNCTION RAILWAY, 105
GREAT NORTHERN RAILWAY
  Parliamentary campaign (1845/46), 73 et seq
  Traffic agreement with M.R. (1857), 163
  Competition with M.R. (1860), 170

INDEX

G.N. breakdown unit *(1858)*, 165
Modifications at King's Cross *(1858)*, 164

HARBOROUGH, LORD
'Battle of Saxby bridge' *(1844)*, 76
HITCHIN JUNCTION
Land dispute *(1857)*, 156
HUISH, CAPTAIN MARK, 133
HUDSON, GEORGE
Biography, 57
Director of N.M.R., 63
Chairman of M.R. *(1844)*, 66
Through carriages to London *(1844)*, 66
Parliamentary campaign *(1845)*, 71
Derby conference *(1846)*, 84
Special Budget express *(1848)*, 87
Resignation *(1849)*, 95
HUTCHINSON, WILLIAM E.
M.C.R. Traffic Supt. *(1840)*, 33
M.R. Chairman, 261

KENTISH TOWN
Origins, 190
Works for London extension begun, 209
Loco. sheds built *(1866)*, 211
Importance of station *(1870)*, 279
KEN WOOD
Preservation of, 188
KING'S CROSS (G.N.R.)
M.R. trains reach *(1858)*, 164
KING'S CROSS (MET.)
Remodelling of junctions proposed *(1864)*, 237
M.R. trains reach *(1868)*, 249
KIRTLEY, MATTHEW
Biographical, 89
Loco. Supt., B.andD.J.R., 45
Loco. Supt., M.R., 89
Loco. policy *(1844)*, 90
Death of *(1873)*, 299

LEEDS
Hunslet Lane station *(1840)*, 50
LEICESTER
Station, M.C.R. *(1840)*, 32
Leicester and Bedford Railway *(1845)*, 80

Leicester and Bedford Railway *(1846)*, 83
Leicester and Hitchin Act *(1847)*, 84
Leicester and Hitchin Act *(1853)*, 144
Leicester and Hitchin Extension opened *(1857)*, 158
LOCOMOTIVES, PRE-1844
MISCELLANEOUS EARLY LOCOS.
'Birmingham', B.andD.J.R., 43
'Boston', B.andG.R., 115
'Bury', No. 65, 108
'Comet', L.andS.R., 19
'England', B.andG.R., 105
'Goliath', L.andS.R., 93
'Great Britain', B.andG.R., 122
'Leicester', B.andG.R., 109
'Liverpool', L.andS.R., 93
'Philadelphia', B.andG.R., 106
'Southampton', B.andG.R., 109
'Spetchley', B.andG.R., 109
'Victoria', B.andG.R., 106
'Victory', S.H.andR.R., 50
'William Gwynn', B.andG.R., 115
'W. S. Moorsom', B.andG.R., 110
M.C.R. CONTRACTORS' LOCOS. (PRE-1840)
'Aphrite', 'Etna', 'Fox', 'Mersey', 'Navy', 'Rob Roy', 'Trent', 'Vivid', 27
M.C.R. LOCOS., 1839/40
'Ariel', 'Hawk', 'Sunbeam', 29
'Bee', 'Hercules', 91
'Leopard', 33
N.M.R. LOCOS.
60 and 61 (Stephenson), *(1840)*, 52
74 (Stephenson o.6.0), 91
MIDLAND LOCOMOTIVES, 1844 et seq
Summary of loco. stock *(1844)*, 91
New locos. ordered *(1846)*, 92
New locos. ordered *(1847)*, 93
Crampton locos. ordered *(1847)*, 93
Summary of loco. stock *(1844/49)*, 94
MIDLAND LOCOS. REBUILT, 1846-50
Nos. 70 and 71 rebuilt *(1846)*, 92
No. 70 sold *(1847)*, 93
No. 291 condemned *(1849)* 136
Nos. 145 and 146 rebuilt *(1850)*, 136
MIDLAND RAILWAY STANDARD LOCO. CLASSES
Nos. 1 - 24 (2.2.2) *(1859/61)*, 179
25 - 39 (2.2.2) *(1863/66)*, 179
26 (2.2.2) *(1848)*, 88
60 - 65 (2.2.2) *(1848)*, 88

60 - 65 (800 class 2.4.0) *(1870)*, 128
66 - 69 (convertible 2.2.2s) *(1848)*, 124
66 (800 class 2.4.0) *(1870)*, 128
67 - 69 (890 class 2.4.0) *(1874)*, 128
80 - 85 (2.4.0) *(1862)*, 170
156 class 2.4.0s *(1866)*, 300
170 - 199 (2.4.0) *(1867)*, 246
204 - 209 (4.4.0.T.) *(1868)*, 248
230 - 239 (2.4.0.T.) *(1868)*, 246
360 series 0.6.0. *(1854)*, 291
690 - 695 0.4.4.T. *(1869)*, 283
780 - 799 0.4.4.T. *(1870)*, 291
800 - 829 (2.4.0) *(1870)*, 276
880 - 889 (0.6.0.F.T.) *(1871)*, 292
890 - 909 (2.4.0) *(1871)*, 299
1070 - 1089 (2.4.0) *(1874)*, 299
LONDON AND BIRMINGHAM RAILWAY
Rugby junction *(1840)*, 35
L.C.D.R.
City Junction Line *(1866)*, 281
M.R. services to L.C.D.R., 283
L.N.W.R.
M.R. coal traffic at Rugby *(1852)*, 141
Negotiations with M.R. *(1852)*, 138
Third line opened *(1859)*, 141
LONDON AND YORK RAILWAY, 1844/46, 70
METROPOLITAN RAILWAY
Proposed additional powers, 236
Traffic Agreement *(August, 1867)*, 245
Midland Junction officially inspected, 246
J. Fowler criticises 230 class tanks, 247
MIDLAND COUNTIES RAILWAY
Proposed *(1833)*, 22
Parliamentary campaign *(1836)*, 23
Opened in sections
Nottingham - Derby *(1839)*, 29
Long Eaton - Leicester *(1840)*, 33
Leicester - Rugby *(1840)*, 35
Red Hill tunnel, Trent Bridge, 31
Mandamus, writ of *(1843)*, 60
MIDLAND RAILWAY
Through coaches to Euston Square, L.andB.R. *(1844)*, 66
Through trains to King's Cross (G.N.R.), 164

LONDON EXTENSION
Projected *(1862)*, 185
Selecting site for terminus, 187
Parliamentary campaign *(1863)*, 195
South Construction Committee, 205
Engineers preliminary report *(1864)*, 204
Land purchased, Surveyors, 206
Engineers joint report, 207
Construction begins, 209
Opened for goods traffic *(1867)*, 230
Local passenger services *(July, 1868)*, 249
Main Line services *(October, 1868)*, 270
NORTH LONDON INCLINE, 1868, 230
NORTH MIDLAND RAILWAY
Surveys for, 45
Parliamentary campaign *(1836)*, 46
Construction begins *(1837)*, 47
Opened in sections
Derby - Masborough *(1840)*, 51
Leeds - Derby *(1840)*, 52
NOTTINGHAM STATION *(1839)*, 28
NOTTINGHAM, NEWARK AND LINCOLN BRANCH, 78

OCTUPLE AGREEMENT, 133
OMNIBUS 'BRITISH QUEEN' *(1839)*, 28
OVEREND AND GURNEY BANKING FAILURE *(1866)*, 257

PULLMAN, GEORGE MORTIMER
At Derby, 303
PULLMAN PALACE CARS FROM THE U.S.A.
Trial runs *(January, 1874)*, 304
Exhibition run (London to Bedford) *(21st February, 1874)*, 305
Trial run (Derby - St. Pancras) *(17th March, 1874)*, 305
Cars placed in service on M.R. *(1st June, 1874)*, 305
Miller automatic couplings, 306
Names of early cars, 306

RAILWAY MANIA
Appearance of *(1844)*, 64
Climax *(1845)*, 74
Collapse of mania *(1846)*, 76

INDEX

ST. PANCRAS
Historical origins, 188
Prebendal Manor (A.D. 603), 190
Old Parish Church, 190
Old burial ground, 241
Cholera *(1866)*, 239
St. Pancras Goods Station
Land purchased *(1859/61)*, 167
Opened *(1865)*, 228
Reconstructed *(1866/67)*, 229
Opened *(1867)*, 230
St. Pancras ale warehouse *(1865)*, 228
PANCRAS EXTENSION
Contract let *(February, 1866)*, 233
Construction work begun, 235
ST. PANCRAS BRANCH
Project of 1862 rejected, 194
Revised project *(1864)*, 236
ST. PANCRAS BRANCH TUNNEL
Under construction *(May, 1866)*, 240
Officially inspected, 247
Opened for traffic, 249
ST. PANCRAS COAL BASIN, 284
ST. PANCRAS STATION
Site for, 188
Barlow's designs for station shed, 253
Site cleared *(1866)*, 256
Contract for ironwork *(1866)*, 256
Brickwork begun *(1866)*, 256
Economy drive *(1866)*, 257
Crash programme *(1867)*, 259
First rib erected *(1867)*, 260
Station opened for traffic *(1868)*, 270
ST. PANCRAS HOTEL
G. G. Scott's design *(1865)*, 255

Construction abandoned *(1867)*, 260
Construction resumed *(1869)*, 265
Clock Tower under construction, 265
Hotel opened *(1873)*, 267
SHARNBROOK, Bank and Viaduct, 148
SOMERS TOWN
Origins and development, 191
Eastern part demolished *(1866)*, 235
SOUTH MIDLAND RAILWAY, 80
SPECIAL TRAIN
Euston Square - Gateshead *(1844)*, 67
STENSON, WILLIAM, 17
STEPHENSON, GEORGE AND ROBERT, 18 et seq
STEPHENSON, G.
Death of *(1848)*, 94
STONEBRIDGE BRANCH B. AND D.J.R., 41
SYSTON AND PETERBOROUGH BRANCH, 76

TOTTENHAM AND HAMPSTEAD JUNCTION RAILWAY, 286
TRETHEWY, HENRY, Land Valuer 144

VIGNOLES, CHARLES, Engineer, 22

WARDEN TUNNEL, Bedfordshire, 145
WELLINGTON, DUKE OF, 39
WHITBREAD, WILLIAM, 84

YOLLAND, COL. W. (R.E.), 193
YORK
Railway Committee, 58
YORK AND NORTH MIDLAND RAILWAY *(1840)*, 45 et seq